ARCHAEOLOGY OF BABEL

ARCHAEOLOGY OF BABEL

The Colonial Foundation of the Humanities

SIRAJ AHMED

Stanford University Press
Stanford, California

Stanford University Press
Stanford, California

Printed in the United States of America on acid-free, archival-quality paper

Library of Congress Cataloging-in-Publication Data

Names: Ahmed, Siraj Dean, author.
Title: Archaeology of Babel : the colonial foundation of the humanities /
    Siraj Ahmed.
Description: Stanford, California : Stanford University Press, 2017. |
    Includes bibliographical references and index.
Identifiers: LCCN 2017028137 (print) | LCCN 2017045915 (ebook) |
    ISBN 9781503604049 (electronic) | ISBN 9780804785297 (cloth : alk. paper) |
    ISBN 9781503604025 (pbk. : alk. paper)
Subjects: LCSH: Imperialism and philology. | Philology--Political
    aspects--History. | Humanities--Methodology--History. |
    Literature--History and criticism--Theory, etc.
Classification: LCC P41 (ebook) | LCC P41 .A37 2017 (print) | DDC 407--dc23
LC record available at https://lccn.loc.gov/2017028137

Typeset by Bruce Lundquist in 10.25/15 Adobe Caslon Pro
Cover design by Rob Ehle. Photograph courtesy of Shirin Abedinirad.

For Yashi Ahmed

CONTENTS

ACKNOWLEDGMENTS

A preliminary version of this book's introduction was published in *Critical Inquiry* 39 (Winter 2013), © 2013 by The University of Chicago. Thanks to Richard Neer, W. J. T. Mitchell, and *CI*'s editorial board for being receptive to an unusual argument and asking me to push it further.

Though I lack the words to express it, I know how fortunate I've been to have an editor as perceptive in all things as Emily-Jane Cohen. Thank you for taking my ideas seriously in the beginning and giving them the time they needed to develop (I promise not to miss another deadline).

The students in the CUNY Graduate Center class I taught on "Critical Method and Colonial Law" modeled a theoretical open-mindedness I'd otherwise assume was no longer in fashion. I wish I could talk to academics like them for the rest of my life.

Sunil Agnani, Alice McGrath, Tim Alborn, Boris Maslov, Ilya Kliger, Kristina Huang, Bill Warner, Madeleine Dobie, Chris Hill, Chris Bush, Daniel O'Quinn, Elaine Freedgood, Dohra Ahmad, Chris Taylor, and Anjuli Raza Kolb gave me opportunities to present this project. Audiences at Brown University, Birkbeck College, University of London, the CUNY Graduate Center, the University of Pennsylvania, Columbia University's Maison Française, Columbia's Heyman Center for the Humanities, the University of Toronto, and New York University offered helpful feedback. Particular thanks to Betty Joseph, Sandra MacPherson, Ben Baer, Gauri Viswanathan,

Michael Allan, Tanya Agathocleus, Nancy Yousef, Suvir Kaul, the late Srinivas Aravamudan, Stathis Gourgouris, Ania Loomba, Ajay Rao, Veli Yashin, Joseph Massad, Moustafa Bayoumi, Paul Narkunas, Frank Crocco, Shireen Inayatulla, Sandra Cheng, and Claudia Pisano for their comments on these and other occasions. Informally, Teena Purohit responded to my inchoate ideas with wise advice. Stanford's external readers provided penetrating analyses both before I began the manuscript and after I had finished it. Shoumik Bhattacharya read the whole manuscript, expertly, in draft. It has greatly benefited as well from Christine Gever's awe-inspiring command of English, among other languages, and eagle-eyed editing skills. With equal expertise, Gigi Mark shepherded this book through Stanford's production process, and Stephanie Adams guided the press's effort to promote it.

I (really) couldn't have finished this book without a year-long Award for Faculty from the National Endowment for the Humanities, and I couldn't have received that fellowship without the support of Walter Blanco, Michael Dodson, and Tim Watson. Grants from CUNY's Research Foundation enabled me, among other things, to consult William Jones's manuscripts in the British Library and the National Library of Wales and to retranslate his many French translations of Hafiz in Aix-en-Provence. I'm deeply grateful to Olivier Coutagne for helping me with the latter task. An award from CUNY's Office of Research helped with publication costs.

The photograph of Shirin Abedinirad's stunning installation *Babel Tower* on this book's cover is used with her kind permission. I'm indebted to Rob Ehle, once again, for his beautiful artwork.

Sincere thanks also to Madeleine Dobie, Janet Sorenson, Chandan Reddy, Anna Neill, Bhavani Raman, Sanjay Krishnan, Claudio Pikielny, Adam Pikielny, Noah Pikielny, Paula Loscocco, Jessica Yood, Terrence Cheng, Earl Fendelman, Dierdre Pettipiece, Mario DiGangi, Carrie Hintz, David Richter, Gerhard Joseph, Ashley Dawson, Watson Brown, Carlos Austin, Jim Bain, Don Buerkle, Rohan Deb Roy, Hussaina Amina, Aminath Rahmah, Riyaz ur-Rahman, Fahima Farook, Ahmed Salahuddin, Rukaiya Salahuddin, Maryam Salahuddin, Aysha Haji, Noora Hameed, Rifa Hameed, Fathi Hameed, Maryam Abdul Cader, Mohamed Hussain, and Sharafa Sirajudeen for their support. Though the miles between us now prevent it, I wish I could linger with Nigel Alderman on another contemplative walk.

My parents, Syed and Muthu Ahmed, knew long before I did what an unwise career choice this would be but still now treat my single-mindedness with the deepest generosity and love.

I've dedicated this book to my sister, Yashi Ahmed, whose daily conversations (and perpetual joyfulness) keep me sane. She also happens to be the academic whose ethics I most admire, one who stubbornly treats science as a source of elegance and wonder, despite the corporate university's demands.

ARCHAEOLOGY OF BABEL

PROLOGUE

The research that led to this book began with a still-disregarded detail of English and comparative literary history. A late eighteenth-century British polymath single-handedly translated the most influential works, arguably, of the Persian, Arabic, and Sanskrit traditions. Displaying a mastery of Asian tongues even more improbable then, Sir William Jones published nuanced renderings of Hafiz in 1771, the *Mu'allaqāt* in 1782, and *Śakuntalā* in 1789. Though spread across two decades, these translations were part of a unified project: Jones intended them to revolutionize European poetry, releasing it from the grip of *ancien régime* neoclassicism. Just as he had hoped, Romantic writers both inside and outside England located radically different aesthetics in the works he translated and turned to them as models for their own poetry. Goethe in particular immersed himself in these works before he formulated the idea of *Weltliteratur*.

But if the seminal place of Jones's translations has been largely overlooked, they point to an even more disregarded history. Before they became part of Romanticism and world literature, these translations were the products of British colonial rule. Jones published each of them alongside philological studies that served the East India Company conquest of Bengal. These studies—including the first colonial grammar of an Asian language, codifications of both Muslim and Hindu law, and the discovery of the Indo-European language family—helped lay the groundwork for the philological revolution.

In fact, they disseminated its cardinal principles: language pertains to history, not divine providence or the laws of nature; each language produces its own history; and the history disclosed by literature belongs to national peoples. But the relationship between colonial rule and the philological revolution has been excised from disciplinary histories of the humanities. Hence, even postcolonial scholars have come around on the question of philology, insisting in ever larger numbers that it is, as Jones always suggested, a politically progressive method.

Many of those discussed in the Introduction and Conclusion to this book have, in fact, called for a return to philology. One irony of this call is that the philological revolution precipitated an epistemic transformation so vast that it has, in fact, never ceased to define the humanities. A second irony is that the new philology became so widespread and powerful precisely because of its own colonial history. The present study returns, therefore, not to the protocols of philology but rather to this suppressed history. As this focus makes clear, the new philology's global force lay in its singular capacity to comprehend every language, literature, and legal tradition—and hence to provide Europeans transhistorical and suprageographic knowledge about the colonized (among much else). The new philology was, in other words, the perfect method for both comparative scholars and colonial states. As Jones's work attests, philology's centuries-old claim to be emancipatory is itself a colonial legacy.

Philology had become entwined with the idea of human liberation even before the eighteenth century. From the late seventeenth century, linguists began to break with the idea of a universal grammar and to study languages historically instead. A century later, philosophers reconceived languages as archives of national spirit. Precisely these lines of argument enabled the East India Company to claim that its grammars of native languages and its codes of native law contained the popular will of its colonial subjects in opposition to the arbitrary power of despots, judges, and priests.

But Company scholars did not merely propagate a mutation in European knowledge; they adapted it to the demands of colonial rule. They used it not only to undercut clerical power but also, much more broadly, to obscure the diverse ontologies of texts that typified manuscript cultures. Before colonial rule, texts had not defined the law but rather served diverse functions within it: pedagogic, mnemonic, commentarial, and even contemplative. When the Company published certain manuscripts as the historically authentic version of the law, it disembedded these texts from all such practices, where they had undergone constant metamorphoses. It thus made both *shariʿa* and the *sastras* appear historically arrested and immutable. Jones's legal project explicitly depended on this operation: he demanded a law founded solely, in his words, on "original texts arranged in a scientific method."[1] This demand reflects the ancient philological approach Michel Foucault described in "My Body, This Paper, This Fire": "the reduction of discursive practices to textual traces; the elision of [events;] the retention only of marks for reading."[2] With the aid of the printing press and historical method, the Company made this approach a ruling principle. Texts became vessels of historical knowledge only on the condition that their own historicity be rendered invisible.

Jones's literary translations must be understood as another effect of the same dynamic. Like his legal codes, they each reduced a complex discursive practice to a standardized text. In fact, it is the substitution of a historically authoritative text for heterogeneous manuscripts and performances that constituted Hafiz, the *Muʿallaqāt*, and *Śakuntalā* as literature in the first place and hence instituted non-Western literatures. On a deeper level, though, the abstraction of texts from discursive practices produced historical knowledge in the modern sense: non-European texts enabled European scholars to reconstruct a global map of human history and hence to acquire total historical knowledge. If non-European literature was to free the republic of letters from the fetters of neoclassicism, it would do so, in Jones's view, by helping it think historically in this way. No less than his legal project, Jones's literary project thus required this substitution: he called on scholars across the continent to translate and publish the Oriental manuscripts that lay unstudied in European libraries.[3]

The Romantic category of literature that emerged—according to Jerome McGann, among many others—from Jones's work presented itself as a new literary practice freed from neoclassicism's bias toward privileged speech.[4] Relying on the nascent disciplines of archaeology, paleontology, geology, and, above all, philology, it aspired to read the history inscribed in every object and hence to give each form of life its own speech back. Like the law after its colonial codification, literature after its Romantic reconceptualization became a universal framework of representation, capable of subsuming every other language. The philological revolution against *anciens régimes* in both East and West turned immediately, in other words, into the rule of this historical consciousness, which was consequently identified with human liberation. Philology still possesses that identity in Erich Auerbach's and Edward Said's dialectically opposed concepts of comparatism. Colonialism's first trick is to make language appear to be the colonizer's possession. Its second trick, per Jacques Derrida, is the idea of "liberation," which internalizes the colonizer's concept of language within the colonized.[5] As the chapters that follow demonstrate, this colonial trick explains phenomena as apparently disparate and politically opposed as language-based racism, Islamic fundamentalism, Hindu nationalism, and the global discourses of environmentalism and indigeneity, all of which descend from colonial philology.

The problem for a properly postcolonial literary studies is, presumably, to move beyond colonial approaches to language and literature. Our failure to recognize the new philology as precisely such an approach may prevent us from seeing this problem clearly, much less solving it. Until we recognize the philological shift that began in late eighteenth-century colonial India, we may be condemned to play it out unconsciously, tacitly assuming that historical method and printed texts possess the power to comprehend every other discursive practice. We will observe this assumption program the arguments not just of the new philology's advocates, such as Auerbach and Said, but even of philosophers as diverse as Friedrich Nietzsche, Gilles Deleuze and Félix Guattari, Jacques Rancière, and Alain Badiou, all of whom take for granted philology's endless linguistic reach.

If we rejected this assumption, we might begin to discern the discursive practices philology has, in fact, failed to grasp. We would, in this way, push archaeological method further than even Nietzsche and Foucault were willing to. The point of archaeology is, of course, not to produce historical truth but rather to excavate the premises that qualify knowledge as truth in a given period and the "subjugated knowledges" these premises disqualified.[6] But if so, archaeology—designed by Nietzsche to be a counterphilological approach—should ultimately arrive at discursive practices completely bereft of philological power. This study thus attempts to take both archaeology and postcolonial criticism to their logical conclusion. What falls through the cracks of print and historicism is not, as Foucault implied, discursive practices as such. It is rather those particular practices that are oriented not toward the production of history but rather, we could say, toward its victims—discursive practices that, in other words, cede historical power and embrace an unhistorical existence instead. These practices leave no mark on the historical record and, as a consequence, absolutely cannot be seen from a new philological perspective. Yet, if the promise of postcolonial studies—in contradistinction to Marxism, for example—is to foster the autonomy of unhistorical lives, it must become sensitive to such practices, which alone articulate such lives.

We cannot simply identify these practices with the subalterns of a certain time and place. The practices in question here belong not to subalterns per se but rather to the conscious desire to remain non-elite. For example, each of the works Jones translated came to be identified with one or another type of subalternity: Hafiz with the medieval Sufi mystic, who embodied self-annihilating desire; the *Mu'allaqāt* with the pre-Islamic Bedouin nomad, who embodied nonstatist sovereignty; and *Śakuntalā* with the ancient Indian *adivasi*, who embodied the primordial earth. Mystic, nomad, *adivasi*: paradigmatic figures of unhistorical life—yet each of them was in fact implicated in the exercise of historical power. We need to see through all such subaltern figures to the discursive practices they appear to inscribe but in fact only efface. Hafiz linked his poetry not to Sufi mystics, who were in fact Shiraz's ruling elite, but instead to nameless *faqir*s who took the greatest pains imaginable to separate their lives from the law. Their spiritual path involved, paradoxically, both a ceaseless confrontation with legal authority and an absolute refusal to represent themselves in its terms. Though the *Mu'allaqāt* opposes nomadism to statism, such Bedouin poetry was actually composed for ceremonies of allegiance between tribal leaders and surrounding empires. It is instead the everyday poetry of Bedouin women that rejects the rituals of sovereign power. Devoted to expressing disaffection from male elders, it is heard only by women and youth. Neither composed nor recorded, it exists in singular performances, as evanescent as the feelings that occasion them. *Śakuntalā* counterposes the earth, represented by the sacred grove, to sovereign violence. In fact, though, such groves were produced by Brahman sacrifice, which burned the forests, cleared its *adivasi* and animal populations, and extended royal territory. Yet *adivasi*s also sometimes served as the advance guard of Indo-European expansion. A truly ecological sensibility belonged neither to sacred groves nor to *adivasi*s in general but rather to the necessarily prehistorical refusal of *all* human appropriation—even the placement of anthropomorphic deities—except what was necessary for bare survival.

In each of these examples, the practice that ultimately lends the literary work its meaning is something philology cannot place. Each of these practices not only resisted being recorded but, furthermore, disavowed all philological power in order to pursue a fundamentally different form of life. This point applies not just to the specific works Jones translated but also to the broader fields they helped constitute, including Romantic literature, world literature, and non-Western literatures. These concepts of literature, descending to us from the new philology, tacitly claim that literature inscribes historically excluded languages. But this claim appropriates to literature languages that belong to antithetical practices. Though these practices often inform the new-philological concept of literature, they are categorically disjunct from it: they resist not just literary inscription but historical transmission of any kind. Paradoxically, then, the languages that supposedly distinguish literature in the modern sense can neither be reconstructed philologically nor even located historically. They belong not to historical figures but rather to the discursive practices such figures inscribe—and, in the very act of inscription, always efface. Without fetishizing literature at all, we could insist that something fundamental to it lies outside history and consequently cannot be approached philologically. As Louis Althusser observed, "The invisible of a visible field is [not] outside and foreign[.] The invisible is defined by the visible as *its* invisible, *its* forbidden vision[:] the *inner darkness* of exclusion, inside the visible itself."[7]

But even as they attempt to discern within the history of literature, law, and religion what philology has obscured, the chapters that follow would have been absolutely impossible without the extraordinary erudition and painstaking research of countless philologists working in many different languages and widely disparate traditions. Similarly, even as I claim that many of the postcolonial scholars and European philosophers most admired today remain trapped within the philological mindset, their theories provide the inspiration behind, when they do not form the foundation of, my own arguments. Needless to say, none of us are free, none of us to blame. But the traces within texts of the discursive practices that rejected all linguistic authority return us to a power that is, in my view, much more profound than philology. If we begin to study these traces, we will use literary studies, now inextricably tied to print technology and historical method, to create an opening for the languages they were designed to erase. We might in this way gradually disentangle the postcolonial humanities from their still-unconsidered and hence unresolved colonial legacy. Now more than ever, doing so has become a politically urgent task, as I explain in what follows.

☙

The story of late eighteenth-century colonial philology is an unexamined part of a familiar and ever more pressing history: the reorientation of humanity's relationship with the earth from subsistence to profit; the transformation of rights to its common use into private property. In the British Isles and Western Europe, the commercialization of people's relationships with each other, their own labor, and the land had been occurring since the Middle Ages. As a consequence, English common law had largely subsumed the islands' diverse concepts of common right into an abstract idea of property by the late eighteenth century.[8] The British Empire spread this definition of property—that is, the absolute and unqualified ownership of both territory and its use—first to the Americas and the Scottish Highlands, then eventually to Asia, the South Pacific, and the Antipodes. In the latter contexts, colonial administrators needed, in effect, to recapitulate English history, turning common use into exclusive property, in a matter of years rather than centuries. Hence, in these territories, it was often the law itself, not merchant capital, that first inducted hunter-gatherers, pastoralists, peasants, feudal lords, and so forth into capitalist property. The law's "most ambitious project" to institute English property—according to a no less authoritative work on this subject than E. P. Thompson's *Customs in Common*—took place in India during the late eighteenth century.[9]

Common rights vary widely across time and space and hence tend to be transmitted orally. The "translation" of such rights into the universal, written medium of private property is, according to Thompson, a "central episode" of "global ecological history."[10] The shift from one to the other has led to the earth's unrestrained privatization and pushed us beyond the brink of ecological catastrophe.

Thompson nonetheless concluded his monograph on English enclosure, *Whigs and Hunters*, with a surprisingly impassioned defense of capitalist property law *against* its Marxist detractors. Though it eventually came to legitimize dispossession, property law was used by seventeenth-century merchants, small farmers, and craftsmen as "a defence against arbitrary power."[11] Thompson called the law's "inhibitions upon power" a "cultural achievement of *universal* significance" and an "unqualified *human* good."[12] In contrast to his Marxist colleagues, Thompson emphasized the "very large difference, which twentieth-century experience ought to have made clear even to the most exalted thinker, between arbitrary extra-legal power and the rule of law."[13]

As I observe in my own Conclusion, many scholars have questioned whether there ever was any such difference in Europe's colonies. And Thompson himself acknowledged a colonial exception: "In a context of gross class inequalities, the equity of the law must always be in some part sham. Transplanted as it was to even more inequitable contexts, this law could be an instrument of imperialism."[14] But he tempered even this condemnation: "The rules and rhetoric have imposed some inhibitions on imperial power. If the rhetoric was a mask, it was a mask which Gandhi and Nehru were to borrow, at the head of a million masked supporters."[15] Thompson here extolled the (colonial) rule of law because it supposedly inspired revolution— even if such inspiration masked revolution in colonialism's very image.

The vision of a million rule-of-law masked Indians thus raises questions about the law's "universal significance" and "unqualified human" value that Thompson did not address. First, if the rule of law inhibited "power," did it not therefore limit the political praxis of revolution as well as the ruling classes, and if so, how? Second, is there no salient difference in this regard between colonial law and its metropolitan kin? Thompson considered the law—not religion, print culture, capitalist markets, or even military power—to be the eighteenth century's hegemonic institution. He astutely observed that, due to the previous century's battles against arbitrary power, eighteenth-century English law had its own "history and logic" irreducible to ruling-class ideology: the rule of law was not just a superstructure but itself a material force.[16] But that century of struggle was manifestly not responsible for the institution of colonial law. How can we grasp the colonies' different materiality, history, and logic?

This study concerns the difference introduced by philology, which in late eighteenth-century British India took the place of struggles against arbitrary power in the definition of property. Though Thompson overlooks this fact, the "translation" from common to private rights could not have been accomplished in colonial India without philology, which alone claimed the linguistic and historical competence necessary to reconstruct Islamic and Hindu law. As they rewrote Arabic and Sanskrit legal manuscripts in terms of modern property, colonial scholars aimed less to protect prescriptive rights from extralegal power than to transform the structure of tradition itself. They dictated that, henceforward, authentic tradition would exist only in philologically reconstructed texts and be understood only by historical method. In this way, they eroded natives' capacity to recall the extratextual practices that had helped constitute precolonial traditions and that might otherwise inform anticolonial thought. Perhaps the image of Gandhi and Nehru at the head of a million followers is instructive in this regard. They were both British-trained barristers whose understanding of Indian legal traditions had less to do with indigenous practices than with colonial knowledge, as I explain in the chapters that follow. In any case, though, the aim of this study is neither (like Thompson's Marxist interlocutors) to dismiss nor (like Thompson's Marxist heresy) to defend the rule of law. It is instead to explore the effects colonial law and, even more fundamentally, philology and historical method have had on our very capacity to imagine political resistance.

This book focuses, therefore, on historical method's forgotten colonial history. For reasons already adduced and to be elaborated in much greater detail, this history first took root in late eighteenth-century British India. But though the chapters that follow critique historical method, their intention is not to reject it *tout court*. In fact, whenever they use the term "historical method," they refer only to the language-based approach to humanity's origins and development that emerged with the philological revolution and served as the epistemic foundation of colonial rule. Adapting Theodor Adorno and Max Horkheimer's idea of "instrumental reason" in *The Dialectic of Enlightenment*, we could thus call this method "instrumental philology."[17]

Its fundamental premise is that language is not the reflection of an a priori reality but rather itself originary. The philological revolution presupposed, in other words, that every language shapes the development of the particular people, culture, nation, et cetera that corresponds to it: studying the evolution of the former unlocked the historical truth of the latter. Thompson himself wrote, for instance, that "most Western intellectuals today would unhesitatingly award theoretical primacy to [language] as not only the carrier but as the constitutive influence upon consciousness[;] It has become fashionable to assume that [common people are] in a sense 'spoken' by their linguistic inheritance."[18] Each of the philological revolution's signal innovations—comparative grammar, the divisions of languages into families, and the reconstruction of protolanguages—presupposed that languages were originary (or constituent) in this way. The rigorously historical approach to language that the philological revolution elaborated was thought, furthermore, to comprehend every kind of discursive practice and by extension every language, law, and literature, which would have otherwise remained heterogeneous and incommensurable. Finally, this approach equated the truth of every tradition—those that held power and hence must be critiqued as well as those that existed in its shadow and hence must be brought to light—with written, if not printed, texts. These interrelated premises—the only historical method this book questions—were fundamental to British rule in India precisely because they held the key to knowledge about its colonial subjects.

Yet one cannot overstate this method's broader significance. By virtue of its ability to make definite historical claims about religions and laws, ethnicities and races, traditions and indeed whole civilizations, the new philology helped give rise to the modern humanities. It underpins the authority of text-based academics today as much as it did colonial administrators centuries ago. Even when humanities scholars no longer invoke the new philology, we almost always tacitly presuppose historical premises it has passed down. Such presuppositions are evident not just in literary studies but in religion, jurisprudence, European philosophy, and historiography proper, among other disciplines. But even as the humanities still emphasize historicism, they tend to dis-identify from philology. I hope that calling the object of this book's critique "historical method" will, therefore, help us see ourselves as inheritors of a colonial legacy.

But rather than rejecting historical approaches as such, the chapters that follow try, on the contrary, to dissociate them from their colonial uses. They do so by using literary history, many different forms of historiography, and even philological learning itself not ultimately to produce historical knowledge about a given period or people but rather to understand what such knowledge constitutively excludes. These chapters argue that when we treat textually transmitted languages as originary, we cast out from history all those who did not possess, or did not want, the power to produce texts. Instead of treating textual discourses as originary, I take account of the philological formations—that is, scholarly and sovereign power relations—that produced the texts (and supposedly originary languages) under investigation. Following Nietzsche, I call this counterphilological method "archaeology." An archaeological approach reveals that the texts we now identify with religions, nations, civilizations, and so on are the products not of such generalities but instead of very particular contests over the possession of philological power. Read archaeologically, these texts become palimpsests of such contests, repeated ad infinitum across time. If we reconceived "history" in this way, as an endless series of philological conflicts that have defined and ceaselessly redefine the very terms of our historical imagination, our histories might finally attend to what philology has traditionally obscured: those who were bereft of philological power. Such attention is at the heart of the historical method for which this book calls, one that brushes philology—and, by extension, the postcolonial humanities—against the grain.

I add one final step to this archaeological approach. As I've already suggested, literature comprises not only languages that possessed philological power but also the trace of those that abjured it altogether. The long, final section in each of the book's three central chapters follows this trace. The philological revolution called for the recovery of languages that lay outside the previous history of philological power, languages that had been silenced or marginalized because, for example, of their radically anticlerical or democratic character. This call of course still provides the humanities much of their ethical energy. My book tries to respond to it even more scrupulously than the new philology itself did. It tries to think through, in other words, precisely what discursive practices count as the antitheses of philological power. If we can use literature to help us imagine what philology cannot recover, we might begin to realize both the new philology's highest ideals and archaeology's counterphilological ambitions.

My task is not, therefore, to recover popular traditions from high culture and elitist historiography. I am not a social historian, nor is this book, à la *Customs in Common*, a study of "plebeian culture."[19] As a literary scholar, I'm concerned instead to consider those discursive practices whose negation is the precondition of the new philology, literary history, and the humanities' epistemic authority. What defines the practices I oppose to philological power is not, therefore, their customary character but rather their opposition to textual authority: because these practices without exception shunned literary inscription and historical transmission, they cannot, in contrast to Thompson's customs, be reconstructed historiographically. Yet far from invisible, their traces are practically ever present, if often difficult to see. The precolonial legal and literary traditions studied here do not merely invoke but appear often to have depended on them. And the scholarship on these texts, traditions, and periods frequently alludes to them, though without being able to describe them rigorously. In other words, the discursive practices of those who abjured textual authority, however imperceptible the modern humanities have rendered them, appear to have shaped premodern traditions in ways we can now barely comprehend.

Thompson insisted that those Marxists who reject the rule of law "throw away a whole inheritance of struggle *about* law, and within the forms of law."[20] But the European rule of law hardly exhausts the possibilities for such struggle. The discursive practices I discuss, no less than Thompson's customs, existed at the "interface between law and praxis" and defended local traditions from "the constraints and controls" of the "rulers."[21] But these practices preceded the European rule of law and thus refute Thompson's premise that its institution must be recognized as a "universal" and "unqualified human" good. Thompson hoped studying what he called "customary pre-enclosure consciousness" would prepare the way for the "unlikely advent of a new 'customary consciousness'" in which "material satisfactions remain stable [but] more equally distributed."[22] Yet pre-enclosure custom was itself, as Thompson acknowledged, "parochial and exclusive": it was "the rhetoric of legitimation for almost any usage, practice or demanded right."[23] It follows that the consciousness of the common Thompson wanted to encourage requires practices different from what he studied. Those I have in mind, in contrast to Thompson's customs, never needed "juridical endorsement" because they did not aim to be exclusive.[24]

Some may consider my advocacy of these practices romantic. Such criticism would fundamentally misunderstand their ontology. To romanticize is to reify or idealize a historical entity. My starting point is not history: I did not arrive at my descriptions of these discursive practices by studying an empirical object (nor do my descriptions presume to explain any such object). I arrived at them instead by working back from the philological revolution through various non-Western legal and literary traditions in an effort to discern the traditional practices the new philology cannot see. These practices are, therefore, ideal from the beginning: they are what I posit to be the philological revolution's negative image. Only such an imaginative act can realize the new philology's ambition to recover the languages that prior philology had ignored. More to the point, only those discursive practices that resist textual authority can, it seems to me, fulfill the humanities' own radically democratic—one could say, romantic—ideals.

The conclusion to this study turns to a subject—states of emergency—one might assume belongs to politics today, not the late eighteenth century. In fact, though, the rule of law in colonial India devolved almost immediately into the states of emergency the East India Company imposed on frontier populations. No less than colonial philology, these colonial emergencies facilitated the earth's reorientation from subsistence to profit and from common use to private property. The Company called those natives who did not want to participate in its political economy threats to security; it met their resistance with the circumscriptions of habeas corpus, martial law, and ecological violence.[25] This colonial logic—wherein property and law metamorphose into environmental devastation and emergency—still defines conflicts throughout the peripheries. Within India alone, in places such as Bastar, Kalinganagar, and Kashmir, mining and hydroelectric projects depend on the army's and police's emergency powers, often to kill those deemed terrorists merely "on suspicion."[26] Multinational corporations thus clear forests and villages of *adivasi*s and peasants in order to explode mountaintops or erect colossal dams. Progress here merely returns to colonialism's script, with today's conglomerates playing the merchant company's part.

Studying late eighteenth-century British India can thus help us understand philology's relationship to emergency. Each of this book's central
chapters explores how British scholars attempted to circumscribe legal authority within the colonial state. The transfer of such authority from the
people to the executive is of course the very definition of emergency: the executive (or "sovereign") proclaims the polity to be in danger, suspends the
constitution, and declares unilaterally the extraordinary laws that govern in
its place. On the level of colonial history, therefore, philology both prefigured
and facilitated the institution of emergency. On a deeper level, philology's
affinity with emergency is immemorial. The usurpation of philological power
is the ancient prerogative of priests and clerics, the arrogation of emergency
powers that of sovereigns and kings.[27] But both practices serve to articulate
the law (during, respectively, peace and war)—or, put differently, to preserve
social hierarchy and unequal distribution.[28]

Philology anticipates emergency, finally, because it expresses the ruler's
ambivalence toward language's constituent power. On one hand, the new
philology drew attention to language's "performative" dimension: language
does not describe but rather constitutes reality; language is, as mentioned,
originary, the quasi-mystical foundation of politics and history.[29] But, on
the other hand, the new philology located language's constituent power only
in those texts historical method had reconstructed and explained. Since the
philological revolution, such texts have always been identified with the tradition or literary history under investigation. The most important of the many
examples discussed in this study are, of course, Jones's Islamic and Hindu
legal codes, which the East India Company intended to regulate Arabic's
and Sanskrit's law-making power. States of emergency likewise appropriate
language's constituent power, which they locate, similarly, within sovereign
command or "decision" alone.[30] Like the new philology, states of emergency
presuppose that politics ultimately has no foundation more firm than language but recoil from the radical consequences of this fact.

Yet these analogies between philology (i.e., the methodological foundation of the humanities) and emergency (i.e., the global deposition of
democracy today) are difficult to see because we reflexively consider new
philological concepts of language the very antithesis of extralegal sovereignty.
William Keach has tracked both terms of this opposition back to the late

seventeenth century. In regard to the former, John Locke's *Essay Concerning Human Understanding* observes, famously, that words do not refer, "naturally," to things but rather are "imposed" by people, "arbitrarily," on their ideas.[31] In regard to the latter, his *Second Treatise of Government* argues, just as momentously, that sovereignty must not take the form of "an Absolute, Arbitrary Power over [Men's] Lives and Fortunes."[32] By the Romantic era, these apparently unrelated forms of "arbitrary power"—linguistic performativity and unconstitutional sovereignty—had become diametrically opposed to each other. Whereas the former was believed to join rule to "the represented will" of the people, the latter severs them from each other again.[33] Hence, in Burke's *Enquiry*, language possesses an "immediate affective power" that, in his later works, helps constitute national "habit" and "custom."[34] Similarly, across his works, from the *Lyrical Ballads* to *The Prelude*, Wordsworth opposed the "language really used by men" to "despotick" or lawless power.[35] Blake and Shelley also aligned language's performative dimension—its "visionary power," its capacity "to act"—with "popular power" against British monarchic and imperial tyranny, from the 1780 Gordon Riots to the 1819 Peterloo massacre (when the British state effectively suspended the law and declared an emergency).[36]

At the same time, the Romantics confined language's constituent power within "poetic agency."[37] The Romantic category of literature thus popularized the new philological fallacy that written texts and "the literary" are paradigmatic of radical democracy.[38] This fallacy persists across the humanities, as my Conclusion illustrates with examples from eminent figures in comparative literature, religion, anthropology, history, and even French philosophy. Searching for the antitheses of antidemocratic politics or coloniality, these scholars are limited, in the end, to rehearsing discourses about language and literature inherited from Romanticism and stereotypes about non-Western cultures passed down by colonial philology. In every case, their varied efforts to exit the history of Western politics or colonial knowledge reach a methodological impasse. One way out would follow the faint tracks of those practices that resisted the lure of cultural prestige and sovereign power and that consequently were never recognized as literature or history in the first place.

The point of conflict in any emergency turns, in essence, on the possession of language's constituent power—on the question of who can suspend the constituted law and thus live *autonomously*, in the literal sense of the word. In their debate about emergency, Carl Schmitt assigned this power solely to the sovereign, whereas Walter Benjamin insisted it belongs instead to those who exercise it democratically, whom he called the "oppressed" and the "anonymous."[39] Trained as both a jurist and a philologist, Schmitt argued law philologically, in terms of Europe's hegemonic tongues.[40] In pointed contrast, Benjamin's invocations of the oppressed and the anonymous gestured toward those recognized by neither the law nor philology, those who had lost their economic rights and their place in history, those whose traditions existed therefore in a real, and perpetual, state of emergency. His final essay, "On the Concept of History," explicitly opposes both the protocols of historicism *and* the practice of emergency. It implies that the antithesis of extralegal sovereignty is neither the rule of law nor linguistic performativity but rather traditions that embraced their exclusion from both the law and history, traditions we text-based scholars conventionally ignore. I close the book by studying this essay, trying to grasp, yet again, at a fugitive power that could overcome the politics of philology and of emergency at once.

INTRODUCTION

The Colonial History of Comparative Method

In our culture, which lacks specific categories for spiritual transmission[,] it has
always fallen to philology [*alla filologia è da sempre affidato il compito*] to guarantee
the authenticity and continuity of the cultural tradition. This is why a knowledge of
philology's essence and history should be a precondition of all literary education;
yet this very knowledge is hard to find even among philologists. Instead, as far as
philology is concerned, confusion and indifference reign.

Giorgio Agamben, Infancy and History: On the Destruction of Experience

Philologism is the inevitable distinguishing mark of the whole of European
linguistics[.] However far back we may go in tracing the history of linguistic categories and methods, we find philologists everywhere. Not just the Alexandrians,
but the ancient Romans were philologists, as were the Greeks (Aristotle is a typical
philologist). Also, the ancient Hindus were philologists.

V. N. Volosinov, Marxism and the Philosophy of Language

I know the philologists [*Ich kenne sie*]: I am myself one of them.

Friedrich Nietzsche, "We Philologists"

For more than three decades now, leading scholars across diverse fields of
literary studies have advanced the argument that philology is the indispensable basis of the humanities. These scholars have called for, variously, a *return
to philology* (de Man, 1982; Johnson, 1990; Patterson, 1994; Holquist, 2002;
Culler, 2002; Gumbrecht, 2003; Said, 2004); a *future* or *new philology* (Nichols, 1990; Wenzel, 1990; Restall, 2003; Pollock, 2009; McGann, 2013); a *critical philology* (Mignolo, 1995; Clines, 1998; Harpham, 2009; Brennan, 2014);
and a *radical philology* (Bal, 1987; Gurd, 2005; Mufti, 2010).[1] An irony of the

repeated admonition not to forget philology is that philology has in fact never ceased to be hegemonic in the humanities. Though the Romantic-era philological revolution has been critiqued from various quarters, its central premises still reign supreme: every language undergoes historical change; all knowledge of the human domain must therefore be historical; and historical knowledge presupposes a historically specific understanding of the language being studied.

Disciplinary genealogies of literary studies—such as those written by Michael Warner, Gerald Graff, and John Guillory—argue that early nineteenth-century German linguistics pioneered the new philology, which rose to scholarly hegemony in the late nineteenth-century research university.[2] But these accounts overlook the fact that late eighteenth-century colonial scholars had already reorganized Indian society on a philological model. These scholars learned India's sacred languages (Persian, Arabic, and Sanskrit); decided which religious manuscripts would become authoritative; translated, edited, and printed them; and made their precepts binding law. Tradition suddenly became text-based, standardized, philologically defined, and state-administered. The new philology acquired global reach and authority only because colonial rule reconstructed traditions around the world on a historical foundation.

The invocation of philology as the humanities' necessary basis thus unwittingly hews to colonial policy. Indeed, this book's argument is that the historical mission of philology reached fulfillment with the establishment of colonial law. If so, the study of colonial law should enable us not to continue extending the history of philology indefinitely but to envision an antithetical approach instead.

The prevailing view, expressed most prominently by Edward Said, is that historical method is the essence of secular criticism and hence indispensable for human emancipation. In fact, though, historiographical "science" emerged originally within the walls of the early modern European state and was expected, in the words of Michel de Certeau, to align "the truth of the letter with the efficacy of power."[3] In the colonies as well, sovereign power used historical method to arrogate authority over tradition to itself: the East India Company proclaimed that its legal codes alone articulated Islam's and Hinduism's authentic laws. But religious authority had never been principally textual in precolonial India. It had instead been embodied by clerics who constantly reinterpreted the tradition from within the fold of particular communities. Texts were primarily educational tools in the construction of the cleric's personal authority. Interpretations that no longer formed part of the written canon were said to survive in the cleric's memory, from where they could reemerge when the community needed them. In diametric opposition, the Company used its codes to argue that clerical knowledge and social custom were historically corrupt.

Historical method identified the truth of every tradition with written texts and the meaning of every text with a historically specific and philologically recuperable content. But these traditions were in fact too diverse to be comprehended by any single analytic framework, historicist or otherwise. They need to be understood not in terms of written (much less printed) texts but instead in terms of discursive practices: that is, radically heterogeneous instances of language in use, where both the form of language and its conceptual relationship to reality varied from one tradition to another. In some cases, the discursive practice was primarily oral: for example, the chanting of the Vedic mantras, which was thought to be more powerful than the Gods themselves; or the Sufic recitation of God's name, which made labor a devotional act and a sacred experience. In other cases, the discursive practice was partly scribal: the dharmasastric manuscripts that were considered to be the inscription of sacred discourses but which varied across both time and space; or the *shari'a* manuals that, though now identified with Islamic law, never presumed to be more than one school's historically and geographically limited interpretation thereof. The discursive practice could also be largely performative: not only the embodied authority of Brahmanic and Islamic jurists but also the staging of dramatic and poetic compositions in court, which were often intended to reconstitute sovereign subjectivity itself. Colonial philology reduced or subordinated all these varied practices to the printed text, which would underpin the epistemic authority of the colonial administrator and the modern scholar alike. For Company officials, as for us, historical truth became synonymous with authentic texts.

The problem with this symptomatically philological premise is that texts never correspond to any general history: they are produced not by social collectivities but rather by hegemonic classes. They are, in fact, the joint

legacies of the many elite orders that have succeeded each other in the transmission of tradition across history, long before the advent of colonial rule.
Even in the most ancient civilizations, priest-philologists claimed the singular
capacity to define the true meaning of the sacred language, which was always,
according to Volosinov, "foreign and incomprehensible to the profane."[4] The
legal manuscripts the Company codified were precisely the products of such
philological power. In the very process of marginalizing the native clerisy,
colonial philologists inherited their legacy and disseminated many of their
values. Whenever we likewise take texts to represent history, we make ourselves one more link in an unbroken chain of philological power. Historical
method promised to emancipate humanity from all preexisting forms of clerical authority but in fact extended the reign of such authority. It made itself
the reigning form.

At the inception of every new phase in the history of philology, one form
of philological power marginalized another. Colonial law merely took this
history to its logical conclusion: it attempted to deauthorize *every* other type
of philological power. It is in this sense that colonial law fulfilled philology's
historical mission. It made the new philology the continuation of conquest
by other means. It is no coincidence therefore that Sir William Jones (1746–
94), the late eighteenth-century colonial jurist who codified colonial law, is
also given credit for founding the new philology. A dialectical response to
colonial history must seek, therefore, neither for a return to philology nor
for a future philology but rather for a way out. It would need to search, in
other words, between the lines of the received tradition for what philology
has effaced.

1. The Return to Philology, the End of Weltliteratur

For postcolonial scholars, the most influential call for a return to philology occurred in a lecture that Said originally delivered in 2000 and which
he rethought after the US invasions of Afghanistan and Iraq (published
posthumously as "The Return to Philology" in *Humanism and Democratic
Criticism*). But the postcolonial recuperation of philology via Said has taken
its cue from not just this essay but also his career-long engagement with
Erich Auerbach's work, spanning from his co-translation of "Philologie der
Weltliteratur" in 1969 to his reintroduction of *Mimesis* in 2003.[5] Auerbach

symbolized for Said both the possibilities and limitations of Romance philology or, in other words, traditional approaches to comparatism. On one
hand, Said presented Auerbach's philological method as a model of "secular
criticism."[6] Auerbach's alienation from Germany in particular, nationalism
in general, and orthodoxies of all sorts enabled him to transform humanism,
making it responsive to contingency, exile, and minority experience.[7] But, on
the other hand, Said acknowledged that Auerbach's concept of "literature"
was, nonetheless, "Eurocentric," with its roots in the Christian incarnation
and its first efflorescence in *The Divine Comedy*.[8] Where Auerbach famously
wrote that "our philological home is the earth: it can no longer be the nation,"
Said added an acid qualification: "his earthly home is European culture."[9]

The calls for new approaches to philology, *Weltliteratur*, and comparative
literature that have followed in Said's wake have not directly addressed the
question that underlies his engagement with Auerbach: how can "literature,"
a concept with a strictly European provenance, ever hope to be adequate to
non-European forms of writing? Jacques Derrida observed that "when we
say *literature*[,] we speak and make ourselves understood on the basis of a
Latin root[.] There [is] no world literature, if such a thing is or remains to
come that must not first inherit what this Latinity assumes."[10] He asked,
therefore, what we mean when we say "literature": "Is it only a [mode] specific to the little thing that is Europe? Or else is it already the *Weltliteratur*,
whose concept was forged by Goethe?"[11] In other words, do we understand
our concept of literature to be spatially and temporally bounded, or do we
believe it to be universal instead? Until we address this question, there is
little reason to hope that any "new" comparative literature will do more than
repeat the prejudices of the old.

In this regard, the problem with philology—which Said described as "the
most basic and creative of the interpretive arts"—might be even deeper than
he was willing to acknowledge.[12] Auerbach claimed that his final essays were
responses to the homogenizing force of capitalism and the Cold War:

> [My] conception of *Weltliteratur*[—]the diverse background of a common
> fate—does not seek to affect or alter that which has already begun to occur[;
> it] accepts as an inevitable fact that world-culture is being standardized. Yet
> this conception wishes [to] articulate the fateful coalescence of cultures for

those people who are in the midst of the terminal phase of a fruitful multi-plicity: thus this coalescence, so rendered and articulated, will become their myth. In this manner, the full range of the spiritual movements of the last thousand years will not atrophy within them.[13]

Said described Auerbach's attitude toward the advent of modernity as "melanchol[ic]" and "tragic."[14] But if so, this passage nonetheless reveals that Auerbach had little interest in opposing the global tendencies he described: they are, he insisted, "inevitable" (*unentrinnbar*).[15] According to his own historical vision, *Weltliteratur*—for Auerbach, the product of different cultures entering into "fruitful intercourse"—is not coming into existence but, on the contrary, going extinct: it is now nothing more than "the diverse background of a common fate." Auerbach faced the ongoing extinction of literary diversity with equanimity: his own conception of world literature "does not seek to alter or affect" its predestined passing away. The aim of his philological work was not to protect cultures endangered by global standardization but, on the contrary, to document their end and so turn them into a "myth" that would provide an otherwise standardized humanity "spiritual" inspiration. In Auerbach's work, in other words, philology becomes a New Age religion.

I would suggest that Auerbach accepted the supposed passing away of world literature not despite but because of his philological vocation. Like Said, he placed its origins in the eighteenth century, when philology underwent a fundamental mutation.[16] The European encounter with countless non-European languages and archaic literatures initiated the new philology, which identified the genealogy of every nation with the history of its language.[17] The new philology presumed, as a consequence, to reconstruct not just authentic texts but at the same time the development of different peoples. Philology's task metamorphosed from the recovery of a single tradition—whether Judeo-Christian or Greco-Roman—into the reconstruction of *all* traditions.[18] Hence, in Auerbach's view, the new philology comprehended humanity in its historical complexity and "totality":

Our knowledge of world literatures is indebted to the impulse given that epoch by historicist humanism[, whose concern] was not only the overt discovery of materials and the development of methods of research, but [their] penetration and evaluation so that an inner history of mankind—[of] man unified in his multiplicity—could be written. [T]his humanism has been the true purpose of philology: because of this purpose philology became the dominant branch of the humanities.[19]

In other words, the recognition of human diversity depends, paradoxically, on a single analytic method, which arrogates to itself the privilege of knowing history objectively: "The progress of the historical arts in the last two centuries [makes] it possible to accord the various epochs and cultures their own presuppositions."[20]

From this perspective, literatures bereft of historical consciousness are inherently "programmed to vanish," superseded by a philological understanding capable of containing them all imaginatively even in their material absence.[21] It is, therefore, not only market economies and Cold War politics that render such literatures obsolete but also Auerbach's own methodological premises: "Whatever we are," he insisted, "we became in history, and only in history can [we] develop therefrom: it is the task of philologists [*Weltphilologen*] to demonstrate this so that it penetrates our lives unforgettably."[22]

This chapter argues that the privilege Auerbach and Said accord historical consciousness over every other form—we could call it their shared philological prejudice—begins with their understanding of historical method's own history.[23] "Historicist humanism" originally emerged, in Auerbach's account, from the eighteenth-century realization of the world's linguistic diversity, which made theological approaches to language obsolete. European philologists responded to this realization by attempting to create a narrative of "man unified in his multiplicity."[24] Auerbach presents the history of the new philology, therefore, as a three-term teleology: European secularization naturally produces "historicist humanism," which elaborates, in turn, a single method to comprehend languages, literatures, and traditions in their totality. But this history omits its own colonial matrix: no less than Renaissance humanism, the new philology came into being as the scholarly protocol of sovereign power.[25] Only under this pressure did it engender what Hans-Georg Gadamer referred to as its "universal hermeneutics."[26] In order, therefore, to call Auerbach's and Said's account of philology into question, this book returns to the eighteenth-century moment in which they both located the new philology's origins but which neither explored.

Even those philologists—including Sheldon Pollock and Haruko Momma—who have acknowledged the new philology's roots to lie in late eighteenth-century British India have not teased out the political implications of this fact.[27] The historical approach to language and literature enabled British scholars to reconstruct South Asia's otherwise incommensurable traditions and use them to legitimize colonial power. Said's secular criticism, no less than Auerbach's philological erudition, was silently determined by a related ambition, the dream of a universal discourse that would contain the diversity of tongues—in Auerbach's words, the "fruitful multiplicity" of literatures now in their "terminal phase" (*Endstadium*). This dream took various forms after colonial rule: nineteenth-century philologists such as Ernest Renan and Max Müller dreamt of recovering the original Aryan language, while twentieth-century critics such as Auerbach and Ernst Robert Curtius searched for a scholarly method that would be equally foundational.

But the origins of such dreams were in fact much older: the idea of a universal discourse begins with Babel.

2. The Ruins of Babel, the Rise of Philology

Babel's significance is obscure to us now because its meaning shifted fundamentally in the early nineteenth century, when Hegel reinterpreted the Old Testament chapter in which it occurs (Genesis 11) as the ur-narrative of progress.[28] While the people of Shinar fail to complete the Tower of Babel, their attempt leads, however unintentionally, to their dispersal across the earth and the production of linguistic and cultural difference, which is, according to Hegel, the precondition of historical development. In the process, humanity loses touch, of course, with the language it had spoken before the Tower's destruction and its own diaspora. Hegel had as little interest in that language as he did in every other prehistory, claiming that once Adam and Eve consume the fruit of knowledge, "Paradise is a park, where only brutes [*die Tiere*], not men, can remain."[29]

But before Hegel, from the Middle Ages through the eighteenth century, the dream of a lost divine language had bewitched churchmen and heretics alike. Biblical hermeneutics was an attempt to decipher the signs of that lost language, regardless of whether the exegetes aimed to restore the sacred text concealed within the rabbis' allegedly corrupt Bible or intended instead to contest the Church's own misinterpretations. These attempts to recover the language that preceded the destruction of the Tower culminated in Bishop Lowth's "Lectures on the Sacred Poetry of the Hebrews" (Latin 1756; English translation 1787), which applied the techniques of classical philology to the Old Testament in order to free "Hebraic poetry" from its supposed imprisonment within the synagogue and to recover its sacred power—to recover, in short, the original and "mystically perfect" language.[30] From the Middle Ages to the eighteenth century, at any rate, the importance of Babel lay in its allusion to humanity's oldest tongue—in Umberto Eco's words, "first-born and, consequently, supernatural"—which as the mirror of nature and divine creation would enable humanity to transcend its linguistic confusion.[31]

While Hebrew was generally thought to be the oldest language throughout this period, ancient rumors still circulated of sacred languages as old as or even older than Hebrew and of revelations that had occurred outside the Judeo-Christian tradition, whether from the Magi, Chaldean oracles, Egyptian Thoth cults, or the Pythagorean and Orphic traditions. European colonialism reactivated such rumors, with missionaries and explorers sending detailed accounts of exotic languages from the New World (e.g., Nahuatl) to the Far East (e.g., Tagalog) and greatly expanding the European comprehension of global linguistic and cultural diversity as a consequence.[32] The Europe-wide interest in languages such as these attested to a common desire to replace or at least supplement the Christian scholarly practice of writing "universal histories"—which discounted all literatures outside the Judeo-Christian tradition—with other ways of conceiving humanity's material and spiritual development.

It was, however, a singular event in late eighteenth-century colonial India that definitively transformed Europe's understanding of Babel. In 1783, Sir William Jones—Europe's leading Orientalist and arguably the Enlightenment's greatest polymath—was appointed to the English East India Company supreme court in Bengal. His time there enabled him to add Sanskrit to the remarkably long list of languages—ancient and modern, Oriental and European—in his grasp. Two years after he arrived in Calcutta, Jones made the programmatic declaration that Sanskrit, Persian, Greek, and Latin were descended from a single common language as old as but apparently unrelated to Hebrew. His formulation of what has since

come to be known as the "Indo-European hypothesis" helped European intellectuals rethink their narrative of world history. The belief in Hebrew's
primordial status had led to a unilinear concept of history. The hypothesis of
separate language families suggested instead a ramified genealogy involving
many different but coeval languages, peoples, and histories. Hence, where
Renaissance philology reinforced theories of historical monogenesis, Jones's
scholarship implied that each language constitutes its own history.[33] The
Indo-European hypothesis made "history," in fact, a dimension *inside* language—defined differently by each language's patterns of lexical, syntactic,
and semantic change—and in this way engendered the new philology. It
enabled comparative approaches across (and indeed beyond) the human
sciences, from literature and historiography to religion and jurisprudence—
"the boast," as Said noted, "of nineteenth-century method," the source of a
"quantum expansion [of] European consciousness," in Thomas Trautmann's
words.[34] Müller claimed that as a consequence of the Indo-European
hypothesis "a complete revolution took place in the views commonly enter-
tained of the ancient history of the world."[35]

In the short term, the ten "Anniversary Discourses" (1784–93) Jones
delivered as president and founder of the Royal Asiatick Society of Bengal—
published in the society's annual volume *Asiatick Researches*—reappeared
almost immediately thereafter in pirated editions widely disseminated
across Europe.[36] They contained, alongside Jones's protodeclaration of the
Indo-European hypothesis, comparative studies of languages, literatures, and
mythologies spanning from India to Italy, and they were consumed by European intellectuals "seething with curiosity," according to Raymond Schwab,
about non-European languages.[37] These essays bear in embryo essential
premises of the new philology. First, the nature of a "people" is defined by
the language they speak, as Jones explained in "An Essay on the Poetry of
Eastern Nations": "Every nation has a set of images, and expressions, peculiar
to itself, which arise from the difference of its climate, manners, and history."[38] Second, human difference across space and time can be understood,
therefore, only by means of philological study. After Jones, philology would
produce what Joseph Errington has called "language-centered images of the
deep human past."[39] Homing in on the historicity of linguistic structures, the
new philology claimed to recover traditions with scientific rigor. Its skill in

this regard predestined it to become the foundation of the human sciences. Jones prefigured this transformation a century before the fact: "Grammar is [an] instrument," he explained, "of true knowledge."[40]

Jones's grammatical approach to history formed the basis of nineteenth-century philology, the discipline that transcended the multiplicity of tongues. According to *The Order of Things*, Jones was as important for the new philology's emergence from the seventeenth- and eighteenth-century field of general grammar as Adam Smith was for political economy's emergence from mercantilist theory: though Foucault barely discusses Jones, he is—alongside Smith and the botanist Jussieu—nothing less than *the* transitional figure for Foucault in the development of modern knowledge.[41] After Jones, language ceased to be the medium of knowledge—the veridical discourse of the Enlightenment, the crystalline lens through which one sees the truth—and became instead the privileged object of knowledge. As the founding figures of nineteenth-century philology—Friedrich von Schlegel (1772–1829), Jacob Grimm (1785–1863), Rasmus Rask (1787–1837), and Franz Bopp (1791–1867)—isolated the members of the Indo-European language family and described their peculiar patterns of change, each language acquired an internal history and hence its own type of opacity. Only after the new philology had detached the phenomenon of language from external reference, on one hand, and linear chronology, on the other, could we enter what Foucault referred to as "the order of time."[42] We could call it "historicism" instead: we have already observed Auerbach place it at the heart of philology and accord it the highest methodological privilege. Because the new philology transformed the very terms by which we understand language's relationship to knowledge, its consequences have been, according to Foucault, the most far-reaching of any modern science and at the same time the most unperceived. It replaced Babel's confusion with a critical method that could know humanity across both space and time.

While Auerbach and Said placed the new philology's origins in the late eighteenth century, they located comparative literature's birth in the early nineteenth—like countless scholars writing in their wake—with Goethe's formulation of *Weltliteratur*.[43] A strange choice: however attractive the term, it has never gained conceptual coherence, oscillating even for Goethe himself between a supranational canon of great works, on one hand, and an inquiry into the transnational conditions of literary production, on the other.[44]

Neither idea will take us very far into the history of comparatism: their vagueness reflects, if anything, only how completely the category of "literature" had been evacuated of its prior meanings by the early nineteenth century. The development of experimental science had emptied "literature" (in the classical sense of erudition or book-learning) of its epistemological value, while Kant's third *Critique* had emptied "literature" (in the eighteenth-century sense of beautiful or tasteful writing) of its aesthetic function.[45] Though Goethe has been credited with a deep interest in Eastern literature, he declared that he had left the Eastern style of *West-östlicher Divan* "behind, like a cast-off snake skin," in the very year he created the term *Weltliteratur* (1827).[46]

I suggest we turn to Jones instead: he not only occupies a seminal place in the history of philology but could also justifiably replace Goethe at the beginnings of comparative literature. Within a two-decade span (1771–89), he translated what are, perhaps, the most important works of classical Persian, Arabic, and Indian literature, respectively: Hafiz's poetry (fourteenth century A.D.); the *Mu'allaqāt* (sixth and early seventh centuries A.D.); and Kālidāsa's *Śakuntalā* (late fourth or early fifth century A.D.). Jones's versions were the earliest such translations into any European language, and they had a profound effect on Romanticism in Europe and beyond, shaping, for example, Goethe's original interest in Eastern literature: the *West-östlicher Divan* was modeled on the first and deeply indebted to the second, while the prologue of *Faustus* was modeled on the last.[47] Tracing the genealogy of comparative literature from these translations rather than from Goethe's mere formulation of the word *Weltliteratur* would have a number of ancillary benefits. First, it would force us to explore comparative method's eighteenth-century roots rather than take them for granted, as both Auerbach and Said do. Second, instead of "revolving around the river Rhine," it would return comparatism to its colonial context.[48] And hence, third, it would disclose comparative literature's initial political utility.

While Goethe's scattered speculations on *Weltliteratur* hardly constitute a project for the field, Jones defined the purpose of his translations precisely. They were, first of all, instruments of historical knowledge. He described the *Mu'allaqāt* as "an exact picture" of "the manners of the Arabs of that age."[49] He claimed that Persian poetry, such as Hafiz's *Dīvān*, contains "positive information," which one cannot acquire, for example, about the "unlettered"

Tartars; if one does not study its literature, one can "at most attain a general and imperfect knowledge of the country."[50] And he "present[ed] [*Śakuntalā*] to the publick as a most pleasing and authentick picture of old Hindu manners."[51] In each case, Jones's comments illustrate how profoundly the new philology's historical ambitions motivated comparative literary study. Literature is the expression of a nation—in the case of peoples such as Arabs, Persians, and Indians who supposedly lacked the disciplines of history and philosophy, the only means to know their past. In other words, after experimental science and Kantian critique had hollowed out "literature," philology gave it a new epistemic value. If world literature now occupies an official space on the curricular and scholarly agenda, we would do well, rather than simply to recall that Goethe coined the term, to understand how our approach relates to the original practice.

In large part, therefore, the discipline of comparative literature was born alongside the new philology as an absolutely essential aspect of its method. As it elaborated Jones's approach, nineteenth-century philology would eventually claim that it could subsume and therefore supersede the diversity of tongues. It was the science that would make sense of everything human, turning linguistic confusion into total knowledge. It would become, in this way, analogous to the dream of a divine language, which it would annul and preserve in a higher form. Its authority—which both Auerbach and Said accepted—would ultimately depend on the obsolescence of all other approaches to language. And yet, as the next section argues, the profoundly influential concept of literature inaugurated by Jones's philology was designed less to transcend Babel than, in fact, to extend its legacy—the dispersion of languages fanning out in every direction from there—indefinitely.

3. Aryanism, Ursprache, *"Literature"*

The Indo-European hypothesis famously led to the Aryan myth: nineteenth-century philologists divided the world's first inhabitants into two peoples, those who belonged to the Indo-European family and those who did not. The Aryans' supposed conquest of countries stretching from Western Europe to the Indian subcontinent and their invention of the countless languages spoken across that expanse proved they possessed the prerogative of historical progress. In contrast, the Semite confinement to the Near East and its relatively few languages indicated a spatial and temporal immobility.[52] The Indo-European hypothesis enabled in this way a categorical distinction between Christians and Jews or, in other words, ruling and subject peoples, as Martin Bernal has argued at length in *Black Athena*. But its effect was, more broadly, a new theory of race, in which each language bespoke a unique racial heritage.[53] From the perspective of nineteenth-century philology, variations in grammatical systems reflected differences in racial consciousness. Building on Herder's arguments about the relation between language and race in his *Treatise on the Origin of Language* (1772), Wilhelm von Humboldt declared that European national languages were each an "involuntary emanation of the spirit, no work of nations, but a gift fallen to them by their inner destiny."[54] Hannah Arendt's description of the philological basis of Eastern European nationalism in *The Origins of Totalitarianism* could easily be extended across the globe: these "liberation movement[s] started with a kind of philological revival [whose] political function was to prove that the people who possessed a literature and history of their own [had] the right to national sovereignty."[55] As a consequence of its transhistorical explanatory power, race eventually became the focus of nineteenth-century philological research.

In its first modern iteration, then, the category of race was the unintended consequence of Bengal's colonization, which enabled Europeans finally to decrypt Sanskrit and begin uncovering the prehistory of the people known in that language as the Ārya. Aryanism was almost as fundamental to colonialism as it was to nationalism and fascism. If ruling groups in Europe invoked Aryan genealogies in order to legitimize their rule and distinguish natives from aliens, colonial administrators in outposts ranging from Ireland to Southeast Asia used such genealogies or the absence thereof to produce knowledge about the native populations they governed.[56]

In either case, though, nineteenth-century philologists imagined that if they could reconstruct the morphological roots of the Indo-European language family, they would recover the thought of the early Aryans. The myth of the Aryans involved, in other words, a new, methodologically more sophisticated quest for the Adamic language that preceded the confusion of tongues, when God, nature, and humankind existed in an immediate relationship with each other.[57] Hence, Saussure identified nineteenth-century philology with the "almost conscious dream of an ideal humanity"—he described the Aryans as the "people of the golden age brought back to life by scholarly thought [*par la pensée*]"—and he founded the "science" of semiology in opposition to this false historicism.[58] Scholars who focus on the history of colonial philology have read this nineteenth-century quest back into Jones's work, claiming that he wanted to recover "the language spoken when Adam and Eve were cast out from the garden of Eden" (Errington); the "fundamental unity in human thought, belief and action hidden under the veneer of linguistic difference" (Tony Ballantyne); "ancient wisdom" or "primitive monotheism" (Trautmann).[59]

In fact, though, if Jones set out in search of a primordial language, his philological studies only proved to him that it would never be found. Far from uncovering the common language of our earliest ancestors or even dividing them into separate Aryan and Semitic tribes, Jones uncovered three separate language families: he argued that "the whole earth was peopled by a variety of shoots from the Indian, Arabian, and Tartarian branches," thereby correctly identifying the Indo-European, Afro-Asiatic, and Altaic language families.[60] He claimed that he could not "find a single word used in common by [these three] families" and hence concluded that "the language of Noah is lost irretrievably."[61] However it began, his research staked itself in the end on the irreducible diversity of languages, whose consequences he claimed even he could not fully comprehend: "Thus it has been prove[d] beyond controversy, that the far greater part of *Asia* has been peopled and immemorially possessed by three considerable nations, whom, for want of better names, we may call Hindus, Arabs, and Tartars; each of them divided and subdivided into an infinite number of branches, and all of them so different in form and features, language, manners and religion, that, if they sprang originally from a common root, they must have been separated for ages."[62] Two centuries later, Jones's dazzling twentieth-century counterpart, Georges Dumézil, would reiterate his precursor's conclusions for anyone who still hoped to recover the *Ursprache: les comparatistes* "know that the dramatic, living reconstruction of a common ancestral language [is] impossible, since nothing can replace documents and there are no documents."[63]

In other words, the Indo-European hypothesis demonstrated, once and for all, that the confusion of tongues is humanity's irreversible condition. Jones believed Babel to be an actual event—"the fourth important *fact* recorded in the *Mosaick* history"—and disavowed the possibility of ever recovering humanity's original language.[64] This attitude of acceptance toward the irreducible diversity of languages originated, according to Umberto Eco, George Steiner, and Gérard Genette, in the long eighteenth century, when the interpretation of Babel underwent a fundamental transformation.[65] According to Eco, the eighteenth-century reinterpretation of Babel hinged on Genesis 10 (the chapter that immediately precedes the story of Babel), which suggests that the multiplicity of tongues was *prior* to the destruction of the Tower and must have been therefore humanity's primitive condition. No longer God's punishment, the confusion of tongues can be seen, finally, as a gift rather than a curse. Once it reappears in this way, Eco observes, "the sense [of] Babel has been turned upside down."[66]

In any case, though, Jones did not use philology to realize either the immemorial dream of a divine language or the nineteenth-century vision of a racially pure *Ursprache*. His concern was, instead, to fully embrace the human condition of linguistic confusion. In Jones's hands, philology became a conscious response precisely to this condition. Histories of philology identify Jones as the crucial figure in the emergence of "linguistic science" from "prescience."[67] Even *The Order of Things* presents Jones's work as transitional, as we have already observed, despite the fact that Foucault generally abjured framing the history of science in terms of progress narratives. In Jones's work, according to Foucault, we encounter an "ambiguous epistemological configuration" involving two different concepts of language: on one hand, language as a veridical discourse, the transparent medium of knowledge; on the other, language as a historical system, the opaque object of knowledge.[68] Jones's work, like Adam Smith's, contains "a philosophic duality" at the point of "its imminent dissolution." When the new philology dissolved the Enlightenment's idea of language, it enabled language, Foucault argued, to assume myriad forms. A conceit about Babel tacitly structures *The Order of Things'* discussion of the new philology: "when the unity of [Enlightenment discourse] was broken up, language appeared in a multiplicity of modes of being, whose unity was probably irrecoverable."[69]

Jones's approach to languages preserved Babel's legacy precisely in its recognition, however inchoate, that every language produces its own history. This recognition depends, in turn, on the premise that language does not operate referentially (or, in other words, that every use of language constitutes its own referent). Philology after Jones delineated the meaning of nonreferential (or performative) language—that is, "literature" in the modern sense—by reconstructing the historical system internal to the language or text under study. In other words, the new philology treats all language as "literary"; it is, as a consequence, the only method adequate to literature in this new sense.

In Foucault's account, the concept of "literature" is born, in fact, only after late eighteenth-century philology discloses language's multiple "modes of being."[70] When different modes of language inhabit the same place, they create what Foucault referred to as "an unthinkable space."[71] "Literature" is Foucault's name for the discursive practice and the theoretical concept that occupy this space. He defined "literature" as a mode of language "folded back upon the enigma of its own origin and existing wholly in reference to the pure act of writing"—a linguistic mode that, in other words, makes no reference outside itself.[72] The intimate relation of the new philology and the literary collapses the age-old distinction between history and literature, truth and representation. Jean-Pierre Vernant claimed that historical method is premised on "a sharp and definitive division between the strictly rational approach and the naïve fantasies of the mythological imagination."[73] Even Foucault described "literature" as "the contestation of philology" (though he immediately qualified the opposition: "of which it is nevertheless the twin figure").[74] But from the perspective of the new philology, historical truth and literary representation can, in fact, no longer be disentangled at all. In the original "Return to Philology," Paul de Man emphasized that philology was, in essence, an "examination of the structure of language *prior* to the meaning it produces."[75] In other words, philology refuses, in principle, to isolate "history" from textual form. Jonathan Culler's "Anti-foundational Philology" argues likewise that philology's most profound lesson is the contradiction between its desire to reconstruct history objectively and its attention to linguistic details that do not conform to any such history.[76] De Man's and Culler's points reiterate Foucault's argument that when eighteenth-century philology liberated the mode of language called "literature," it brought history itself into crisis.

Hence, even as Jones presented philology as the instrument of "true knowledge" and described his translations of Hafiz, the *Mu'allaqāt*, and

Śakuntalā as vehicles of historical truth, he also denied that the language of
these texts has any reference, foundation, or origin outside itself. True knowledge therefore existed for Jones largely *inside* literary texts. The language of
Mu'allaqāt, Jones claimed, does not merely express but enacts the nomad's
love of freedom: for the Bedouin, "delighting in eloquence," "disclaim[ing]
dependence on [the] monarch," and "exulting in their liberty" were one and
the same act.[77] Jones's essays "On the Persians" and "On the Mystical Poetry
of the Persians and Hindus" invoke literatures that explicitly reject all external reference. The first essay notes that Sufi writing advises its practitioners
to "break all *connexion* [with] extrinsick objects, and pass through life without *attachments*."[78] The second essay translates the words of Rūmī (1207–73)
to gloss a poem by Ismat Allāh Bukhārī (1365–1426): "[The Sufis] profess
eager desire, but with no carnal affection, and circulate the cup, but no material goblet; since all things are spiritual in their sect, all is mystery within
mystery."[79] As with Arabic poetry, Jones's discussions of Persian and Indian
literatures emphasize the ways in which they reject objective knowledge and
recognize language's performative power instead. Jones's commitment to understand "Asiatick" literature on its own terms forced him, in other words, to
confront the language of "infidels" who do not believe in the preconceived
meanings of words, for whom the word has become dissevered from the
thing and recovered its own creative force. This language, a "mystery within
mystery," prefigures Foucault's definition of "literature."

The connection is no coincidence: it was precisely this concept of language that Jones's essays and translations helped make available to the
Romantic generation and beyond. More than any other figure, Jones inspired
the "Oriental Renaissance" that shaped the modern category of literature, as
Schwab demonstrated at length.[80] Jones wanted European writing to share
Eastern poetry's performative power, which resided for him not in already
constituted relationships between word and thing but rather in the *acceptance*
of linguistic confusion, which necessarily constitutes that relationship anew.
The next chapter argues that Jones considered nonreferential (or "expressive") language the antithesis of authoritative speech. He imagined that the
conscious embrace of such language would move European culture beyond
neoclassicism in particular and despotism in general, every project—like the
mythic one that occurred at Babel—to make a single discourse universal

or quasi-divine. Even scholars who explicitly reject philology often remain trapped in this philological fantasy: the belief that the performative power of language—which the new philology alone can recover—constitutes the antithesis of authoritative speech. One can still resist every hegemony, it would seem, by simply appreciating language's nonreferentiality and endless multiplicity.

So, for example, in Jacques Derrida's *Psyche: Inventions of the Other*, the confusion of tongues becomes the prototypical punishment for colonial projects. If the construction of the Tower accompanied the early Semites' attempt to make their language universal and thus establish an empire, the destruction of the Tower interrupts their "linguistic imperialism."[81] As soon as they express their desire to be a single people with a single tongue (Genesis 11:4), God confounds their idioms, making them mutually unintelligible. He thereby transforms Babel from a colonial project to a figure for "the inadequation of one tongue to another."[82]

Like Derrida, Daniel Heller-Roazen has also observed that Genesis 11:9 redefines Babel as "confusion," thereby itself confounding a noun meaning "the gateway of God" with the Hebrew verb *bilbél* ("to confuse"). Ironically, this single alteration contains God's punishment within itself: when God shatters the original language, he prevents the people of Shinar from communicating with each other and throws them into confusion. Whereas "Babel" had been the quintessentially proper name, since it opened to God's presence, it suddenly became the quintessentially improper (or fallen) word, since it paradoxically signified the noncorrespondence of word and meaning. Answering the human desire for an imperial language, God ensured that no linguistic experience except confusion could ever be universal again. Glossing a passage from the Babylonian Talmud that claims the "air around the [ruined] tower makes one lose one's memory," Heller-Roazen has suggested that each of us still unwittingly inhabits these ruins, fated to forget not just the *Ursprache* but every idiom we have spoken from our first words to the present.[83] Only such forgetting can make languages multiply, or, in other words, allows "all languages to be."[84]

The noncorrespondence of languages that, in Derrida's and Heller-Roazen's readings of the Babel myth, opposes the desire to make any single discourse divine is also the distinguishing feature of the *reine Sprache*, or "pure language," that Walter Benjamin described in his own meditation on Babel's legacy, "The Task of the Translator." In diametric contrast to language treated as a medium of something outside itself, pure language "no longer signifies anything"; it refers only to the "creative word that is the intended object of every language."[85] Pure language presupposes that the confusion of tongues neither can nor needs to be redeemed; an openness to the pure language of any text is, in other words, an approach to the confusion of tongues that, like Jones's philology, does not attempt to transcend it. Benjamin explains that in this approach, "the great motive of integrating the plurality of languages into a single true language [carries] out its work" otherwise: though "individual propositions" from different languages "never arrive at agreement," "the languages themselves [nonetheless] agree" in their common resistance to referentiality.[86]

The opposition between performative language and imperial authority implicit in these interpretations of Babel is made explicit in the work of many postcolonial scholars, as the conclusion to this book demonstrates. For now, we could simply let Bernard Cohn's groundbreaking essay "The Command of Language and the Language of Command" stand for the rest. Drawing on the work of an Indic philologist, Kamil Zvelebil, Cohn argued that precolonial traditions cannot be understood on the model of the sign, the signature, or any other European theory of correspondence between word and thing.[87] In these traditions, language was understood instead to transmit the being of the one who originated it and, consequently, to transform the being of the one who received it. It was, in other words, a material substance and an active force, its simple articulation altering the unfolding of time itself.[88] In Cohn's account of language before colonial rule (as in Foucault's account of "literature" after philology), historical referents can exist, paradoxically, only *within* words themselves.

Yet precisely this account of language and literature had originally been advocated by the colonial philologist par excellence. We need, therefore, to consider the possibility that such concepts (emphasizing performativity, noncorrespondence, nonreferentiality, etc.) are not some lost or forgotten experience of language but rather, in part, colonial artifacts. The next section argues that the understanding of language as essentially nonreferential—and hence recuperable only by the new philology—was itself a colonial strategy.

Put differently, this description of language's ur-form—the mode that precedes every colonial project to make a denotative language predominate—considers itself diametrically opposed to the Aryan *Ursprache* but is no less the effect of colonial philology. Since philology is the only method appropriate to this mode, such descriptions of precolonial languages always lead back, ironically, to philology's absolute authority. For postcolonial criticism, everything is at stake, therefore, in how we understand the archaeology of Babel, of the always colonial project to authorize one or another form of speech. The question this archaeology needs, at last, to address is, what do the philological revolution and its concepts of language and literature themselves efface? To answer this question, we will need to seek, underneath every imperial edifice, neither the *Ursprache* that came before the confusion of tongues nor the original meaning and nature of that confusion, but something altogether different.

4. Colonialism and Comparatism

The recognition of language's "fragmentation" and "dispersion" was an "event," Foucault claimed, that occurred "toward the end of the eighteenth century."[89] But if Jones's formulation of the Indo-European hypothesis initiated a dispersion of language, we must nonetheless recall, unlike Foucault, that Jones sat on the East India Company supreme court; his studies occurred within a colonial context and were meant to serve colonial rule. Even before the Company formally established a colonial administration, its officials understood that a historical approach to the subcontinent's various languages would be the precondition of colonial hegemony. One of the first governors of Bengal, J. Z. Holwell, wrote in 1767: "A mere description of the exterior manners and religion of a people, will no more give us a true idea of them, than a geographical description of a country can convey a just conception of their laws and government. [One must be] skilled in the languages of the [people] sufficiently to trace the etymology of their words and phrases, and [be] capable of diving into the mysteries of their theology."[90] Prefiguring the new philology, Holwell implied that once Company officials understood each Indian language to have its own history, they would unlock the truth of their native subjects. During the final three decades of the eighteenth century, in the wake of Jones's pioneering study of Persian, Company scholars created an extensive philological apparatus for South Asian languages, including textbooks, literary and linguistic treatises, dictionaries, and grammars.[91] These studies formed the groundwork for the numerous legal and religious texts Jones and his colleagues reconstructed from supposedly archaic originals—which in turn enabled the colonial state to claim knowledge about Indian history and present itself as an extension of native sovereignty.[92] The new philology was apprenticed to colonial rule.

In fact, the British colonial government's approach to India was philological in the modern sense: it made native history a dimension internal to language. Company scholars viewed Persian, Arabic, and Sanskrit—the prestige languages of the Islamic and Brahmanic legal canons—as the vessels of Islam's and Hinduism's true histories. Hence, they were able to reduce Indian society, which they found forbiddingly complex and heterogeneous, to a discrete number of legal and religious texts, which they rendered legible and coherent.[93] In the process, they turned native languages into markers of human difference, dividing individuals into groups that had previously not existed and fixing social practices that had been fluid, as Cohn's "Command of Language" argues.[94] In fact, colonial jurisprudence gave natives an ethnological character: it redefined not merely the property relations but even the rituals and beliefs that counted as "traditional."[95]

The colonial utility of philology lay here: because it identifies tradition with texts alone, it provides sovereign power a "traditional" lineage from which native experience itself is exiled. Jones intended his legal codes to achieve this end in colonial India.[96] As he often observed, the "native lawyers and scholars" who had adapted religious law to local circumstances could not be trusted.[97] Jones aspired, as a consequence, to replace their socially embedded authority with the colonial state's transcendent power. He effectively refounded the Hindu and Islamic legal traditions solely on colonial textual authority: not on native experience, therefore, but rather on its destruction.[98] Legal codes enabled the colonial state to overwrite the ungovernable babble of the newly conquered with "the language of the law," as John Comaroff has observed.[99] Jones used the philological skills he developed in his translations of Hafiz, the *Mu'allaqāt*, and *Śakuntalā* to produce versions of *shari'a* and the Dharmaśāstra that would reconstitute native law and have an inestimable effect on Indian colonial and postcolonial history. Nineteenth-century Indians—and eventually colonial subjects around the world, Said included—

would learn to read standardized texts and understand their histories in terms of the scholarly protocols bequeathed to them by colonial philology.[100]

The study of world literature would be more attuned to its own genealogy if it acknowledged the extent to which both its materials and its methods are colonial legacies. Colonial philology disembedded native literatures from their traditions in order to dissever native subjects from their forms of life. It initiated a transformation so massive that no tradition now remains untouched. "Historicist humanism," as Auerbach would have it, authorized this transformation: it argued that philologically reconstructed texts contain the truth of tradition more authentically than people themselves do. The new philology became hegemonic—the basis of both critical method and colonial domination—because it enabled modern institutions to impose analytic and bureaucratic order on multilingual terrains. According to Michael Herzfeld, it "transmuted the polyglot agonies of Babel into a cult of transcendent European erudition."[101]

Colonialism involved the conquest of an epistemic space by means of which precolonial discursive practices were turned—as Ranajit Guha has explained—into "abstract legality."[102] The human sciences have rewritten this act of conquest as the gift of historical sensibility. Its legacy lives on in Auerbach's and Said's commitments to realism and secular criticism, respectively. Auerbach's presupposition that world literature would exist in the future only as a subject of philological scholarship and Said's silence on this score reflect their preference for the new philology over all other approaches to language. In a primer for his Turkish students, Auerbach described philology as an expression of the civilized desire to preserve tradition: "The need to establish authentic texts arises when a people of an advanced civilization become aware of this civilization and want to preserve from the ravages of time the works that constitute its spiritual heritage."[103] But for Auerbach, this "spiritual" heritage comprised texts amenable to historical analysis. The European tradition was intelligible to him only to the extent that it progressively engendered historical thought, thereby fulfilling the figure of Christ's incarnation and realizing, in Hayden White's words, "humanity's distinctive mode of being," that is, historicity.[104] The "real" (or *Wirklichkeit*) with which Auerbach aligned both European realism and his own critical method is, in other words, an effect of the new philology's concept of language-history.

Any new postcolonial comparatism that wants to be adequate to the alterity of precolonial practices but still remain faithful to philological protocols will come to an old impasse, as one could argue both Auerbach's and Said's work did. Like Auerbach, Said considered philology the method by which diasporic scholars avoid "falling victim to the concrete dangers of exile: the loss of texts, traditions, and continuities that make up the very web of a culture."[105] Hence, while Said criticized the Eurocentrism of both Orientalism and Romance philology, he could not question their methodological foundations.[106] Rather than distancing himself from this method, Said advocated it throughout his career.[107] In his view, the new philology laid the foundation for secular criticism, which likewise presupposes that written language provides total access to the human domain.[108]

What remained invisible to Said is the genealogy and politics of secularism itself. It emerged, according to Talal Asad and others, not with the replacement of divine providence by human agency but rather with the removal of divine presence from the material world to a transcendent realm instead.[109] Once the earth has been secularized in this way, it can be exploited without limit. In fact, the term "secularism" began its life as the name for a nineteenth-century political movement that wanted to transform European society in line with industrial capitalism. Secularists contested the Christian Church's traditional authority by reconstructing the law. But if modern law underwrote industrial society in Europe, it served an even more fundamental purpose in the colony: it made the non-European world secular for the first time. One could argue that, in his advocacy not only of humanism but also of secular criticism, Said remained trapped within the very language of colonial rule.

To extricate ourselves from that trap, we would need to begin a colonial archaeology of historical method. Modern literary studies developed not only in academic institutions but also in colonial legal and print cultures; the latter have had much more global influence. At some point, therefore, our critiques of literary studies must venture beyond the walls of the academy and analyze the spread of colonial law across the earth. We may find that the philological revolution has less to do with the nineteenth-century research university than with the reconstruction of indigenous life on a planetary scale: historical method became the epistemic foundation of colonial rule. Like colonial jurisprudence, secular criticism assumes that historical method is the pre-condition of political competence.[110] In contrast, an archaeological approach would not take historical method for granted; it would acknowledge that philology's colonial function was to appropriate and efface—in a word, de-stroy—the diverse discursive practices that preceded it. Hence, we need to see the new philology not as the preservation of tradition, but rather as its destruction. Such an archaeology would trace not only the colonial arrange-ment of knowledge that shaped historical method—and secular criticism as well—but also the precolonial practices that existed outside this arrange-ment. An archaeological project of this kind is, as Agamben has emphasized, philology turned against itself—or "the destruction of a destruction."[111] This project must be part of any postcolonial comparatism to come, whose task involves unearthing the approaches to language the new philology buried in its colonial past.

5. Chapters in the History of the Philological Revolution

During the course of the late eighteenth century, the philological revolution's three major innovations—comparative grammar, the division of languages into families, and the reconstruction of historically unattested protolanguages—developed in conjunction with colonial rule across three distinct phases. Each phase would have profound consequences for both metropolitan and colonial societies.

Phase 1—involving the roots of comparative grammar—redefined the origins of language. The belief that each language possessed its own gram-mar, which could be known only by means of historical method, replaced the premise that every language was a variation on a single universal grammar whose provenance was divine or natural. Jones's wildly successful *A Grammar of the Persian Language* (1771) was a seminal work within this transformation. But its intended purpose was to teach East India Company servants Persian: it helped them appropriate the Mughal Empire's scribal, scholarly, and liter-ary practices and, by extension, its forms of linguistic authority during the first years of colonial rule. It also served as the model for the Company's countless grammars of South Asian languages. Colonial scholars used histor-ical grammar to reconstruct these vernaculars' normative forms, which would become the foundation of modern Indian literatures.

Phase 2—reflecting the same ethnographic impulse that produced the classification of languages into families—invented national literary traditions. The historical approach to texts was thought to disclose a people's sovereign history and hence their national identity. In colonial India, this approach produced the codification first of Islamic and subsequently of Hindu legal traditions. Jones's translations of Islamic legal manuscripts—*The Mohamedan Law of Succession* (1782) and *Al-Sirájiyyah, or The Mohammedan Law of Inheritance* (1792)—purported to contain the historical truth of *shari'a* and hence of the East India Company's Muslim subjects. But these codes were also part of an unprecedented experiment in government, as Cohn and Michael Anderson have observed: the first attempt of any European empire to govern the colonized according to their law. Colonial legal codes became the principal medium of historical knowledge about non-European populations and provided the new philology primary source materials. At the same time, they made cultural difference the central category of modern governance, as Mahmood Mamdani has recently argued.

Phase 3—leading to the reconstruction of protolanguages—began with the idea of Indo-European civilization. The Indo-European hypothesis (1786) posited a common but historically unattested ancestral language from which all the Indo-European languages diverged. Jones's 1794 translation of the oldest Dharmaśāstra, commonly called *The Laws of Manu*, was thought therefore to contain the Indo-European people's earliest concepts. Inspired by Jones's translations of Sanskrit legal and literary texts, European philologists began to "restore" the root words they believed had existed during human prehistory, even before the dawn of civilization. These roots became the indispensable basis of the nineteenth-century philological effort to map human development in its historical totality: they both cancelled out the dream of a divine language and elevated this dream to a much more methodologically rigorous plane.

The constantly rearticulated endeavor to align the interpretation of literature with the principles of the new philology has, therefore, consistently neglected a central fact: these principles are deeply entangled with colonial law. This projects also overlooks a second salient fact: the entanglement of the new philology and colonial law came to encompass—or contaminate—the category of literature itself. In fact, during each phase of late eighteenth-century colonial philology, Jones produced a corresponding translation that would shape world literature.

Phase 1: *A Grammar of the Persian Language* contained "A Persian Song of Hafiz," Jones's translation of Hafiz's masterful *ghazal* known as "The Shirazi Turk." Jones's version would be widely read by Romantic writers from Byron to Emerson and beyond. Jones presented Hafiz's poetry as a model of aesthetic production founded on "violent passion," according to Jones the true source of the fine arts. He argued that the origins of poetry lie not, as per Aristotelian and neoclassical aesthetics, in the imitation of aristocratic speech but rather in diverse expressions of human desire. René Wellek, among others, placed this argument at the roots of Romantic thought.[112] Hence, during this phase, the nascent discipline of historical and comparative grammar helped produce the modern category of literature and "the literary."

Phase 2: In the same year that Jones published his first codification of *shariʻa*, he also translated the *Muʻallaqāt*, the most prized collection of poems in the classical Arabic tradition. Jones intended *The Moallakát* (1782)—with its emphasis on the nomad's autonomy and consequent willingness to war against states and empires—to express his support for the American revolutionaries. Bedouin poetry would remain the prototype, long after the late eighteenth century, of languages that oppose transcendent authority and constitute a different form of sovereignty. The attempt to understand segmentary or decentralized tribal societies—what Deleuze and Guattari would call the "war machine"—during the era of decolonization gave the study of such poetry new life. In any case, though, the ethnographic impulse that divided languages into families led, during this phase, to a connection between national literatures, on one hand, and collective life or "immanent" sovereignty, on the other.

Phase 3: Soon after formulating the Indo-European hypothesis, Jones translated the ancient Sanskrit drama commonly known as *Śakuntalā*. European philosophers and poets from Herder to Goethe declared that Jones's *Sacontalá* (1789) brought them closer to humanity's original language than any other extant literary work. Schwab would consequently call the first decades of the Romantic period the "*Shakuntala* Era."[113] The Romantic reading of *Śakuntalā* prefigured the nineteenth-century philological desire to reconstruct the language that precedes the historical record and to recover, by extension, the original form of humanity's habitation on the earth. Hence, during this phase, the idea of an Indo-European civilization and of historically unattested protolanguages transformed the very concept of the origin and thus formulated an axiom that still governs the humanities: language does not reflect any other a priori reality but is itself "originary."

The late eighteenth-century emergence of the new philology thus occurred in three phases, each of which was intimately tied to colonial rule and each of which has outlived the eighteenth century. First, European philologists historicized the origin of language; second, they nationalized literary traditions; and third, they recovered the prehistorical roots of language. Each phase engendered a correspondingly long-lived fantasy: philological methods would reconstruct the primordial languages of desire, the collectivity, and the earth and thus give birth to new literary practices. The dream of recovering these three languages—which correspond, we could say, to psychoanalysis, Marxism, and ecocriticism—has not only survived into the present but assumed manifold scholarly and creative forms.[114]

The Romantics believed, in any event, that Jones's translations captured the historical origins of human desire, society, and speech itself. They took these works, like those of Homer and the bardic poets, to be the voice of the people before the rise of priestly and despotic power. They consequently made Hafiz, the *Mu'allaqāt*, and *Śakuntalā* archetypes of a Romantic (i.e., counterhegemonic) concept of literature. But each of these works was in fact part of a hegemonic tradition. The historical function of these traditions was precisely to define desire's legitimate expression, the tribe's acceptable speech, and the earth's sacred discourse. Hence, in each case, the exclusion of alternative discursive practices—if not the expropriation of other forms of life—constituted the tradition. Precisely when Hafiz presumes to speak for desire, the *Mu'allaqāt* for the tribe, and *Śakuntalā* for the earth, they conceal their own constitutive exclusions. The new philology's attempt to locate counterhegemonic languages within the literary tradition itself only reinforced this process of exclusion. To fulfill the new philology's original aspirations, we would need a different approach.

Its first step would be to study the history of philological power itself. The next three chapters study the colonial history of the new philology. They respectively analyze each of its three phases and in this way undertake an archaeology of the philological revolution in general and its concepts of the literary, the immanent, and the originary in particular. These concepts are largely responsible for the ideologies of the literary text, the aura that consequently attaches to literary studies, and the scholarly aspirations that, by extension, tacitly program the postcolonial humanities still today. Yet, as this archaeology reveals, philological method itself ensures that the very languages the humanities reflexively seek—desire (or "the literary"), collectivity (or "the immanent"), and the earth (or "the originary")—will remain always outside their reach.

Archaeology is itself, of course, a mode of historical understanding. But in the chapters that follow, it turns historical method against itself. These chapters delineate historical method's own historicity, its political instrumentality, and the alternative concepts of truth it marginalized along the way. They use historical method, in other words, to explore its own unacknowledged colonial history. Though the approach here is archaeological, the goal is Gramscian: to open oneself to the forms of consciousness one's own professional education has rendered subaltern. Such openness presupposes an "ab-use" of one's education—hence the necessary reliance on historical method.[115]

Only after each chapter has worked through philology's colonial history does it turn to the literary works Jones translated during the corresponding phase. In contrast to the Western reception of these texts, this study refuses to make them the antitheses of Western power. It rejects, in other words, facile oppositions between the non-European and the European, tradition and modernity, or the precolonial and the colonial—where the former term is imagined to be counterhegemonic. Even in their precolonial forms, Hafiz's poetry, the *Mu'allaqāt*, and *Śakuntalā* were shot through with various forms of philological power. This study's approach to precolonial literature—no less than its approach to colonial philology—is therefore archaeological. It treats literary texts as palimpsests of the historical process by which certain discursive practices seized, and others lost access to, linguistic authority. We could consider this the second step of a counterphilological approach.

The languages that never possessed linguistic authority belong, however, not to literary texts but rather to the discursive practices these texts appropriate. The rhetoric of nonnormative desire in Hafiz, nonstate sovereignty in

the *Mu'allaqāt*, and the prehistoric earth in *Śakuntalā* each contain the trace
of languages that were not recorded and that consequently resist philological analysis. The final steps of a counterphilological method would therefore
follow this trace. They would, in other words, reflect on the practices—the
counterhistorical labor—that philology must, ironically, always efface. Such a
mode of reflection would attempt to turn literary study toward those whom
it has previously only excluded, those for whom the tools of scholarship were
never intended. Only in this way could comparative or "world" literature finally realize the new philology's universalist and egalitarian aspirations.

Conclusion

In Auerbach's hands, philology pretends to know much more than the historical archive can attest: it presumes to unfold the "inner" history of the human
mind as such, from the Homeric period forward.[116] Auerbach and Said both
privilege the term "history" precisely because it encompasses, in their view,
the full range of emancipatory thought and action—what Auerbach called
"counteractivity."[117] But historical method inevitably reduces human activity and political praxis solely to what the written record can represent. In
other words, it confounds the struggle for emancipation with conflicts that
occurred largely within the literate and clerical classes alone. For Auerbach
and Said, history is, for all intents and purposes, the product of those who
can write and, further, produce permanent written records.[118] And literature
is, of course, the most valuable—or, in Said's words, the "most heightened,"
"rewarding," "complex and subtle"—expression of human experience.[119]

Auerbach's inner history of mankind records, moreover, only those moments that set off the gradual emergence of historical consciousness. For
Said also, to be secular or worldly is, explicitly, to think historically. One
demonstrates one's worldliness only by reading in a philological way, elucidating the relationship between text and its historical—or, more importantly,
geographical—context.[120] In sum, history as Auerbach and Said conceive it
can thus only render invisible those who were not entitled to write, to bequeath
their writing to future generations, or to acquire historical consciousness.
Though we now identify both Auerbach and Said with the interrogation of
scholarly orthodoxies, the general authority accorded to literate subjectivity
and to philological knowledge remained, for them, beyond question.

The postcolonial scholars who have called for a return to philology intend to correct its Eurocentrism, which is abundantly self-evident in Auerbach's *Geistesgeschichte*. In Pollock's view, for example, the humanities should pursue a "global knowledge" of precolonial philological practices.[121] In Aamir Mufti's view, the burgeoning field of world literature needs to recognize itself as the product of colonial Orientalism, which reduced the "formerly extensive and dispersed cultures of writing" that existed outside Europe "to narrowly conceived ethnonational spheres."[122] In either case, the effort to turn philology against its colonial history comes to rest on the recovery of literary formations that, albeit non-European, were nonetheless hegemonic. These formations were not necessarily any less contaminated by power than colonial knowledge is. However oppositional such scholarly projects may appear, they nevertheless remain trapped within the trajectory of philological power.

Because that trajectory now tacitly circumscribes critical method in the humanities, we will be able to rethink our approach only by working through philology's terms. Its general premise, across its geographically and historically diverse forms, is that authoritative languages, particularly written ones, stand for a given tradition as such. The new philology added a second premise: only a historical understanding of such languages counts as knowledge. A dialectical response to the history of philology would turn, therefore, on two antithetical premises. First, a given tradition comprises not only the languages that were authoritative but also those that were unable or unwilling to leave a mark on the historical record. Second, it is consequently impossible to reduce any tradition to an object of historical or philological knowledge.

To move beyond philology's first premise, we would need to value the languages of those who do not possess authority *and* who do not pursue it. For a discursive practice to be truly counterhegemonic, it cannot merely reject some given form of authority. It must resist authority as such, including, first of all, its own disposition to become socially authoritative. Such a discursive practice, which fully embraces an unhistorical life, may never occur in an unmixed form. But however impure and fleeting, it nonetheless not only exists all around us but also points the way beyond the desire for philological power. If we searched for it between the lines of every text and tradition, we would forget philology and fulfill the new philology's counterhegemonic vision at the same time.

This is, obviously, not a proposal that comparatists and postcolonialists are likely to accept: we are habituated to value literary discourses that have enjoyed some measure of global success. Even the contemporary study of anticolonial and radical literature focuses, inevitably, on revolutionary parties, tricontinental congresses, and aesthetic manifestos. If we do not want to fall unwittingly into the trap colonial philology set for us, we will need to take a step back from all such attempts to define what is revolutionary. This trap leads us to mistake forms of textual authority for counterhegemonic languages, as Robert Young and Michael Denning do in the privilege they grant Marxist literature or as Auerbach and Said did in their advocacy of philology.[123] Needless to say, this observation is meant not to dismiss these remarkable scholars but, on the contrary, to honor their aspirations, which the philological mindset forecloses in their own work. The languages that resist historical power lie not in specific traditions, even communist and anticolonial ones, but in every moment within any tradition when those who lack authority reinterpret the tradition in the name of their excluded experience instead.

If we want to move beyond philology's second premise, we must no longer pretend to possess historical knowledge about languages that are not part of the historical record. To study what philology has itself absented, we obviously cannot appeal to the authority of philological protocols. But literary texts gesture toward precisely these languages whenever they appropriate them or, on the contrary, record their erasure. These traces of powerless speech give us the occasion to imagine carefully what cannot be historically attested: the different forms opposition to philological power can take. This paradoxical project—to study languages that were never recorded in the first place—has the virtue, ironically, of abiding by the new philology, which, at least in principle, considered *every* language to be worthy of scholarly scrutiny and which consequently inspired heterodox scholars such as Auerbach and Said.

But apart from this, it also has a practical value. We live now in a global state of emergency. According to Achille Mbembe, Nasser Hussain, and Bhavani Raman, colonial rule pioneered this condition. Colonial law devolved into martial law, in fact, almost immediately: European empires codified native law, it would seem, only so that they could suspend it by sovereign decree. Emergency is now primarily treated as a political and juridical condition. But I would emphasize that it is, first of all, a discursive practice, whereby the sovereign circumscribes language's performative power within his own speech. He arrogates the right, univocally, to suspend the constitution and to declare the laws that govern in its place. We literary scholars have not, to my knowledge, come up with a critical method that opposes emergency, even though it is now the practice that expropriates language's creativity. Those who abjured historical power understood history itself to be an emergency, placing every nonsovereign form of life under threat. But they treated this precarious condition as an opportunity: not to become desperate for historical authority but, on the contrary, to practice living outside its grip.

THE LITERARY

The Persian Imperium and Hafiz, 1771 A.D.–1390 A.D.

Introduction

During its eighteenth- and nineteenth-century emergence, the new philology presented itself as an epistemic and political advance over previous methods. It understood language to be a historical phenomenon and claimed it could consequently recover, within the history of any language, the forms of that language that preceded the inevitable process of its corruption and decay. The humanities in general and the recent calls for a return to philology in particular tacitly accept claims such as these at face value: our general premise is that historical method is adequate to the full range of possibilities that language and literature contain.

Hence, if we wanted to understand the disciplinary limits of the humanities today, we could begin by interrogating the new philology's progressive claims. According to the common consensus, the new philology comprised three fundamental innovations: the invention of comparative grammar, the classification of languages into families, and the reconstruction of historically unattested protolanguages.[1] This chapter and the two that follow excavate the roots, respectively, of these three innovations, demonstrating that each of them originally served colonial rule. During colonial philology's first phase, East India Company scholars used the nascent discipline of historical grammar to begin reconstructing the languages and literatures they encountered in South Asia. Historical grammar introduced the new philological principle

that, at its essence, language operates nonreferentially. It thus helped produce the definition of literature to which we still cling: an aesthetic practice
attuned to language's performative (or "literary") power. Canonical works
from the Persian, Arabic, and Sanskritic traditions immediately became
prototypes of literature in this Romantic and modern sense. In fact, only
after the advent of colonial rule—as European scholars began to reinterpret
non-European verbal art according to this standard—could such a definition of literature appear universally valid. Our concept of literature must be
understood, therefore, as the product of colonization. Its effect, if not its underlying logic, has been to globalize new-philological values while effacing
the antithetical practices that helped constitute precolonial traditions.

Like the two that follow, this chapter views the new philology, in other
words, less as a methodological breakthrough than as another phase in the
intertwined histories of scholarly and sovereign power. This perspective reveals that the philological revolution's epistemic consequences have been
diametrically opposed to its claims. Any return to the new philology will, in
other words, only reinforce the limits it has placed on our concept of literature and its role in social resistance.

On the eve of the East India Company's 1765 conquest of Bengal, Persianate
empires—the Mughals, the Safavids, and the Ottomans—stretched across
South Asia, the Middle East, and North Africa. In each of these empires,
Persian was the language of polite culture, a primary medium of scholarly
discourse, and the model for all other literary languages.[2] It is no coincidence, therefore, that the pioneering text of colonial philology was William
Jones's *A Grammar of the Persian Language* (1771). Though largely forgotten
now, Jones's *Grammar* was wildly successful in late eighteenth- and early
nineteenth-century Europe. Its success was, in Garland Cannon's words,
"immediate" and "phenomenal," securing Jones's reputation as Europe's leading Orientalist.[3] It went through six editions over the next three decades and
nine total—as well as multiple translations into other European languages—
before it was finally superseded.

The *Grammar* was part of a far-ranging transformation of European
philological thought that had been under way, in much less widely read

works, for more than a century. Scholars across the continent had rejected the previously widespread premise that language's origins were either divine or natural and placed them within the confines of secular history instead. The focus of language study in Europe gradually shifted from the universal grammar that supposedly underlay every language to the historically specific grammar that distinguishes each language from all the others. But the new discipline of "historical grammar"—Antonio Gramsci's name for this philological transformation—involved a reconceptualization not only of language but of human nature itself, which was increasingly understood in terms not of universal rationality but of historical difference instead.[4] Historical grammar thus became the authoritative method for understanding not just language but, more broadly, the secular domain as such. Hence, however obscure historical grammar has since become, it nonetheless partially constitutes the modern humanities' foundation.

At the same time that Jones's *Grammar* played a part in philology's transformation, it also served a more practical function: to teach the agents of the East India Company the courtly forms of Persian; enable them to appropriate the scribal, scholarly, and literary practices of the Persianate empires; and hence endow them with those empires' sovereign aura. The *Grammar* inducted Company servants into Persianate gentlemanly culture and thus released the Company from its reliance on Persian-educated natives. The first attempt of a British philologist to reconstruct the study of an Asian language and literature on a colonial foundation, the *Grammar* marked the beginning of an epochal shift in the hegemonic forms of both philological and political power in the Indian Ocean world, as the clerks, scholars, and administrators of European corporate power replaced the Persianate elite. Eventually, colonial scholars would use historical grammar to study all of South Asia's vernacular languages, reconstruct their normative forms, and thus begin to modernize Indic literature. In this way, historical grammar laid the groundwork for colonial knowledge as well.

The *Grammar*'s importance lies, though, not only in these two interrelated events—a new science of language that gave the colonial state cultural authority over the colonized—but also in a third. In one of the many curious constellations within Jones's polymathic lifework, the *Grammar* introduced an urtext of European Romanticism: "A Persian Song of Hafiz," a translation

of the fabled fourteenth-century poet's masterful *ghazal* "The Shirazi Turk."
Jones's version would be widely read, praised, and cited from the date of its
original publication well into the twentieth century and frequently included
in anthologies of British period verse. Jones considered it, like the many other
Hafiz poems he translated into both English and French, a model of poetry
founded on passion rather than imitation. In the century that followed the
Grammar's publication, Western writers from Goethe to Nietzsche would
identify Hafiz's poetry with Dionysian desire and hence with the potential
revitalization of European culture. They would thus extend the *Grammar*'s
own aesthetic project, invoking the example of Hafiz as they attempted to
overturn the rules governing the European republic of letters.

Hence, by studying Jones's Hafiz, we can begin to undo a complex
historical knot. The new science of language informed both the colonial
reconstruction of non-European literatures and the aesthetic revolution
against neoclassicism. Once the phenomenon of language was understood
to reflect neither divine providence nor natural laws but instead human subjective diversity, the neoclassical demand that art imitate an objective world
became untenable. In the essays on aesthetic philosophy he published at the
same time as the *Grammar*, Jones famously renounced the principle of imitation altogether. He argued that the fine arts' primordial foundation lay not
in the imitation of nature but rather in primitive humanity's expression of
"violent passion": art originated, according to Jones, in languages that inten-
tionally articulate subjective states rather than those that presume to make
external reference. M. H. Abrams would place Jones's "expressive theory of
poetry" at the roots of Romanticism. But the fundamentally nonreferential
language intrinsic to violent passion—meant to illustrate that human subjectivity and speech precede and create the "objective" world—distinguishes
not just the Romantic category of literature but, of course, our idea of "the
literary" as such.

In short, then, "literature" is tied to historical grammar. This concept
emerged, per Foucault, only after eighteenth-century grammarians began
to demonstrate that every language is incommensurable with all others and
hence fundamentally performative: "[though] there has of course existed in
the Western world, since Dante, since Homer, a form of language that we
now call 'literature'[,] the word is of a recent date, as is also, in our culture,

the isolation of a particular language whose peculiar mode of being is 'literary.'"[5] In Foucault's lyrical account, "literature" is, at its roots, nothing but the conscious embrace of language's performative power: "At the moment when language becomes an object of knowledge, we see it reappearing in a strictly opposite modality[,] where it has nothing to say but itself, nothing to do but shine in the brightness of its being."[6] As this quotation attests, the embrace of language's performative power is one source of the aura—not to say fetishistic value—that still attaches to the study of literature today.

To the extent that we remain transfixed by this aura, we still accept the new philology's premises about "the literary." First, if literature is, by definition, nonreferential, it encompasses the secular domain even more completely for that reason. Its refusal to imitate any univocal reality enables the modern practice of literature—as Jacques Rancière has argued—to include all languages equally, not only those of every people and period but even those inscribed and waiting to be deciphered within all inanimate objects.[7] Second, as it liberates language's performative power, literature effectively dissolves every rule, law, and false metaphysical principle: in Foucault's words, literature "leads language back from grammar to the naked power of speech, and there it encounters the untamed [*sauvage*], imperious being of words."[8]

Hence, scholars from the late Enlightenment to contemporary postcolonial studies—including Foucault, Rancière, and many others discussed in this chapter and in the Conclusion—have consistently adduced a binary opposition between the conscious embrace of language's performative power, on one hand, and the forms of Western rationality (academic, juridical, political, etc.) they want to critique, on the other.[9] Whereas the latter distinguish the history of the West over the last three centuries, the former characterizes, according to the terms of this binary, archaic and non-European traditions. In fact, more than any other figure, Hafiz came to signify the supposedly convention-shattering and spell-binding force of performative language.

What should no longer pass without notice is that our concept of the literary has its own colonial matrix and logic. By virtue of its singular capacity to recover every language's performative power, the new philology appeared to make native literary traditions transmissible—even absent the material contexts that had given them their meaning. Hence, European philologists effectively reduced non-European verbal art to this idea of the literary: in the late eighteenth and early nineteenth centuries, they treated Asian works as models of performative language; by the late nineteenth century, they were more likely to deem such works aesthetic failures by the same measure. In either case, though, the hegemony of the literary within the realm of verbal art enabled Western scholars to exercise authority over non-Western traditions. To the extent that this concept now defines the universal essence of literature, it does so only because it began to colonize these traditions in the late eighteenth century. Even as it claimed to be the only type of language that could completely encompass the secular domain and abolish every metaphysical truth, the literary actually effaced the discursive practices that preceded colonial rule and served, unmistakably, as one of colonial philology's most effective tools. Hence, one of the most recent calls for a return to philology—Werner Hamacher's *Minima Philologica*—explicitly equates philology with the incomparable within each language.[10]

One could argue that the power of precolonial literary traditions lay not in the literary but precisely in its antithesis. For example, even as Hafiz's work does indeed aspire to a language that embraces every aspect of material life and opposes every metaphysical law, it implies that this language categorically cannot be textual. In fact, Hafiz famously refused to write his poetry down. On one level, Hafiz's poetry could not be abstracted from its performance (within local court culture). It needed to be a completely sensual—as opposed to merely textual—experience because its very point was to transform its audience's physical being, exploding the narrow limits of human desire in order to disclose within each listener an infinitely expansive (hence "divine") desire. It was designed, in other words, to turn the courtier's desire for social power into an altogether different desire and power. Precisely for this reason, Hafiz's poetry existed, on an even deeper level, in a fundamentally antagonistic relationship with textual culture—which was, for Hafiz, inextricable from the desire for public recognition and social authority. The language of his poetry was modeled not on literature or even on the literary but, in diametric opposition, on forms of life devoted to overcoming all such desire. The archaic—and indeed divinatory—power of Hafiz's poetry was thought to lie precisely here: not in its dependence on the literary but, on the contrary, in its connection to those now invisible realms textual culture had appropriated and effaced. Hence, any attempt to reactivate this power would need to begin, first of all, with an archaeology of the literary itself, this supposedly oppositional discourse that was bequeathed to us, in fact, by European philological power.

1. The Colonial Grammar of "Literature"

The historical facts passed down to us about the poet known by the pen name Hafiz are largely unverifiable. One detail, though, is unquestionably true: during the course of his lifetime, Hafiz became the acknowledged master of the *ghazal*, a genre of poetry that thematizes the pain of the poet's separation from the object of his or her desire. With roots in sixth-century Arabia, it spread, with Islam, to Southeast Asia in one direction and Andalusia in the other. It continues to shape both the classical and the popular traditions—musical as well as literary—of this tricontinental expanse.[11] Its cultural consequences are, for this reason, beyond reckoning. After the first translations of Hafiz into English and German in the late eighteenth and early nineteenth centuries, the *ghazal* would become a popular genre in these languages as well. The inspiration behind Goethe's *West-östlicher Divan*, Hafiz's *ghazal*s were consequently key to the original conceptualization of *Weltliteratur*. But even before the publicity the *West-östlicher Divan* brought Hafiz in the West, his work—as the preeminent model of the Islamic world's most influential literary genre—was a global phenomenon with few historical parallels.

In Hafiz's own time, though, and in the centuries before his transformation into a figure of world literature, the power of his poetry was thought to extend, in fact, *beyond* the farthest reaches of this world. Hafiz was known as "the tongue of the unseen" (*lesān-al-ḡayb*). His *Dīvān* (or collected poems) was said to be suffused by a secret knowledge of the mysterious force that rules human destiny and the stars alike—rivaled, in this regard, only by the Qur'ān. The early Sufis took seriously the Qur'ān's status as God's word and immersed themselves in its language.[12] Passages from the Qur'ān became the interpretive key through which they understood their own experiences, a phenomenon Paul Nwyia called, in an often-quoted formulation, the "Qur'ānization of memory."[13] Sufi poets—Hafiz in particular—alluded to and elaborated the significance of Qur'ānic passages even when they did not cite them directly. Thought to unfold the Qur'ān's hidden meaning, Hafiz's *Dīvān* was itself treated, therefore, as a kind of divine revelation.

Precisely because Persian speakers believed Hafiz's *Dīvān* partook so completely of the Qur'ān's sacred and revelatory nature, they entrusted the *Dīvān* with the mnemonic, cognitive, and interpretive functions they otherwise invested only in the Qur'ān and often studied the former text with a care normally reserved for the latter. In fact, they went even further, not only memorizing Hafiz's poetry and invoking it proverbially in everyday conversations, practices that have continued into the present, but even using it for divination (*tafā'ul*). People across the Persianate world, from Turkey to South Asia, would open Hafiz's *Dīvān* at random and seek for auguries of their own future in the radically polysemous language of the poem they found there, which they felt free to interpret after their own fashion. The omens they discovered would shape their choices as well as the behavior of family members and colleagues.

But when William Jones included "A Persian Song of Hafiz" within his *Grammar*, he brought Hafiz to the West as the vessel of a different knowledge. In Cannon's view, the *Grammar* initiated the scientific study of language in the West, dividing language into the categories of morphology, syntax, and phonology—though such terms were not yet available to Jones.[14] Éva Jeremiás has located, alternatively, an inchoate historical linguistics within the *Grammar*. According to her, it accurately placed Persian within a larger typology of languages, prefiguring the comparative techniques that subsequently led to the Indo-European hypothesis.[15] Lyle Campbell has focused on Jones's insistence—first articulated in the *Grammar*—that languages are of scholarly interest only because they contain, more completely than any other medium, the respective histories of different nations. He has consequently described Jones as the precursor of the nineteenth-century scholars such as Wilhelm von Humboldt and Max Müller who used philology to construct the modern categories of racial difference.[16]

Leading historians of the philological revolution—including Foucault, Hans Aarsleff, John Guillory, Sheldon Pollock, and Haruko Momma, among countless others—have also credited Jones with its founding in one regard or another.[17] But placing Jones at the source of scholarly disciplines that evolved, stage by stage, only decades after his death can obscure his distinctive approach to the history of language. Contrary to Cannon's claims, it lay not in the *Grammar*'s scientificity or systematicity. Labrosse's Persian grammar (1648), on whose analysis Jones drew, had already described most of Persian's major morphological features.[18] Neither was it the *Grammar's* historicism. In fact, Jones's work has less in common with the comparative method of historical linguistics and the new philology than that of a number of his predecessors and contemporaries across Europe, including Llhuyd (1707), Sajnovics (1770), Proyart (1776), Kraus (1787), Edwards (1787), and Gyarmathi (1799). Earlier scholars—in particular, Jäger (1686)—had even articulated more systematic formulations of the Indo-European hypothesis than Jones did.[19] His imprecise hypothesis gained traction while their more methodologically rigorous studies were overlooked only by virtue of Jones's extraordinarily prominent position within the late eighteenth-century republic of letters. Nor should Jones be conflated with the philologists who produced Aryan race theory, which draws on the Indo-European hypothesis but does not otherwise connect to Jones's work.

On one hand, the *Grammar* was, like the work of the seventeenth- and eighteenth-century scholars just cited, indeed part of a gradual and expansive shift from universal to historical grammar. The former's roots lay in medieval scholasticism, which was concerned to delineate the universal logic—the rationality God had gifted man—supposedly embedded within every language.[20] This project reemerged in the universal grammar of Scaliger, Sanctius, and, after Descartes, the Port Royal school: if all languages reflect the same mental structures, each must follow the rules of a single, universal grammar. These rules were supposedly set forth in the 1660 *Grammaire générale et raisonnée* (or *Port-Royal Grammar*), which defined orthodox linguistics for the next century. From the perspective of universal grammar, in short, all languages named the same a priori concepts and were, as a consequence, fully interchangeable and translatable. Ironically, the *Port-Royal Grammar* took only Latin and French into account: since all languages were governed by a single grammar, there was no reason to consider any others.

But Europe's colonial ventures gave the continent's scholars access to a much broader array of languages across both space and time and thus spurred the development of historical grammar.[21] At the same time, the disavowal of a priori analyses in favor of empirical approaches by Locke, among others, also encouraged the historical study of language and, by extension, of human nature itself. The discovery of the planet's linguistic diversity together with the development of empirical methods led, ultimately, to one of the new philology's guiding principles, namely, that languages, far from being semantically interchangeable, were in fact completely incommensurable. Hence, in the *Grammar*'s preface, Jones emphasized that his work "refrain[s] from making any enquiries into [universal] grammar."[22]

But Jones's *Grammar*, like his other early philological studies, was also part of another project: to open European letters to the literary practices it had abandoned. If the concept of universal logic—a priori and abstract—had circumscribed European grammatical thought, an encounter with Asia's classical literatures would, Jones believed, finally give European intellectuals a wider understanding of humanity's historical and geographic diversity. Jones's aim in this regard was to recover the "uncorrupted" language of every literary tradition—in other words, *all* the world's languages that existed before the advent, or within the interstices, of despotic law and arbitrary government.[23] Only grammar can recover the "ancient purity" of languages because of its unique capacity to disclose their historical content and to delineate their emergence and decline.[24] In "The History of the Persian Language"— an essay Jones intended to include within the *Grammar*—he observed that though "the transition appears rather abrupt, from *the history of Monarchs* to *the history of mere words*, and from the revolutions of *the Persian Empire* to the variations of *the Persian idiom*[,] *a considerable change in the language of any nation is usually effected by a change in the government*; so that *literary and civil history* are very nearly allied."[25] Scholarly attention to the "literature of Asia," Jones observed in the *Grammar*, would enable one to understand "by what degrees the most obscure states have risen to glory, and the most flourishing kingdoms have sunk to decay"; to "trace the human mind in all its various appearances, from the rudest to the most cultivated state"; and thus to "unlock the stores of native genius."[26]

Jones hoped that, by delinking philology from universal logic and orienting it toward "native" genius's countless forms instead, he could make it serve an emancipatory project. If philologists studied the historical conditions that enabled a given nation's unique spirit to flourish and those that led to its decay, they would help spread "the light of liberty and reason" within Europe, where, according to Jones, it had largely been extinguished.[27] In the view of Jones and his politically subversive contemporaries, the study of the Orient's "native," "original," or, in other words, "uncorrupted" languages would arrest European civilization's cultural decline. The terms Jones uses here, "native" and "original languages," correspond in more than superficial ways to the concept of "native" or "aboriginal languages" that the Marxist linguist V. N. Volosinov associated with "living speech in its limitlessly free, creative ebb and flow."[28] Volosinov contrasted such everyday use of language by native speakers with the "foreign" word, with languages, in other words, that "entered upon the scene with alien force of arms and organization": think here of any purely scriptural, liturgical, and/or bureaucratic language as well as every colonial language.[29] In diametric opposition to native speech's performative power, such languages "systemize" and "singularize" word meaning and thus produce transcendent "authority," "power," "holiness," and "truth": they play a "dictatorial" role in cultural production.[30] The opposition here—implicit in Jones, explicit in Volosinov—is between the political energy late eighteenth-century revolutionaries called "constituent power" and its principal adversary, constituted power.[31] The first names people's originary capacity to constitute a body politic, the second the appropriation of this power by social and political institutions. In Jones's view, "original" languages and the Oriental literatures he translated were aligned with the former, neoclassical aesthetics with the latter. If grammar had immemorially fixed the meaning of languages (such as Sumerian, Vedic Sanskrit, Homeric Greek, Qur'ānic Arabic) that had ceased to be demotic but still underpinned sovereign and/or clerical authority, Jones's work implicitly opposed this conservative function by recovering language's creative power instead.[32]

The *Grammar* thus marks the beginning of what would become Jones's overarching aesthetic project: the recovery of Asian languages in their "pure" forms as alternatives to European cultural and political decay. Though the *Grammar* participated in the philological revolution (and disseminated it to the colonies), its historical importance lies, in other words, not only there: it also helped constitute the modern category of "literature." Historical grammar presupposed that languages are incommensurable and, as a consequence, that each language's meaning is, ultimately, performative, not denotative. The modern category of literature defines "the literary" as the conscious embrace of this performative power. We can understand Jones's often-quoted explana-

tion of his translations in terms of this category, which took nascent form in
his work:

> Our *European* poetry has subsisted too long on the perpetual repetition of
> the same images, and incessant allusions to the same fables[:] it has been
> my endeavour for several years to inculcate this truth, that, if the principal
> writings of the *Asiaticks* [were printed] and if the languages of the *Eastern*
> nations were studied in our great seminaries of learning[,] a new and ample
> field would be opened for speculation[;] we should be furnished with a new
> set of images and similitudes.[33]

What European writers have to gain from "the images and similitudes" of
Eastern poets is more, though, than a set of new tropes. Whereas European
writing is, according to Jones, *"the likeness of a likeness,"* "Eastern poetry" does
not represent something else but instead realizes *"that rich and creative invention, which is the very soul of poetry."*[34] Jones wanted European literature to
share, in other words, Eastern poetry's performative power. He considered
performative language to be not only ontologically prior but also intrinsically
opposed to constituted power. Jones thus articulated the concept of literature that still shapes the widespread belief in its supposedly radical potential.
Jones made Hafiz the model of this concept (and, by extension, one origin of
world literature), thus dissociating his work from Persianate traditions.

2. From the Persian Imperium to the British Empire

Yet Jones published the *Grammar* when he did because he realized that the
British conquest of Bengal—now "the source of incredible wealth to the merchants of Europe"—had suddenly increased the economic value of Persian,
which had long been the Mughal Empire's primary political as well as poetic
medium.[35] Persian maintained these roles even after the Mughals lost Bengal
because the East India Company initially preserved Mughal institutions and
forced its junior servants (or "writers")—who were responsible for creating
the Company's archive of official records—to learn Persian. In fact, many
required the specialized knowledge necessary to read the formal documents
Mughal officials used to communicate with each other. In the preface to the
Grammar, which Jones envisioned as a textbook for Company servants, he
described the convergence of British imperial history with his own cultural

project: "The languages of Asia will now, perhaps, be studied with uncommon ardour; they are known to be useful, and will soon be found instructive and entertaining. [The] manner and sentiments of the eastern nations will be perfectly known; and the limits of our knowledge will be no less extended than the bounds of our empire."[36]

But the utility of Persian went far beyond British India, as Jones fully recognized. Persianate elites held power not merely in India but, as mentioned, across Central Asia and the Middle East as well. The *Grammar* could help British merchant corporations, therefore, operate across this vast territory: "There is scarce a country in Asia or Africa from the source of the Nile to the wall of China, in which a man who understands Arabic, Persian, and Turkish may not travel with satisfaction, or transact the most important affairs with advantage and security."[37] In fact, the Levant (or "Turkey") Company—responsible for British trade to Egypt, the Middle East, and the Ottoman Empire—joined the East India Company in encouraging Jones's work on the *Grammar*. Jones sought the patronage, furthermore, of continental courts and learned societies, emphasizing that "all Europe [would] in a few years reap the benefit" of the *Grammar*, his address to both sovereigns and scholars testifying to the *Grammar*'s simultaneously political and cultural project.[38] Because its publication coincided with a far-reaching transformation of imperial power in Asia, Jones was in an unprecedented position to disseminate Persian literature to civil servants in India as well as to intellectuals in Europe.

Both aspects of the *Grammar*'s project, literary and political, depended on the appropriation of Persianate linguistic authority. As the court language, both administrative and literary, of the Delhi Sultanate (1206–1526), Persian had been an imperial language in India long before the Mughals.[39] The sultans brought Persian literature to South Asia along with Persian court scholars to educate the native elite. As a consequence, in the sultanate and Mughal courts as throughout the Persianate empires, courtiers proved their status by their membership in Muslim gentlemanly (*sharif*) culture, their mastery of the Persian literary tradition, and their capacity to compose verse in the same manner. According to Tariq Rahman, "Persian was the language of the powerful, of the exercise of power itself, when the British arrived on the scene."[40] As mentioned, the *Grammar* enabled the Company, wherever possible, to replace native clerks, scribes, record-keepers, and secretaries with British writers. Jones's preface emphasizes the *Grammar*'s place in this pro- totypically colonial transformation, what Bernard Cohn called the conquest of "epistemological space": "It was found highly dangerous to employ the natives as interpreters, upon whose fidelity [the East India Company ser- vants] could not depend; and it was at last discovered that they must apply themselves to the study of the Persian language, in which all the letters from the Indian princes were written."[41] Wherever it was not possible to replace natives, the Company incorporated them into the lowest levels of its own administration. For these natives, Persian literacy remained a prerequisite of public employment, and they consequently continued to study Persian even after its elimination as an administrative language in the late 1830s.

After the Company's court of directors recommended the *Grammar* to Company servants, it introduced countless British colonists to the study of Persian as well. Jones had illustrated the *Grammar*'s rules with poetic cou- plets from "classical" Persian, the medieval literary dialect of Shiraz (which he called "the Athens of Persia").[42] He considered Hafiz the "most elegant" poet in the Persian tradition and consequently quoted and translated his work ad nauseam in the *Grammar*.[43] He aimed, in this way, "to facilitate the progress of [Persian] literature" among Europeans.[44] Studying Hafiz did in fact become one method by which Company servants learned classical Persian, proved their own politesse, and hence acquired the qualifications necessary to ascend the Company ladder: those who mastered the language most completely moved more quickly to positions of power. Many of the nineteenth-century English translations of Hafiz published in British India demonstrated precisely such mastery. British administrators created personal libraries of Persian literature in the original language and spent their leisure absorbing Persian poetry, reserving for Persian the same scholarly attention European intellectuals applied to Greek and Latin. The cultural value they attributed to Persian realized Jones's aspiration to make this language the source of an alternative classicism. Hence, for British colonists as well as na- tive subjects, Persian maintained its cultural prestige long after it had lost its administrative function.

Company scholars augmented the *Grammar* with books about Persian scribal and Mughal administrative practices as well as dictionaries, language textbooks, and numerous translations from the original language, historiographical as well as poetic. Together with the *Grammar*, these works effectively initiated the European field of Persian studies. When the Company created Fort William College (est. 1800) to educate its newly arrived servants, it founded a chair in Persian—anticipating both Oxford and Cambridge in this regard—and made the college's Persian Department its most prestigious. Once British scholars realized Persia's extraordinary importance to the empire in the early nineteenth century, Persian studies began to explode.[45]

But even as colonial statesmen and soldiers alike treated Persian literature as another classical tradition, it also meant something altogether different to them. In this also, their encounter with Persian followed Jones's design. I have argued that Jones published the *Grammar* as part of a larger project to transform European poetry. It may be more accurate to say, though, that he wanted to turn his readers into something other than what they were, to make them no longer European at all or, at least, more than merely European. When he described Persian as a "branch of literature" whose progress he hoped the *Grammar* would facilitate, Jones used "literature" in a sense now largely lost to us. From the late seventeenth century, "philology" had denoted not a specifically historicist approach to language and texts but rather scholarly book-learning, "literature" the amateur version of the same.[46] During this time, the spheres of "philology" and "literature," on one hand, and of poetry, on the other, had not yet been separated from each other: the former were thought to shape the latter and consequently blurred into it. Professional and, even more, amateur literary study were meant, in other words, to reorient poetic production: Jones's work attests to the late eighteenth-century constellation of these now separate and often opposed concepts, book-learning and belles lettres. When Jones was elected to Samuel Johnson's Club after the *Grammar*'s publication, Johnson himself sent Governor-General of India Warren Hastings a copy of the *Grammar* with the comment "that literature is not totally forsaking [us] will appear from [this] book."[47]

Many of the British colonists who studied Persian would indeed go on to write *ghazal*s themselves. Following the formal convention by which the poet would weave his pseudonym (*takhalluṣ*) into the *ghazal*'s final couplet (*maqṭa*) as both his signature and, if possible, a semantic element—a convention whose most artful practitioner was the poet with the pen name Hafiz—these colonists assumed Persian, Arabic, and Urdu aliases. Alexander Heatherley became "Azad" (Persian for "free"); George Puech "Shor" (Urdu for "noise"); General Joseph Bensley "Fana" (Arabic for the verb "to pass away" or "cease to exist").[48] The last *takhalluṣ* alludes to the negation of the self considered to be the necessary condition for divine union in Islamic mystical thought: it is said to originate from the Qur'ānic verse "All things in creation will suffer annihilation [*fānin*], and there will remain only the face of the Lord in its majesty and bounty."[49] In their *ghazal*s, Company servants strove to become Sufis. The *Grammar*'s true progeny, they appeared to testify, if not to the existential transformation of European life, at least to the epistemic transformation of European and world literature, an aesthetic revolution that occurred, ironically, under the aegis of colonial rule.

But when Jones, Company Persianists, and generations of colonial officials ascribed prestige to classical Persian in general and to Hafiz's work in particular, they extended, after their own fashion, the literary prejudices of the Persianate elite who preceded them.[50] Hafiz's *Dīvān* was, in the words of Shahab Ahmed, "the most widely-copied, widely-circulated, widely-read, widely-memorized, widely-recited, widely-invoked, and widely-proverbialized book of poetry in Islamic history."[51] The Mughals immersed themselves in the work of Sufi poets and made Hafiz a paradigm for South Asian court poetry. In Mughal India—from where more commentaries on the *Dīvān* issued than from even Persia itself—as subsequently in British India, the study of Hafiz formed part of the Persian curriculum that enabled one to become fluent in the language of the elites and hence in the idiom of power. Thus, however true to Hafiz's spirit colonial officials such as Heatherley, Puech, and Bensley believed themselves to be, their understanding of his work was mediated, like our own, by many layers of imperial culture, from the emergence of Persianate ruling classes across Western, Central, and South Asia through the Delhi Sultanate and Mughal courts to the British Empire and European philology. Here, we witness the extent to which the sudden formation of a supposedly counterhegemonic Romanticism grew, in fact, directly from the centuries of sovereign and philological power that preceded it. The Hafiz we have inherited—via the British colonial rule—is an imperial legacy through and through.

3. The Passions of Literature:
Hafiz, 1771 A.D.

Jones had himself paraphrased, he claimed, nearly three hundred of Hafiz's
ghazals.[52] He published fifteen complete verse translations in three different
languages: besides "A Persian Song of Hafiz" in English, there were thirteen
much more nuanced translations in French, and even one in Greek. Though
the *Grammar* contains only one complete verse translation, "A Persian Song" is
by far Jones's most influential. The original poem, known as "The Shirazi Turk,"
is considered, even within Hafiz's dazzling oeuvre, to be particularly brilliant.
To translate Hafiz's dense metaphors, Jones expanded the poem from nine couplets to nine sestets, the first famously beginning: "Sweet maid, if thou would'st
charm my sight, / And bid these arms thy neck infold; / That rosy cheek, that
lily hand, / Would give thy poet more delight / Than all Bocara's vaunted
gold, / Than all the gems of Samarcand."[53] Jones would republish the poem the
following year in his *Poems, Consisting Chiefly of Translations from the Asiatic
Languages*; *The Annual Register* of 1772 reproduced the poem again, testifying
to its immediate popularity. Eventually, the work of Byron, Shelley, Thomas
Moore, and Swinburne, among others, would bear traces of Jones's poem. The
Hafiz vogue it created would engender countless further translations, in German as well as English, that would leave their marks on the poetry, among
many others, of Goethe, Emerson, Thoreau, Whitman, Longfellow, Melville,
and Tennyson, who studied the *Grammar* in order to read Hafiz in the original.
Engels would do the same, updating Marx on his progress: "It is, by the way,
rather pleasing to read dissolute old Hafiz in the original language[,] and, in
his grammar, old Sir William Jones likes to cite as examples dubious Persian
jokes, subsequently translated into Greek verse in his *Commentariis poeseos asi-
aticae*, because even in Latin they seem to him too obscene."[54]

Scholars have long recognized the seminal place of "A Persian Song"
within Romantic Orientalism. A. J. Arberry emphasized that of Jones's "various important contributions" to the nascent field of Persian studies, none
was "more far-reaching in its consequences" than his translations of Hafiz.[55]
Vivian de Sola Pinto's claims for "A Persian Song" went further: "The once
famous lyric called "A Persian Song of Hafiz" [may be] one of the chief
sources of that dream-world of Oriental pleasure which haunted the imagination of so many English poets of the early nineteenth century."[56] Michael

Franklin has gone further still: "Romantic Orientalism is born [within] the pages of [Jones's] Persian grammar."[57]

But though these scholars confine Jones's translation within the ambit of Romantic Orientalism, one could argue that Orientalism was constitutive of Romanticism *tout court*. For Jones and the Romantics who followed his lead, poetic language found its exemplary form less in Europe than in the Orient. The redefinition of poetic language that Jones presented in "On the Arts, Commonly Called Imitative"—an essay published one year after the *Grammar* within the same volume that reprinted "A Persian Song"—would soon become a Romantic axiom. This essay rejected the Aristotelian "assertion [that] *all poetry consists in imitation*" and argued instead that poetry originates in "a strong, and animated expression of the human passions," in particular "the violent passions."[58] But if poetry's origins lie in such passions, refined poetry requires "the greatest calmness and serenity of mind" and must, as a consequence, reflect on these passions from a distance.[59] Three decades later, Wordsworth's "Preface to *Lyrical Ballads*" would formulate this theory more evocatively: "Poetry is the spontaneous overflow of powerful feelings: it takes its origins from emotions recollected in tranquility."[60] But Jones's emphasis was on the violence of the passions that produce poetry: "*original and native poetry*" is "*the language of the violent passions*"; "*genuine poetry*" is "some vehement passion [expressed] *in a common voice*."[61] And the prototype of poetry in this sense lies in archaic and Oriental writing: Jones claimed that his definition of "what true poetry *ought to be* [also] described what it was really *was* among the *Hebrews*, the *Greeks* and *Romans*, the *Arabs* and *Persians*."[62] Like the archaic, Eastern poetry—which Jones believed to be expressive, not imitative—is closer to the "first language of man" and as a consequence to the elemental sources of human creativity:

> In some *Mahometan* nations; where [the imitative arts of] *sculpture* and *painting* are forbidden by the laws, where *dram[a]* of every sort is wholly unknown[,] the pleasing arts, of *expressing the passions in verse*[,] are cultivated [with] enthusiasm. [Poetry's] greatest effect is not produced by *imitation*, but by a very different principle; which must be sought for in the deepest recesses of the human mind.[63]

According to the scholarly literature, Jones's programmatic declaration of "the expressive theory of poetry" turned eighteenth-century aesthetic philosophy on its head, describing art in terms no longer of the spectator and judgment but rather of the artist and "creativity."[64] As almost every scholar discussing Jones's poetics has recounted, M. H. Abrams considered "On the *Arts, Commonly Called Imitative*" to be the first systematic articulation of Romantic aesthetics and Jones the first writer to disavow completely the neoclassical principle of imitation in favor of a Romantic emphasis on creativity.[65] The *Broadview Anthology of British Literature* reiterates Abrams's claims: according to its Romanticism volume, Jones's "theories of poetry and poetic inspiration [had] an immeasurable influence on the development of the Romantic movement." This volume concludes the preface to its William Jones section: "Any comprehensive study of Romantic poetry should begin with his work."[66]

Actually, though, Abrams misstated Jones's argument. As a consequence, his account of the "expressive theory of poetry"—like those of the countless scholars, such as Charles Taylor, who depend on him—empty it of its provocation.[67] According to Abrams, Jones believed that lyric was "the original poetic form" and wanted to make it "the prototype for poetry as a whole."[68] In fact, Jones described lyric as only one of poetry's original forms, which are unified not by any single genre but only by their shared basis in violent passions. Jones's point was not, furthermore, to replace neoclassicism's formulaic imitation of Greek and Latin tropes with the "emotional intensity," per Julie Meisami, of lyric poetry.[69] It was instead, much more ambitiously, to overthrow altogether the "classical order of representation" that ruled the fine arts.[70] Within this order, the principle of imitation tied the arts to aristocratic forms, to the languages of the only men supposed capable of political praxis. Ultimately at issue for Jones and the Romantics was not the expression of emotion per se but instead the effort to disentangle art from socially privileged speech, from the social hierarchies they believed had defined the fine arts since Aristotle.

Hence, Jones intended his "expressive" theory—his emphasis, more precisely, on the *performative* power of "original" languages—not only to evoke a more historically and geographically inclusive concept of humanity but also to be politically subversive: such languages alone fully inhabit humanity's constituent power: "Thus will each artist gain his end, not by *imitating* the work of nature, but by assuming her power."[71] It was precisely with this "natural" power that neoclassical art, in its studied artificiality, had lost touch: "considering [art to be originally expressive] will set the refinements of modern artists in their true light[;] no man, truly affected with *love* or *grief*, ever expressed the one in an *acrostick* or the other in a *fugue*."[72] To the extent that they enact the "violent" passions that predate political corruption, expressive languages are aligned with popular against autocratic power.

The Romantic opposition to social privilege is embedded within Jones's very use of the word "literature," which acquired an additional semantic layer—over and above the one already discussed—at this time. While Johnson's *Dictionary* still records the older sense ("learning; skill in letters"), texts by Voltaire, Lessing, and Herder from 1751 to 1767 employ *littérature* and *Literatur* in a modern sense: to refer not just to the socially exclusive knowledge possessed by the cultivated individual but also to the total body of written works, whether in a given language, a particular period, or across human history as such.[73] This definition of literature arrived in Scotland and England slightly later: it is evident, for example, in Adam Ferguson's *Essay on the History of Civil Society* (1767) and in the earliest volumes of Johnson's *Lives of Poets* (1779). Raymond Williams considered this concept—concerned not to privilege any single genre, language, or tradition but to treat them all as sources of historical knowledge—to be the product of the late Enlightenment.[74] Yet colonial Orientalists such as Jones—including Alexander Dow (1768) and Warren Hastings (1785)—had used "literature" in precisely this sense as early as writers in Britain. According to Vinay Dharwadker, they "were at the forefront of European scholarly thought about the category of 'literature.'"[75]

These Orientalists intended their reading of texts across genres, languages, and religions to produce a comprehensive knowledge of human nature and development and consequently an epistemic revolution within—and against—European civilization. They sought, in other words, to know both human desire in its original state, before the advent of autocracy, and all the diverse paths history had taken from there. In their view, neither end of this spectrum—neither desire in its purity nor history in its complexity—could be known if one remained wholly within the horizons of European civilization.

The Orientalist study of "literature" both as the inclusive category of texts written across history and as language's originally performative power influenced the Romantic reconceptualization of "literature" as the deepest form of verbal art, encompassing the language of not just the aristocracies but every form of life. In other words, colonial philology informed the Romantic pursuit of languages and forms of life that existed before, outside, or on the margins of the historical record. In each of these Romantic dreamworlds—whether archaic, medieval, rural, illiterate, Oriental, et cetera—the power of language resides in its performative, not denotative, aspect.

Jacques Rancière has argued that the Romantic concept of "literature"—"the radical democracy of the letter that anyone can grab hold of"—places all modes of representation on an equal footing.[76] In fact, though, this concept privileges one mode above all others: historical understanding. Whether it drew its inspiration from archaic or from Oriental poetry, the post-Romantic practice of "literature" depended on philological reconstructions. When it invoked forms of life, human or not, beyond philology's grasp, it depended on philology's sister disciplines—archaeology, paleontology, and geology—that could tell, respectively, architectural, evolutionary, and geologic time. Like philology, each of these new methods gave semantic depth to previously silent objects. If neoclassical art claimed mimetic truth or verisimilitude, the new practice of literature staked a superior claim: it possessed the unique capacity to read and give voice to the otherwise mute languages inscribed in "life"—that which precedes law and politics—itself. "Democratic literarity," according to Rancière, "spells the absence of any boundary between the language of art and that of ordinary life": "what literature pits against privileg[ed] speech [is] writing seen as a machine for making life talk[:] speech written on the body of things, taken from the sons and daughters of the plebeians; but also speech that is not offered by anyone, that does not answer to any desire for meaning but expresses the truth of things the same ways fossils or striations in rocks bear their written history."[77] Hence, regardless of the commonplace opposition between fiction and history, the language of literature could emerge henceforward only from historical consciousness, as *Mimesis* tacitly insists. Literature is, in other words, a counterhistorical practice that cannot fully acknowledge the forms of historical authority—including colonial philology—on which it depends.

This is not to suggest that Romantic writers were unaware of the paradox. Romantic poetry is, on the contrary, full of "things longed for but never really seen," images of fugitive experience the poet pursues but consciously fails to capture.[78] They testify to the poet's recognition of his own imprisonment within forms of desire that have been produced by writing itself and, for this reason, cannot be fully realized. Nonetheless, the Romantics' very desire for affective and linguistic models outside the classical tradition suggests how deeply determined they were by the transformation of grammatical thought embodied in Jones's work. The concept and practice of literature that followed this transformation was less an openness to the East and silenced others than one manifestation of philological power's latest phase, still organized around historical knowledge. Regardless of Rancière's claims, modern literature is not the democratized representation of previously "mute speech" but rather its aesthetic expropriation.

The transformation of grammatical thought that underlies the modern concept of the literary had consequences far beyond the domains of literature and aesthetic philosophy. It also legitimized colonial rule's arrogation of control over native tradition: because the colonial state possessed historical knowledge about native languages, literatures, and laws, it could reject or subordinate the authority of native philology *tout court*. The grammars, dictionaries, textbooks, and translations colonial scholars published enabled them to reconstruct the most widely spoken native languages, not just in South Asia but across the empire, and to claim, at the same time, that each of these reconstructions merely restored the proper form of the language in question. Hence, regardless of its counterphilological roots, historical grammar eventually became a form of philological power whose global reach was much greater than that of any prior phase.

4. Nietzsche and "World Literature"

"I am afraid we have not got rid of God," Nietzsche famously observed, "because we still have faith in grammar."[79] In his view, theological habits of mind emerge from the false belief—as old as ancient Greek and Indian thought—in the metaphysical reality of semantics and syntax. Glosses of this passage fail to mention, though, that Nietzsche was not calling on us to treat meaning and order as linguistic constructs. Such an attitude produces nihilism, the mirror image of metaphysics, the inevitable outcome of all previously sacred entities losing their essential significance: "In the beginning there was the great disaster of an error, the belief that the will is [a] *faculty*. These days we know that it is just a word."[80] Nietzsche referred the linguistic organization of the world neither, like early modern proponents of universal grammar, to an eternal faculty nor, like late nineteenth-century philologists, to the dead letter. He identified it instead with the endlessly active and affirmative energy he called "the will to power." Though this drive to realize singular desires has no metaphysical stability, it is nonetheless, in Nietzsche's view, always historically present. Texts and traditions are of interest to him, therefore, only to the extent that they manifest this power's operation.

I would emphasize that Nietzsche's will to power carries the echo of Jones's "violent passions" and their constituent energy. In fact, though the scholarship on Nietzsche has largely overlooked this fact, his overarching project—to transcend Europe's millennia-long tradition of metaphysical thought—is symptomatic of the Oriental Renaissance. A century before Nietzsche, Jones had already discussed the idea that "Creation was rather an *energy* than a *work*," which, in contrast to Nietzsche, he claimed had been pervasive in ancient Indian, Persian, Egyptian, and pre-Socratic thought and had survived among "the most enlightened" modern philosophers.[81] The Oriental Renaissance was precipitated precisely by European philologists' efforts to undo the metaphysical faith in universal grammar. Nietzsche's thought merely took historical grammar, the Hafiz vogue, and the Oriental Renaissance to their logical conclusion. For Nietzsche as for Jones, in other words, emancipation from European knowledge depended on an encounter with the Orient. Nietzsche's private correspondence attests, in the most compact terms imaginable, to this connection: "I want to live for [a year or two] among Muslims, specifically where their faith is now most severe: *thus will my judgment and my eye for all things European become sharper.*"[82]

A few years after confessing to his amanuensis this yearning to live among the faithful in Tunisia, Nietzsche presented his lifework as preparation for the return of Eastern thought:

> To wait and to prepare oneself [for] strange faces and voices[;] to *overcome* everything Christian through something supra-Christian[;] to reconquer southern health and hidden powerfulness of soul; step by step to become more comprehensive, more supranational, more European, more supra-European, more Oriental[,] for the Greek was the first great union and synthesis of everything Oriental, and on that account the *inception* of the European soul, the discovery of *our "new world"*: whoever lives under such imperatives, who knows what *he* may not encounter one day? Perhaps—a *new day*![83]

This entry from Nietzsche's notebook recapitulates the Oriental Renaissance. Like Jones's "On the Arts, Commonly Called Imitative," it claims that the Orient—to which it also assimilates Greece—constitutes both the lost origin and the revolutionary future of European civilization. It aligns itself with this origin in pointed opposition to classical and neoclassical culture. It suggests that modern Europeans must now "reconquer" their origin, appropriated even in the ancient world by antithetical forces: the one who does so will become "comprehensive," effectively absorbing the whole history of civilization into himself.

Nietzsche used Hafiz, more than any other Oriental figure, to mark Europe's limits: he invoked Hafiz's name throughout his late work and even, like colonial Orientalists from the late eighteenth century forward, wrote poetry in Hafiz's honor.[84] Hafiz was for Nietzsche the absolute antithesis of the two primary currents, Christianity and Romanticism, that composed the problem of "Europe" as he conceived it. Whereas Christianity is the ethical and Romanticism the aesthetic expression of *ressentiment* (or hatred for the material conditions of human existence), Hafiz's work sacralizes life in precisely the sense previously described, the "bare life" that precedes law and politics. Hafiz's poetry reflects his capacity to experience "the highest and most illustrious human joys, in which existence celebrates its own transfiguration."[85]

Nietzsche continually returned to this opposition. The fifth book of *The Gay Science* invoked Hafiz in the process of answering the question "What is Romanticism?" Here, Hafiz reappears "blissfully jesting," an artist who creates from "gratitude and love," "super-abundance," and an "overflowing energy [pregnant] with the future."[86] Hafiz's poetry is an "art of apotheoses": it deifies, in an absolutely amoral fashion and without prejudice, every element of the human realm.[87] Nietzsche contrasted it with the *ressentiment* of the "disinherited" and "underprivileged" who "*must* destroy, because what exists, and indeed all existence, all being, outrages and provokes him."[88] The following year, the third essay of *The Genealogy of Morals* used Hafiz to answer a related question, "What is the meaning of ascetic ideals?" Here, Nietzsche placed Hafiz among "the best and brightest" of "healthy and cheerful mortals" who completely embrace their human condition ("between 'animal and angel'"), experiencing it not as "one of the arguments against life" but rather as "one *more* of life's charms."[89] The premise that literature (of a certain kind) alone can completely embrace life programs Nietzsche's passages on Hafiz as clearly as it does Rancière's *Politics of Literature*, different as these two philosophers are from each other. The translation of Hafiz into European languages heralded, in Nietzsche's view, a future Romanticism based—in diametric opposition to Schopenhauer's and Wagner's poverty—on the superabundant creativity of desire. The allusions to Hafiz began to multiply: *Beyond Good and Evil*, *Nietzsche contra Wagner*, the notebooks, and so on.

Nietzsche aligned Hafiz with Dionysus, the foreign god who, the archaic cults claimed, had arrived from the Orient. The "superabundance" of Hafiz's poetry was—as Nietzsche noted in *The Gay Science*—"Dionysian."[90] The Dionysian principle was, in turn, a more precise name for Europe's suppressed origin and its revolutionary future. During the period in which Hafiz was a motif in Nietzsche's work, the Dionysian became the antithesis no longer just of the Apollonian but, much more momentously, of both Christianity and Romanticism. The Dionysian energy that is the source of art in Nietzsche's schema accepts the violence intrinsic to the material world and directs it against any entity that confines desire: he who "is richest in the fullness of life, the Dionysian god and man, [can afford] even the terrible deed and any luxury of destruction, decomposition, and negation."[91]

In diametric opposition, Christian morality turned violence *against* desire.[92] "Romantic pessimism"—which Nietzsche called "the last *great* event in the fate of our culture"—took Christian morality, in turn, to its limit.[93] Schopenhauer's and Wagner's generation represents the complete supersession of material life by cultural production; they turn their own hatred of life "into a binding law and compulsion."[94] But Nietzsche foresaw a subsequent and final stage in the dialectical history of desire. Because European civilization's desire to destroy life had become total and pervasive by the late nineteenth century, its own destruction would inaugurate a new epoch, the return of Dionysus on a continent-wide scale: "[Dionysian pessimism] comes! I see it coming!"[95] Like Jones's "violent passion," Nietzsche's Dionysian principle no less than his "will to power" names desire at the moment of its emergence—constituent power, an always revolutionary event.

Nietzsche claimed that this principle was largely invisible to philological understanding: "Here is the great depth, the great *silence*, in all matters Greek—*one does not know the Greeks* as long as this hidden subterranean entrance lies blocked with rubble. Importunate scholars' eyes will never see anything in these things."[96] The Dionysian—subsequently overcome by the successive forms (e.g., Apollonian, Christian, Romantic) of European textual authority—remains as only a trace within Greek art. Its recovery required, therefore, a revolutionary philology, a revolution against the history of philology, an archaeological approach that would destroy the layers of philological power that had determined European self-understanding. In the days after his breakdown, before friends brought him from the South back to the North, Nietzsche signed his "madness letters" with a new pseudonym: "Dionysos."[97]

Yet, though Nietzsche aligned his understanding of Hafiz and Dionysus with a revolutionary future, it was, in fact, a philological legacy. For example, the idea that Christ and Christianity were dialectical appropriations of Dionysus and the Dionysian religion, respectively, descended from Hölderlin, Schelling, and Creuzer, among many others.[98] And the association of Hafiz with Dionysus descended from Jones himself, who referred to Hafiz as "the Anacreon of Persia."[99] The Romantics picked upon this association and presented Hafiz in bacchanalian terms. The rejection of imitation and the identification of passion as the basis of artistic creation, which recur in Nietzsche as well as Jones, had their own antecedents, in both recent European philology (Vico and Bishop Lowth) and ancient Epicurean philosophy (Lucretius).[100]

And in the *West-Eastern Diwan*, as the Napoleonic Wars drew to a close, Goethe had already called on European letters to revitalize itself by turning to Hafiz and Islamic poetry, thereby echoing Jones's *Grammar* and prefiguring Nietzsche's *Gay Science*. Here are the opening verses of the poem's first books ("Hegira" and "Lied und Gebilde"):

Thrones are shattered, empires shaking:
Flee to the pure East, and there

. . .

Love, wine, song are waiting for you,

. . .

Origins of humankind,
And that simple lore I'll find
Which they learnt, unschooled, God-given,
Dropped in earthly tongues from heaven.

. . .

Alien thraldom they rejected.

Hail, glad early youth of man,

. . .

In their words a power unbroken

Dwelt, for all their words were spoken.

. . .

In the baths and taverns too, Häfiz, I'll remember you,

When some sweetheart lifts her veil,

Shakes her scented locks; the tale

Of our whispered love shall fashion

Even the Huris' hearts to passion.

. . .

Let the Greek make shapes of clay

. . .

To rejoice his sight.

But our pleasure is to plunge

In the Euphrates' stream,

Dipping, drifting to and fro

Through its liquid dream.[101]

The connections between passion, Oriental poetry, and constituent power—
and hence the underlying premise that literary expression, properly practiced,
precedes politics and opposes autocracy—are particularly pronounced in
this text at the roots of world literature. The opposition here, as in Jones,
is between an expressive art, which possesses performative power ("In their
words a power unbroken/Dwelt, for all their words were spoken"), and an
imitative one, which is merely denotative and hence does not ("Let the
Greek make shapes of clay/[To] rejoice his sight"). Goethe presented this
opposition in the same terms Jones used in his passage on the "*Mahometan*
nations" that cultivate poetry but forbid sculpture and the fine arts. Only
expressive art lies at—or before—the very origins of civilization ("Origins
of humankind/[I'll] find"; "Hail, glad early youth of man"), is truly aligned
with constituent power ("Alien thraldom they rejected"), and, as a consequence, also points toward the future.

Hence, far from either an effaced origin or a revolutionary future, this centuries-old concept of the literary—still responsible, in part, for the aura that surrounds literature—is a new-philological construct. Though Nietzsche's invocations of Hafiz are meant to signal his break with the European tradition, they follow strictly in its tracks. The fantasy of becoming "supra-European" accompanied the rise of comparative method and world literature. Nietzsche patterned his lifework, in other words, on the prototypical quest of the new philology, which believed itself to be dismantling the prior history of philological authority in order to recover the primordial human creativity that such authority had appropriated and deformed. But this epistemic revolution ended up only reinforcing philological authority in a reconstituted form. Despite their own counterphilological ambitions, Jones, Goethe, the Romantics, and Nietzsche remained captivated by the new philology's trick: with the emergence of historical grammar, philologically transmitted texts and traditions became embodiments of historical difference. In other words, our alternatives to the history of philology are, perversely, always its own products. Historical grammar's effort to recover the uncorrupted form of every language from its *written* record—and, in this way, to define normative use in the present—reinforced and naturalized the different phases of philological power that had created that record. In his centrality to the court cultures of the Persianate empires, Hafiz was, for example, practically a civilization-founding figure. Each of these empires—including the Ottomans in Turkey, the Safavid and Qajars in Persia, the Timurids in Central Asia, and the Mughals in India—were, as Leonard Lewisohn has noted, "Hafizocentric" and treated the *Divan* itself as a type of "miraculous scripture."[102]

Nietzsche not only recognized such paradoxes but also understood he could not extricate himself from them—hence the epigraph from him that begins this book: "I know [the philologists]: I am myself one."[103] But however much Nietzsche ironized philology, his very dream of an epistemic revolution—and the limits that defined his dream—was tacitly governed by it. Like Jones and the Romantics, Nietzsche attempted to oppose the philology of his day and, indeed, the whole history of European philology but could not oppose philological authority as such. One cannot stress this distinction enough: Nietzsche's own training prevented him, despite his best intentions, from brushing traditions against their philological grain. The history of philology must be understood—precisely as Nietzsche suggested—in terms of an endless series of appropriations. But what lies before or at the origins of this history is, ultimately, not the Dionysian. This principle—the "superabundance" and "overflowing creative energy" of desire—was in fact integral to Western philology long before Nietzsche. A truly constituent politics would need, therefore, to conceive the exclusion at the origins of European civilization and neoclassical culture in terms very different from those we have inherited from Jones, Goethe, and Nietzsche.

Historical grammar sutured precolonial to colonial forms of philological authority. The prescriptive and universal grammars that respectively defined Islamic and European language study before colonial rule were fundamentally normative practices. Historical grammar was originally premised, as Gramsci noted, on the "uselessness" of normative grammar.[104] Yet historical grammar emerged at a specific historical juncture: the moment when singularly centralized state structures began to govern exceptionally large and heterogeneous territories. Gramsci identified this moment with the rise of nation-states, but one could argue that it belongs to the emergence of modern empires instead.[105] In either case, though, despite its opposition to the normative rules that defined language use, historical grammar only ended up reproducing such rules, as Gramsci emphasized: "Since the study of languages as a cultural phenomenon grew out of political needs[,] normative grammar ha[s] exerted an influence on historical grammar and on its 'legislative' conceptions."[106] Historical grammar remained, therefore, the site of linguistic struggle: the official languages it created effaced discursive practices that would have otherwise threatened the concentration of linguistic authority. Historical grammar's ultimate effect was less to eliminate the normative implications of grammar than to give them a historical foundation.

Another name for the language that wins the struggle within historical grammar for hegemony is—as Gayatri Spivak has observed—"literature."[107] Once the authority of this language exceeds the sphere of the nation, it becomes a part of "world literature." Criticizing the criteria David Damrosch used to include texts within this category, Spivak has commented: "What is selected out [i.e., excluded from Damrosch's "World Literature"] is the space of subalternizaton that must be disavowed for a polity to function."[108]

In other words, the institutional imperatives behind the development of world literature parallel the political logic of historical grammar: both function to marginalize discursive practices that do not conform to its ethos. The disciplines of the new philology and world literature are exercises in "subalternization." No longer legible within scholarly frameworks, the practices they silence survive only as the substance of subaltern consciousness.

Many different empires, from the Timurids to the British, used Hafiz's poetry to reinforce their own power and prestige. In the process, they inevitably rendered many of languages that originally informed Hafiz's work subaltern. The existing scholarship on Hafiz has failed to delineate this process, that is, precisely how his work originally opposed the imperial formations within which it was composed and how it was also, from its very origins, forced to be complicit with such formations. If, in contrast to this scholarship, we could discern the trace of such subaltern practices between the lines of Hafiz's work, we might finally liberate ourselves from the new philology's authority and, at the same time, keep faith with its heterodoxy.

5. Sovereign Law and Sacred Life:
Hafiz, 1390 A.D.

Jones presented "A Persian Song of Hafiz" as the model of a poetry founded not on the imitation of neoclassical values but on the expression of passion. The poem thus became an early model of what we now call the "literary," a language that embraces its own performative power. About Hafiz, Jones simply observed that "the *Persian* poet was too sincere a lover, to *imitate* the passions of others"; what pleased Jones most about the poem he translated was its "wildness and simplicity."[109] The interpretations of this poem and of Hafiz in general from Jones's translation to the twentieth century and beyond—including Hammer-Purgstall, Bell, Arberry, Hillman, Meisami, and Dabashi, among many others—have tended to emphasize Hafiz's hedonistic and secular tendencies as the ground of his opposition to Islamic orthodoxies.[110]

And indeed, in Hafiz's work no less than in the new philology, the form of life that cannot be encompassed by the legal and political spheres—"life" in Niezsche's and Rancière's sense—is precisely what is in question. But once we recognize the extent to which new-philological approaches have determined Hafiz's reception, we will see that his vision of this life—as well as of desire, the human domain, and poetic experience—is fundamentally different from the new philology's. "The literary" does not in any way correspond to this vision, nor does Hafiz's work place any particular value on literature. In fact, his work purposefully turns away from the written record toward the forms of life it cannot see: it is only this unseen life, Hafiz's *ghazals* suggest, that is truly exterior to the law. Hafiz's own discursive practices were, as a consequence, antiliterary to their core.

Scholars who insist that Hafiz was secular suggest that "the libertine" encapsulates his heterodoxy; those who acknowledge his Sufic learning emphasize "the mystic" instead. In fact, though, far from opposing the law, both these figures were aligned with fourteenth-century elites. Shiraz's rulers depended on the taxes they received from the "booming business" of the brothels, bars, and opium dens the libertines frequented.[111] Hence, libertinism was, in general, officially encouraged, not suppressed. The libertines not only financed the government but were themselves often servants of and paid by those in power. On the other hand, Shiraz's Sufi masters came, invariably, from its aristocracy, which remained on intimate terms with its foreign rulers. Sufism eventually shaped the agricultural, commercial, bureaucratic, and even legal practices of the new states and empires that developed across the Islamic world just before the advent of European colonialism. Colonial states consequently came to depend on the cooperation of Sufi masters, whose shrines often possessed vast swathes of agricultural property and thus commanded large followings.

Hafiz was himself deeply implicated in the political and economic structure of Shiraz. For example, though well known for mocking the orthodox morality of the judges (*qāżi*) and jurists (*faqīh, mofti*, etc.) who controlled the law, he did not hesitate to praise the most powerful of these figures, Shiraz's chief judge (Qāżi al-Qozat), whenever he patronized Hafiz's poetry.[112] That patronage was itself the product of the Qāżi's landed property, often so expansive that it encompassed many villages within its boundaries. The Qāżi would accumulate massive private estates by rack-renting peasants, forcing many of them to flee their land and placing those who remained under even greater pressure. Such fortunes not only provided the patronage for court poets such as Hafiz but also funded the religious infrastructure—comprising Shiraz's numberless shrines, madrasas, and mosques—that Hafiz attacked.

Hence, understood in historical context, the mere fact that Hafiz mocked the political and religious elite—or that libertines and mystics appear to be revolutionary characters in his writing—means little: such rhetoric merely conceals a deeper complicity. In fact, Hafiz's poetry itself makes this complicity clear. Far from sparing Sufis, more than a third of his *ghazals* criticize them, presenting them, regardless of their "cloaks of poverty," as institutional figures who pursue profit and power.[113] Hafiz condemned even the figure of the *ḥāfiẓ*—those who, like himself, had memorized the Qur'ān and were entrusted with its recitation—in exactly these terms.

In diametric opposition to Jones's concept of the literary, Hafiz emphasized that worldly desire is inseparable from temporal power and, as a consequence, always already inscribes the law. Poetry for Hafiz is therefore in no sense identical to the performative language that actualizes passion. The desire for worldly objects, the affective attachment to the human domain, is, on the contrary, precisely the problem to which his work responds. His poetry's very goal is to help its audience transcend—or transform—this desire, to protect all those who listen to it from the pathology of power. In contrast to Romanticism's "natural supernaturalism," Hafiz was concerned not to replace sacred with secular authority, or vice versa, but rather to oppose authority as such. He did so from a cultural position that cannot be disentangled from the particular forms of power and authority that governed Shiraz. Both poles of this contradiction—the conceptual rigor of his opposition and the historical depth of his complicity—have been largely overlooked by the scholars who extol his work. Despite what the Hafiz industry would claim, his work opposes power in the name not of desire per se but only of a desire that does not want power. The essence of Hafiz's art lies in this invisible desire, which physical entities and philological approaches alike only obscure.

Hafiz's poetic practice thus explicitly disavowed the authority not just of written texts but indeed of everything history attests. There is, for example, no possibility of a definitive edition of his *Dīvān*: Hafiz could not be bothered to write his compositions down because—according to anecdotes told by his contemporaneous biographer Muhammad Gulandam—he spent his leisure reciting the Qur'ān instead.[114] And though his work is, as mentioned, full of Qur'ānic allusions, Hafiz understood even the Qur'ān to comprise not a written text but instead the fourteen semantically different recitations (*qirā'āt*) produced by its fourteen early reciters (*qurrā'*), each of whom imagined the Qur'ān's unmarked vowels in a unique way. The word *qur'ān* in fact means recitation, and like Hafiz's own work, the Qur'ān's original and still often preferred form is not a written text but an oral performance wholly from memory. Like the *Dīvān*, the Qur'ān was textualized only posthumously, and the authenticity of its orthodox recension is thus equally open to question.[115] Hafiz commented in regard to the relationship of his own poetic achievement to the Qur'ān's variant recitations: "All I've done has come from the grace/And *embarras des richesses* of the Qur'ān."[116] Hafiz chose his pseudonym because, as mentioned, he had memorized the Qur'ān. But he claimed to have memorized not any single recitation but all fourteen, the embarrassment of riches to which he refers: "No *ḥāfiẓ* in the prayer-niche dome of the heavens can ever know/The blessings I have had from the wealth of the Qur'ān."[117] Within the tradition of Qur'ānic exegesis, the Qur'ān's polysemous language—comprising both exoteric (*ẓāhir*) and esoteric (*bāṭin*) layers—is considered one of its "miraculous features."[118] Whereas the conventional view held each *sura* (or chapter) of the Qur'ān to contain four such layers of meaning, the medieval scholar al-Zarkashī claimed that every word within the work contained twenty distinct layers in itself.[119]

According to Hafiz, those who renounce the world alone gain access to these mysteries. His own *ghazal*s disclose their meaning only on the same condition. As a court poet, Hafiz addressed his *ghazal*s to sovereigns but nonetheless insisted that he would acknowledge them only if they first "humbly abased themselves [at] the threshold of this door."[120] Because the *ghazal*'s formal rules are so stringent, any audience immersed in the *ghazal* form—such as the court connoisseurs who composed the audience for Hafiz's poetry—would have had a sophisticated understanding of what was rhetorically and syntactically possible as they listened to the poet complete each couplet.[121] When he did so properly, he defeated the audience's expectations, suddenly expanding the semantic possibilities of the tradition and, by extension, his audience's consciousness. Hafiz intensified this dimension of the *ghazal*: his performances were less texts than *events*, the production of an experience designed to transform the audience's desire, as we shall see, from human to divine and thus sever its consciousness from the power relations that produced it.

In any case, though, the meaning of the *ghazal* resided not in a text but rather in a series of extratextual relationships philology cannot easily reconstruct.[122] Herein lies the irony of the attempt, common across Persianate empires, to use Hafiz's work to model the rules of normative grammar. His performances purposefully subverted precisely these rules. They depended on amphiboly (in Arabic and Persian, *īhām*), a phrase that contains more than one grammatical possibility and hence that means multiple things at once.[123] *Īhām* enabled Hafiz's metaphors to register the secular and spiritual realms simultaneously, both this world and its absolute annihilation. Hafiz emphasized language's grammatical indeterminacy in order to free his audience from grammar's otherwise inescapable hegemony. He aimed, no less than Nietzsche, to free language from grammar (and logocentrism) altogether but, unlike Nietzsche, did not look for such languages within the written record. He knew the philologists but refused to remain one.

The *ghazal* Jones translated happens not only to be one of Hafiz's most masterful but also, ironically, to illustrate how poorly our concept of "the literary" fits Hafiz's work and the discursive practices on which he modeled it. But before we analyze this *ghazal*, we will need to consider the form in general. Its common theme is the grief that attends the awareness of one's inescapable separation from the object of one's desire; in the *ghazal*, the beloved is always absent. Whereas the absent beloved is political revolution in the anticolonial *ghazal*s of the twentieth-century Urdu master Faiz Ahmad Faiz, it is sacred experience in Hafiz.[124] Desire pervades Hafiz's *ghazal*s, as all Western commentators from Jones forward have recognized. But whereas they have tended to understand Hafiz's desire as Dionysian, it is in fact the expression of a Sufic ideal. The desire (*'ishq*, or "love") expressed in Hafiz's *ghazal*s has less to do with human passion than with its overcoming. Sufic *'ishq* is a kind of disease: its root (*'a-sha-qa*) refers to an ivy that chokes any plant it entwines.[125] In other words, this concept of *'ishq* implies that the desire for divine consciousness lies within every desire for a particular object and, if properly elicited, will shatter the latter desire and unveil itself.

In Hafiz's *ghazal*s, therefore, *'ishq* operates dialectically. If the obsessive quality of desire forces us to forget all objects but one, Sufic *'ishq* takes desire to its logical conclusion. It emancipates desire from *every* object. It leads, in other words, from every particular passion to "pure love" (*'ishq-i pak*), an all-embracing love of existence as such—from secular desire to sacred experience.[126] The human (or historical) domain is important here, ultimately, because it contains, concealed within itself, the desire to transcend its own limits. Hence, the *ghazal*'s explicit objects of desire—wine as well as the absent beloved—are also vehicles for the spiritual quest along which the *ghazal* guides the listener—that is, the esoteric path (*ṭarīqat*) that abolishes exoteric knowledge (*sharī'a*) in order to arrive at divine truth (*ḥaqīqah*) and gnosis (*ma'rifa*) instead.

We can now read the opening couplet of "The Shirazi Turk," here translated verbatim: "If that Tartar, that fair-skinned Turk of Shiraz, gets hold of my heart / I'll give Bokhara and Samarkhand for the Indian-black mole on his cheek."[127] On an exoteric level, the couplet claims that Hafiz would sacrifice the richest cities in the world for a single blemish on the face of his absent beloved. But within the lexicon of Sufi esotericism, the "Shirazi Turk" (*turk-i shirazi*) figures the object of pure love and the sun—that is, a light that can set fire to the self, a desire beyond self-object dualism.[128] The Shirazi Turk therefore stands, at the same time, for same-sex desire and divine union (*ittiḥād*). As a blemish, the Indian-black (*khāl-i hindū*) mole on his face symbolizes, again on an exoteric level, something the world denigrates. But *hindū* also has esoteric connections to the planet Saturn (*zuhal*): both are the watchmen, the latter, as the outermost planet, guarding the mystery of the universe. Hence, the *khāl-i hindū* is, all at once, the beloved's blemish, a sunspot (thought to be caused at that time by planetary transits across the sun's face), and a metaphor for the cosmic mystery that cannot be seen, much less solved, within the confines of this world. What the world judges to be a mere blemish thus holds the key to this mystery—or, in other words, to divine union. It is to unlock this mystery, to satisfy *this* desire, that Hafiz would sacrifice the world. The poem begins, in short, with an act of world renunciation (*zuhd*)—a refusal to accede, above all, to the world's judgments—as the precondition of pure love.

In fact, the words commonly read as "libertine" and "mystic" in Hafiz's poetry carry much more historically precise meanings, referring not to libertinism and mysticism per se but rather to those in particular who renounced the world. The term for the former, *rend* (pl. *rindan*), alluded to those who not only frequented bars, brothels, and opium dens but, furthermore, sought infamy and notoriety. The tradition of Sufi poetry that immediately preceded

Hafiz linked the figure of the *rend* to a loose Sufi order (or *ṭarīqat*, the same word used for the esoteric path) called Qalandariyya, based on extreme poverty, the renunciation of all property, itinerancy, the rejection of society, and the refusal to engage in its economic reproduction to any extent.[129] But the *qalandar* (literally, "uncouth") was identified, above all, with uniquely shocking forms of social deviance, including nudity (or appearing strange in other ways, such as wearing woolen sacks or animal hides; shaving off all facial hair including their eyebrows; or encircling otherwise naked body parts, including their penises, with iron collars, bracelets, belts, and rings), the use of narcotics, engaging in forms of nonreproductive sexuality, and self-mortification. They nonetheless helped spread Islam across the Middle East, South Asia, North Africa, and Andalusia and are still today venerated as saints. Both the *rend* and the *qalandar* became spiritual figures in Persian poetry, despite or perhaps precisely because of their associations with debauchery, with the emergence of the *ghazal* in the late eleventh and early twelfth centuries.

The *qalandar*s were linked, in turn, to another *ṭarīqat*, the Malāmatiyya ("the path of blame"), which originated in late ninth- and early tenth-century Persia.[130] By the late tenth and eleventh centuries, the Malāmatiyya involved the self-conscious transgression of legal prescriptions as well as social conventions—an absolute hostility, in other words, toward juridical and clerical authority. For the *malāmatī*, the sacred and the law were mutually exclusive. The esoteric wisdom contained within divine union had priority over the exoteric—or discursive—knowledge articulated by the law. One's union with the divine thus effectively abolished the law, freeing one from its grasp. To prove this freedom, the *malāmatī* broke laws as blatantly as possible and thus courted society's "blame" (*malama*). In fact, if anyone attempted to honor them as saints, they would, according to colorful anecdotes, scandalize that person in the most vulgar ways imaginable, even at the risk of breaking the law in order to do so. They drew their inspiration in this regard from the Qur'ānic verse that described Muhammad and his companions as those who "struggle in the path of God and do not fear the blame of any blamer."[131]

Only after we understand the precise historical resonance of Hafiz's own terms for the libertine and the mystic can we read one of "The Shirazi Turk"'s central couplets: "Though you revile and curse me, yet I will pray for you;/ for bitter answers well become those sugared, ruby lips."[132] The couplet articulates an axiom of Hafiz's philosophy: he who refuses to judge opens himself to judgment. Against sovereign law, Hafiz here counterposes an older concept of sacred life in which one's identification with those who have been judged and condemned—the supposedly unsavable—alone leads one to salvation: "God did not send his Son into the world to judge the world, but to save it."[133] In other words, if one wants not to judge but to save, one has no choice but to place oneself directly in the path of juridical authority and expose oneself to its judgment. Hence, in the Gospel of Nicodemus, Jesus responds to the question with which Pilate examines him—"Is there not truth on earth?"—by emphasizing the truth's opposition to secular authority: "Those who tell the truth are judged by those who have authority on earth."[134] About this episode Giorgio Agamben has observed: "He—who has not come to judge the world but to save it—finds himself, perhaps precisely for this reason, having to respond in a trial, to submit to a judgment"; Jesus nonetheless "does not want to escape [this] judgment."[135]

The truth Jesus tells—exactly like the *haqīqah* to which every *tarīqat* should lead—testifies "*in* this world" to a kingdom "not from this world": it attests "*in history and in time* to the presence of an extrahistorical and eternal reality."[136] The higher truth—for Jesus, the *qalandar*, and the *malāmatī* alike—is that we are, in fact, ultimately unjudgeable and hence already have access to salvation. The kingdom to which this truth testifies belongs not to this world but to those it has deemed unsavable, those who no longer have any place in history. Yet, as Agamben notes, "the juridical order does not allow itself to be inscribed [into] the order of salvation nor the latter into the former"; "earthly judgment does not coincide with the testimony of truth."[137] The manner in which Jesus conveys his testimony—not the half-human, half-divine being attributed to him posthumously—is, therefore, the real paradox and mystery of his life. "How can one testify," Agamben has asked, "to the presence of a kingdom that is not 'from here'?"[138] How can one testify, in other words, to that which cannot be historically attested?

Kierkegaard provided an answer: "A witness to the truth [is] a person who is flogged, mistreated, dragged from one prison to another[,] then finally is crucified or beheaded or burned[,] his lifeless body thrown away [in] a remote place[,] unburied."[139] This testimony must occur not in words but in the sacrifice of this world, which alone demonstrates one's acceptance that one belongs not to it but to another. The *qalandar*s not only engaged in self-mortification but in fact courted their own deaths and treated themselves, furthermore, as if they were already dead, in accordance with the hadith that one should die before one's death.[140] Such self-sacrifice constituted a "mystery" in the original sense of the word, which referred, as in the Eleusinian mysteries, not to a secret doctrine but rather to a "sacred drama," that is, the interruption of "human" experience with a "divine" happening.[141] The mystery of the truth-teller who opens himself to judgment but nonetheless refuses to speak in the law's terms or to defend himself in any way: however ineffective this act might appear, it suddenly unveils another kingdom hidden inside this one, making the human domain and divine consciousness correspond. In other words, it implies that everything else judged unsavable might also have access—precisely by virtue of its illegitimacy within the human domain—to a much deeper power. Anyone who observes such an act is thus also delivered from the former to the latter. This transformation is, of course, precisely the point of Hafiz's performances, hence the alignment of his poetry with the other-worldly power of those who sought blame: "Let's be faithful and endure blame, and be happy / For in our *ṭarīqat*, it is blasphemy to take offense."[142]

This power might be, at the same time, the very basis of an alternative politics. The preceding Agamben citations are from a book, *Pilate and Jesus*, that, though written immediately after the end of the decades-long *Homo Sacer* series, returns to an early—and particularly riveting—instance of the basic conflict, between sovereign power and bare life, that the series treats. According to the original volume in the series, the constitutive exclusion of bare life from every juridical order offers the "key by which not only the sacred texts of sovereignty but also the very codes of political power will unveil their *mysteries*."[143] In any case, though, once sovereign power takes the form of biopolitics, we can no longer assume an opposition, to any extent, between human desire, on one hand, and "the deployment of power," on the other.[144] At this point, the defense of "bodies and pleasures" that we have observed in Jones, Goethe, Nietzsche, and Hafiz's Western specialists (and that Agamben attributes to Foucault) can no longer found a politics against existing power relations, if it ever could: "nothing in [the body] or the economy of its pleasure seems to allow us to find solid ground on which to oppose the demands of sovereign power."[145] A politics that truly opposed such power would need instead, in Agamben's view, to disavow the premise that life must be disciplined by heteronomous law (or biopower) to *any* extent: "This biopolitical body [must] be transformed into a form of life that is wholly exhausted in bare life."[146] This disavowal is, for Agamben, the precondition of any effort fundamentally to rethink political praxis (as opposed to the reconstitution of sovereign power).[147]

One could argue that the *malāmatī*s and, even more starkly, the *qalandar*s were engaged in precisely this effort. By refusing, in the most rigorous ways conceivable, to circumscribe life within any existing legal structure, they intended to open the space of human action once again. For the *qalandar*s in particular, one's salvation depended on one's capacity completely to reject human culture in the forms it then took.[148] But this rejection entailed not social withdrawal but instead a ceaseless confrontation with this culture: the *qalandar*s self-consciously created a "social wilderness" within society.[149] Their aim was not to constitute an alternative polity but rather to engage in a permanent revolution against the one at hand. This polity depended on the emergence of the institutionalized Sufi master (*shayk*) previously mentioned, who made the promise of salvation a socioeconomic enterprise. By means of juridical works, clerical biographies, historical surveys, and conduct manuals, they created official norms for salvation that shaped the behavior of their followers and served the interests of allied sovereigns. It was in response to this particular complex—which practiced a form of biopower *avant la lettre*—that the *malāmatī*s and *qalandar*s attempted to negate all laws and thus make their worldly selves pass away. The invocation of "the libertine"—that is, of the *ṭarīqat*s followed by *malāmatī*s and *qalandar*s—in Hafiz's *ghazal*s needs to be understood, more precisely, as a critique of the very complex that would eventually align itself with European colonial rule.

Within the *Homo Sacer* series's many volumes, only one, *The Highest Poverty*, locates a form of life that consciously sought to liberate itself from religious law. Not coincidentally, this form of life belonged to a medieval renunciatory movement. Not only were Christian monastic and Sufi mendicant orders coeval, both originating in the first centuries of the second millenniumA.D., but their shared vows of extreme poverty were reactions against the new forms of urban and merchant capital that had emerged in the Italian city-states and the Islamic caliphates alike. In fact, Christian and Sufi movements were connected at this time by the Eastern trading routes that terminated in Venice's and Genoa's ports.[150] According to *The Highest Poverty*, in any case, the Franciscans attempted "*to realize a human life and practice absolutely outside the determinations of the law*": "perhaps for the first time, what was in question in the movements was not the *rule*, but the *life*, not the ability to profess this or that article of faith, but the ability [to] practice joyfully and openly a certain form of life."[151]

In Agamben's narrative, such attempts falter whenever monastic communities cease to induce their rules from their very form of life and instead deduce them from already written texts, when, in other words, they pass from "the rule-form of life to the rule-text."[152] The failure of the Franciscans in particular to achieve "a human existence beyond the law" lies, furthermore, in their ill-considered effort to argue before the Church that their "abdication of every right" was legally justified, that their attempt to live beyond the law could somehow be lawful.[153] In both these regards, the *malāmatī*s and *qalandar*s were, needless to say, much more radical. Considering spirituality an internal state compromised by every desire to manifest itself externally, they left little in the way of a written record.[154] They tended not to record their own lives; what little they wrote circulated only among themselves. Our knowledge of them now comes, ironically, largely from Sufi clerics who condemned them as criminals and heretics.

One of Hafiz's couplets observes: "Around the tavern door the reprobates of God—*qalandar*s—swarm / They withdraw and they bestow the diadems of Empire."[155] As this couplet demonstrates, Hafiz located in the *rend* and the *qalandar* a power more fundamental than sovereign authority. This power—the desire for union—silently governs everything in the universe, both visible (e.g., the movement of the planets and the stars) and unseen: the esoteric path that refuses to testify to its truth in the idiom of power. When fully realized, as in the Sufic figures of the *rend* and *qalandar*, this desire dissolves every object and every law, in order to embrace the forms of life they have judged unsavable. It is by virtue of this desire—which treats constituted power as a prison—that Hafiz's *Dīvān* was considered, before colonial philology, "the tongue of the unseen." Hafiz's poetry was modeled, in other words, on forms of life and language that did not care to be historically attested and cannot now be philologically reconstructed. It is no accident that, exactly like the *malāmatīs* and *qalandars' ṭarīqat*s, Hafiz's *ghazal*s, which intended to defy normative grammar, also avoided their own transcription. In each case, the resistance to representation's limits reflected a desire to keep the experience of life open. Hafiz's *ghazal*s were designed to liberate precisely this desire in their audience, to make them, in other words, *malāmatīs* and *qalandar*s as well. Like so much of Islamic art, they intend to sublate human desire from the material to the divine realm by revealing the sacred character of mundane life.[156]

In fact, when Hafiz invokes his *takhalluṣ* at the end of each *ghazal*, it functions both as an imperative and a vocative: it both commands the listener to inhabit a different consciousness and addresses him as if he already has. By its end, in other words, the *ghazal* has, ideally, turned each of its listeners into a *ḥāfiẓ*. Ḥāfiẓ is, in fact, one of God's names: in the Qur'ān, he is often called "Ḥāfiẓ of everything."[157] The root of *ḥāfiẓ* (*ḥ-f-ẓ*) means, among other things, "to protect, guard, preserve" and "to follow, observe, comply with (an oath, covenant, divine command)." In line with the former meaning, God is the "Ḥāfiẓ of everything"—the one who preserves and protects *all* being—by virtue of the boundlessness of his creative love. As a *takhalluṣ*, Ḥāfiẓ thus connects these two senses of the root: it commands the *ghazal*'s audience to fulfill their sacred covenant with the divine by safeguarding everything that has existed and thus to partake in divine consciousness. But if at the end of each poem every listener is potentially addressed as a *ḥāfiẓ*, we can respond to this call only if we first realign our consciousness with "the unseen" (*ghayb*). We would comprehend, in this way, the esoteric meaning both of poet's pen name and of his lifework ("the tongue of the unseen").

Only if we do so will we be able, furthermore, to appreciate the final couplet (the *maqṭa*) in any of his poems, where his signature always appears. Here is the conclusion of "The Shirazi Turk": "A *ghazal* have you composed and pearls threaded, so, Ḥāfiẓ, come and bravely sing:/The heavens over your verse scatter the necklace of the Pleiades."[158] In Sufi poetry, "pearl" (*durr*) refers, among other things, to a substance at the bottom of the sea and, esoterically, to the cosmic realm that lies beyond the reach even of Saturn.[159] The Pleiades (*'iqd-i thurayyā*) are a star cluster that lies, of course, past the furthest limits of our own universe as well. This *maqṭa* suggests that any *ḥāfiẓ* who sees, hidden in the words of this *ghazal*, pearls and the

Pleiades has passed through the visible universe and can now view its mystery in a different light. Hafiz's *ghazal*s enable one to perceive, in other words, not just the visible spheres but the source of the cosmic mystery, the invisible force that governs the movement of every sphere: it is by virtue of this capacity that his *Dīvān* was used in divination across the Persianate world. The force that moves all things is, of course, the divine love that originally made them and still embraces each—that which the world denigrates as much as that which it esteems—equally. Hence, "the unseen" every *ḥāfiẓ* must safeguard has a double sense: it is both that divine love and that denigrated thing; the beloved and the blemish on his face; the one who comes to save and the one who cannot escape judgment; the higher truth and its intransigent refusal to testify in the language of the law. In each case, the former is sacred only by the virtue of its relationship to the latter (and vice versa). *Ḥāfiẓ* names the one who searches for and is able to recognize divinity in this intertwined love and anonymity.

Indeed, if every *ḥāfiẓ* must align himself with the unseen, the pen name "Ḥāfiẓ" is another word, paradoxically, for self-annihilation. It manifests a kingdom where judgment—and hence self-regard—are no longer possible. Contrary to the many imperial appropriations of as well as more recent scholarship on Hafiz's poetry, it is thus modeled on the practices not of Persianate power but instead of the politically disenfranchised. The *malāmatī*s and *qalandar*s' illicit acts were designed to undermine their own desire for a "good" name (*jāh*) because they believed this desire turned the *ṭarīqat* toward hypocrisy.[160] In precisely the same vein, one of Hafiz's *ghazal*s describes his own illicit acts as attempts to escape the limits of ethics and hence of the self: "I'm the one who is the talk of the town for love-making. / It is I whose sight is not polluted by seeing 'evil.' // I have drowned my image worshipping wine / That I might destroy the idolatry of the self."[161] The *qalandar*s were committed, much more uncompromisingly than Hafiz himself, to the belief that life itself (before and outside the law) is unjudgeable and sacred. For this belief, they were themselves judged, criminalized, executed, and always rendered subaltern.[162]

On an even deeper level, the *takhalluṣ* Ḥāfiẓ in itself joins the Word and indeed name of God to human language. In another volume of the *Homo Sacer* series, *The Sacrament of Language*, Agamben has observed that, according to Jewish esoteric thought, divine language and human speech communicate their properties to each other via "the name of God."[163] The proper name thus first contains the crossing of the human and the divine (the *communicatio idiomatum*) subsequently attributed to the Christian incarnation. Walter Benjamin's "On the Language as Such and on the Language of Man" expands on precisely this point. According to this early essay, after the Fall, language ceases to communicate irreducibly particular experiences—or, in other words, to operate according to proper names—and becomes the medium of judgment instead: "the abstract elements of language [are] rooted in the word of judgment. [In] the Fall, man abandoned immediacy in the communication of the concrete—that is, name—and fell into the abyss of the mediateness of all communication."[164] Judgment suddenly intervenes between (otherwise sacred) life and (all-too-human) language. God's Word had previously foreclosed the very possibility of judgment: "The Tree of Knowledge stood in the garden of God not in order to dispense information on good and evil, but as an emblem of judgment over the questioner. This immense irony marks the mythic origin of law."[165] "Mythic" here corresponds to the concept of mythic violence—that is, sovereign law—in Benjamin's "Critique of Violence." Opposed to mythic violence is "divine," or revolutionary, violence, which seeks to destroy not a particular legal order but sovereign law as such. In this essay, as in the encounter between Christ and Caesar narrated by Agamben, the divine exists *only* in its confrontation with the law: if it judges anything, it judges only judgment (or the law) itself. The "immense irony" of judgment is, therefore, that it violates God's Word, which originally prohibited not the commission of evil but rather the question of "good" and "evil" itself. Before the Fall, this question—or, more precisely, the paradigmatically human knowledge to which it leads—alone was evil.

For Hafiz likewise, judgment is the only sin the Qur'ān recognizes: "I said to the master of the tavern: 'Which road is / The road of salvation?' He lifted his wine glass and said, / 'Not finding fault [*'ayb*] with others.'"[166] The categories of good and evil overturn God's Word and transform it into sovereign law; it is this perverse genealogy that Hafiz's poetry also identifies and attempts to reverse, in order to make divine speech audible and sacred life visible, once again, within the human domain. He chided his competition: "You writers who write such bad poems, why do you envy Hafiz so much? / His grace of speech that people love comes entirely from God."[167]

Conclusion

The Western reception of Hafiz reflects the broad project of cultural transformation that the philological revolution precipitated. From the late eighteenth century forward, this project attempted to resist the main trajectory of European development, which, it believed, obscured the ontological priority and primordial creativity of human desire. Its belief that Hafiz's unqualified affirmation of desire was the source of an alternative aesthetic followed in the tracks of Jones's *Grammar*, which considered such an affirmation art's lost origin and revolutionary future. Jones's seminal premise was that the "expressive" (or nonreferential) language of desire is not just historically prior but also intrinsically opposed to constituted power. Historical grammar claimed that it alone could comprehend the historical specificity of such language—a claim the widespread call among postcolonial scholars for a return to philology tacitly accepts. It is also by virtue of this claim that Jones, Goethe, Nietzsche, and British colonial administrators imagined they could enter directly into Hafiz's *Dīvān* and appropriate its peculiar power. In any case, though, Jones's argument about expressive poetry remained influential long after the eighteenth century. On one hand, it defines our concept of literature and "the literary," which is precisely the conscious embrace of language's performative power. On the other, it programs how scholars across the humanities and social sciences understand the antithesis of colonial knowledge, as I suggest in the Introduction and demonstrate at greater length in the Conclusion. Its influence is evident as well in the definition of modern literature put forth by Foucault's early essay "Language to Infinity": that is, a language "that appropriates and consumes all [supposedly divine and referential] languages in its lightning flash."[168]

At the same time, though, this cultural project also possessed a colonial utility. Because historical grammar possessed singular access to every language's historical truth, it legitimized the colonial state's control over literature, law, and tradition and undermined the authority of all competing approaches. It enabled the colonial state, furthermore, to acquire knowledge about the governed simply by studying their languages and texts. This chapter has argued, in diametric opposition to the postcolonial premise that new-philological approaches are inherently oppositional and even emancipatory, that they were instead the instrument of colonial rule and remain the latest stage of philological power. If we hope to conceive a truly *post*colonial approach, we would need first to make this instrumentality visible. Until we do, we will fail to acknowledge, much less address, literary studies' own colonial legacy. In this regard, philology is precisely what we must now bring to crisis.

In diametric opposition to the history of philology, Hafiz refused to valorize texts or textual traditions. Though his *ghazals* are utterly immersed in material life, they nonetheless aim, in fact, to transcend the human domain altogether. In its place, they privilege the practices of world renouncers who, in the name of sacred life, lived in a ceaseless confrontation with sovereign law but refused to represent themselves in its terms. Hence, in Hafiz's view, the power that is both prior and opposed to the law exists not in texts but only in the esoteric consciousness they conceal. Even as literature appropriates this power, it reflects a contrary impulse: "literature" is precisely the name for the desire to leave a mark on the historical record. Perhaps the literary always exists, therefore, in an intimate and violent relationship with antithetical practices. In any case, we cannot even begin to understand what is most provocative for literary studies in whole traditions now called "literature" or even misappropriated as the very model of "the literary" if we do not first acknowledge the presence within them of discursive practices that were, for the most profound and urgent reasons, fundamentally opposed to the very production of literature. Such practices, and their otherworldly power, may help us reconsider what politics could mean today.

THE IMMANENT

Shariʿa *and the* Muʿallaqāt, *1782 A.D.–550 A.D.*

Introduction

In response to the widespread demand that comparative and postcolonial literary studies return to philology, the previous chapter began instead to excavate philology's own colonial history. While extending the same archaeological project, this chapter shifts the site from colonial linguistics to colonial jurisprudence. Whereas the former prefigured comparative grammar, the latter heralded the ethnographic impulse that would lead to the classification of languages into families. Texts and traditions would henceforth be understood in terms of national histories and, for a time, of racial typologies. Late seventeenth- and eighteenth-century linguistics had isolated a secular domain it wanted to disentangle from every theological presupposition. It insisted, furthermore, that only the study of languages, each incommensurable with all others, could comprehend the secular domain in its temporal and spatial diversity. Taking place wholly within this newly delimited domain, colonial jurisprudence sought, more narrowly, to define the immanent traditions of the East India Company's Muslim and Hindu subjects. Its premise was that such traditions could be found only in their canonical texts. The spread of colonial codification around the world—and the frenzy of postcolonial constitution-writing that began even before independence was granted—would make this premise a global fact.

The identification of a culture's canonical texts and its immanent principles eventually became as fundamental to the methods of literary history
as it was to those of colonial rule. We can trace its genealogy here. Hegel's
Lectures on Aesthetics famously identifies the "epic"—or the "absolutely
earliest books" of "every great and important people," including the Old
Testament and the Qur'ān—with the people's "originary spirit."[1] Lukács's
Theory of the Novel adapts this argument to bourgeois modernity. Its premise
is that in advanced capitalist societies, in contrast to ancient and medieval
nations, immanent principles are no longer self-evident: "the immanence of
meaning in life has become a problem."[2] Once such principles are no longer
immediately given, they must be sought. Yet in postindustrial society as in
pre-, with Lukács's novel as with Hegel's epic, it is literature alone that is
entrusted with the task of articulating society's immanent truths. This argument was made axiomatic by two exceptionally influential studies published
in 1983. In Benedict Anderson's *Imagined Communities*, textuality and immanence become absolutely inextricable: the novel, the newspaper, and print
culture in general *produce* the immanent experience of national belonging
in both its temporal and spatial dimensions.[3] Immanent meaning becomes,
in this way, wholly "imagined." In Ernest Gellner's *Nations and Nationalism*, standardized literatures, which textualize otherwise popular knowledge,
are the preconditions of industrial education, national homogeneity, and
hence the modern state form.[4] In each case, texts set forth the collectivity's
immanent principles, whether passively, in the case of antiquity, or actively,
in the case of modernity. Scarcely less than the identification of literature
with the supposed power of "literary" language, the putative presence within
canonical texts of a given culture's immanent truths is fundamental to the
aura that attaches to literary studies today.

But however self-evident this premise now appears, the identification of
authoritative texts and immanent traditions has only served to obscure—
indeed, turn inside out—their actual relationship. It is precisely for this
reason that the confusion of one with the other emerged in colonial philology at least as early as it did in literary studies. We need to keep in mind,
contrary to this new-philological fallacy, that texts played fundamentally
different roles in the constitution of collective life before colonial rule. To
the extent that *shari'a* had been an immanent tradition, it turned not on

the production of authoritative texts but rather on practices that defended communities from the dangers of textual authority. Colonial jurisprudence substituted the former for the latter, state-adjudicated legal codes for pre-colonial pedagogic, hermeneutic, and ritual practices. Substitutions such as this cleared the way for the new philology's hegemony—and the confusion of textuality with collectivity—on a planetary scale. Retracing this historical trajectory, the following account finds its way back to the discursive practices that colonial and postcolonial ideologies of the text have eclipsed.

∽

The appropriation of Persianate discursive practices was merely the first phase of the East India Company's attempt to establish cultural hege-mony in its colonies. Though the Company had initially founded its rule on Mughal institutions, Governor of Bengal Warren Hastings soon called for colonial law to be based on native religious traditions instead. His "Plan for the Administration of Justice" (1772) proposed the institution of civil courts that would apply *shari'a* to Muslims and the Dharmaśāstra to Hindus in all aspects of private law.[5] Parliament made Hastings's plan offi-cial with the 1781 Act of Settlement. Whereas the Company's original policy of a dual government—partly British and partly Mughal—required Com-pany servants to learn Persian, the Mughal Empire's bureaucratic language, its subsequent decision to replace Mughal institutions with what it claimed to be more ancient Islamic and Hindu legal traditions would eventually lead Company scholars to learn Arabic and Sanskrit as well.

Though he had not yet set foot in India, Sir William Jones was consulted by members of Parliament about the Hastings plan before they enacted it.[6] Like Hastings, Jones insisted that *shari'a* and the Dharmaśāstra be the basis of colonial law, but he did not believe native clerics could be trusted to ad-minister it impartially. After he arrived in India, his distrust only grew. He consequently formulated an alternative plan, "The Best Practicable System of Judicature," designed to undermine clerical authority: he would use his own knowledge of Arabic and Sanskrit to create native legal codes in English that would have authority over native jurists. Whereas Jones intended *A Gram-mar of the Persian Language* to marginalize the Persianate elite who ran the Mughal administration, he wanted his codes of Islamic and Hindu law to marginalize the Arabicate and Sanskritic clergy who controlled religious law. The Company's decision to found its colonial rule on native law and, ultimately, on codified texts brought both Arabic and Sanskrit within the purview of colonial philology, leading to the first widespread translation into English of texts in these languages.

Even more importantly, Jones's codification of *shari'a* and subsequently of the Dharmaśāstra—the British Empire's initial attempt to rule non-English people according to their law—was part of a groundbreaking experiment in the history of governance. In the Americas, colonial law was largely an extension of the British constitution, indigenous populations having been enslaved, displaced, or exterminated. In Ireland, British settlers likewise pacified the native population by dispossessing them of their land and turning them into tenants on Protestant-owned plantations.[7] Hence, as Bernard Cohn observed, "the invention of [the colonial] state in India was without precedent in British constitutional history."[8] Jörg Fisch has gone even further, explaining that, before Jones's codes, there had been "no serious European endeavor to develop jurisdiction over an indigenous population according to their own law."[9] After the British Empire's pioneering development of "indirect rule," cultural difference would become the central category, according to Mahmood Mamdani, of both modern governance and social scientific thought.

This rearrangement of colonial rule's legal foundation—from the Mughals' Persianate institutions to the Company's Arabicate and Sanskritic codes—corresponded to a pivotal development in the new philology. As the new philology's first phase, historical grammar, helped erode the widespread belief in language's divine origins, it spurred the new philology's second phase, which, adapting Anderson's terms, we could call "national lexicography." Its basic principle was that languages belong not to God but rather to their native speakers; they express not the vertical relationship that links the human to the divine but rather the horizontal relationships that bind people to each other.[10] National lexicography located a politically urgent wisdom in the depths of every language: the collective beliefs, values, and practices that had emerged organically from its speakers' shared history together. Hence, during the new philology's second phase, philologists working within each of Europe's national languages expended extraordinary labor to recover and reconstruct the sovereign spirit they believed to be inscribed within it.

"Language became," according to Said's *Orientalism*, "less of a continuity between an outside power and the human speaker than an internal field created and accomplished by language users themselves."[11] The new philology was an emancipatory method for Said by virtue precisely of this premise. The following quotation from Said would be no less true—or biographically telling—if it referred not to Ernest Renan but to Said himself: "Whenever he discusses language and philology, whether at the beginning, middle, or end of his long career, he repeated the lessons of the new philology, of which the antidynastic, anticontinuous tenets of a technical (as opposed to a divine) linguistic practice are the major pillar."[12] Here, tacitly emphasizing the reason he himself always defended the new philology, Said explained the relationship of its first phase to its second. When philology rejected language's "divine" origins, it made itself a weapon against every ideology that claimed "dynastic" authority. If there is nothing outside the secular domain, no sovereign discourse can be transcendent. Sovereignty is legitimate only when it is immanent to people's collective lives, to the "internal field created" unconsciously "by language users themselves."

As this passage from Said suggests, the scholars who now call for a return to philology give it credit, at least implicitly, for this epistemic (and political) shift—from the vertical and autocratic to the horizontal and democratic—that supposedly followed from the rejection of language's divine origins. The new philology thus appears to be at the very roots of the concepts—collectivity, immanence, horizontalism—that govern leftist thought, perhaps now more than ever. But, in contrast to these scholars, I would question whether such a shift actually took place, much less whether the new philology deserves credit for it. Though Anderson does not himself make this point, *Imagined Communities'* historical narrative suggests that the new philology was trapped within a larger cultural transformation that both enabled and limited its capacity to think such concepts.

In short, print preceded the new philology and circumscribed its understanding of the collective and the democratic within the historically irresistible shape of the nation. When print capitalism and the Protestant Reformation spread textual culture beyond the Latin reading public, Europeans began to base their identities on horizontal relationships, per Anderson, for the first time: they understood themselves each to be part of the people who came from the same blood, shared the same traditions, and, above all, spoke the same language as they did.[13] Of course, print and Protestantism had, in fact, fabricated these national languages ("English," "French," "German," and so on)—which existed at first *only* in print—from otherwise mutually unintelligible dialects, thus creating markets and mobilizing populations that otherwise would not have existed. But if the nation could not predate print, once it had been called into being no dynasty could match its political power: witness the career of the Dutch Republic and the English Commonwealth, print capitalism and the Protestant Reformation's first progeny, also the earliest nation-states.

By the time Anderson's "philological-lexicographic revolution" took place in the nineteenth century, with scholars compiling dictionaries and grammars of Europe's national languages and histories of its national literatures, the belief that sovereignty must be immanent to people's collective lives had already become inseparable from the struggle for *national* liberation.[14] Once print had reduced Europe's countless dialects to a few national languages, the nation became, in effect, the only legible collective formation. "Literature began to be felt," in René Wellek's words, "as a particularly national possession, as an expression of the national mind, as a means toward the nation's self-definition."[15] The "ultimate locus of sovereignty" had indeed become human "collectivity," but this collectivity could be understood, perversely, only as the "speakers and readers" of national languages.[16]

My point here is not to extend the long (and honorable) tradition of critiquing the nation's pretensions to inclusivity. I focus on the idea of the nation merely because it is the first kind of community that could be apprehended only by means of print.[17] Whereas the nation's exclusions have received their fair share of criticism, the relationship of the nation's false claim to be inclusive and its fundamental dependence on print has not. But if the nation's imagined reality relies on print technology, the nation's imaginative limits must be imposed, in large part, by that technology. To understand why the nation form is constitutively exclusive, we should consider, in other words, the forms of life print technology is structurally unable to represent. If we did, we might begin to explore the limits not only of the nation but of every effort to think horizontality after the emergence of print. This chapter argues, in any case, that the limiting factor in our ability to conceptualize collective life and immanent sovereignty is not the hegemony of the nation, which no longer determines scholarly thought, but rather the hegemony of print, which in most cases still does. Our concept of the national-popular has been abstracted from "tradition" and "already existing conditions" precisely because, as Gramsci argued, it has been defined by modes of inquiry, like literary history, based solely on printed texts.[18]

This argument—that print circumscribed philology's concepts of the collective and the immanent—will make more sense once we shift our lens from Europe to the colonies. Though Anderson dated the "philological-lexicographic revolution" to nineteenth-century Europe, where it was instrumental to nation-building, it was already in place in late eighteenth-century India, where it was no less important for colonial governance. British rule claimed that its philologically reconstructed legal codes contained the sovereign principles immanent to their subjects' histories. But the very point of colonial rule is, by definition, to eliminate immanent and collective forms of sovereignty. Legal codes served this purpose precisely: they replaced the discursive practices by which local communities had always appropriated received tradition. These codes consequently satisfied colonial rule's basic demands: to wrest authority from such communities, eliminate endogenous sources of social change, and place sovereign power beyond popular contestation. Hence, the substitution of printed texts for the practices that had previously articulated collective life was even more abrupt in the colonies than in Europe. This substitution became, if not the quintessential colonizing act, an invariable element of modern colonial regimes. In the process, colonial philology created a fundamental misunderstanding of *shari'a* that has persisted, as we shall see, to this day—not just in the West but in the Islamic world as well.

The colonial history outlined here has much to teach us about literature. Colonial law is, in fact, part of the same philological formation that gave rise to the modern concept of "literature." As Jones's career illustrates, the codification of law and the reconceptualization of literature could even stem from the same scholars, in the same place, at the same time. In 1782, the year he published his first translation of a *shari'a* manuscript, Jones also translated the *Mu'allaqāt*, arguably the most influential collection of poetry within Arabic literary history.[19] Jones's translation would soon take its place at the origins of world literature as well, famously shaping Goethe's *West-östlicher*

Divan and Tennyson's "Locksley Hall," among other works. No less than colonial law, "literature" in its modern sense was aligned with "the voice of the
people" as opposed to the language of the elites.[20] Jones insisted, for example,
that the *Mu'allaqāt* articulated Arab society's ancient spirit of freedom, that
is, their willingness to rise up against the states and empires that surrounded
them. Jones's translation marks the beginning of a scholarly tradition that has
read into the Arabic poetic canon an expression of the immanently sovereign spirit—and, subsequently, the historically arrested development—of the
Arab people. As Vinay Dharwadkar has argued, the British reconstruction of
Persian, Arabic, Sanskrit, and numerous vernacular works in late eighteenth-
and early nineteenth-century colonial India laid the still-unacknowledged
groundwork for the all-encompassing but profoundly reductive categories of
national literary history.[21]

This chapter argues, therefore, that world literature does the same work as
colonial law. The former misrepresents native literary traditions in precisely
the same way the latter misrepresents native legal traditions, replacing precolonial discursive practices with printed texts. It serves in this way to obscure,
if not expropriate, the constantly evolving process by which communities
transformed tradition in response to their own changing circumstances. As
the previous chapter observed, the modern concept of "literature" aspired to
attribute aesthetic value and cognitive substance to every language equally.[22]
But its historically antagonistic relationship to the discursive practices that
precede it reveals this concept's internal contradiction.

As a consequence of this history—the emergence of print capitalism
and the new philology and their global dissemination by means of colonial
law and world literature—scholars have lost touch with the practices that
gave precolonial traditions their life. When we imagine collectivity or immanence now, we can no longer make reference to such practices. This inability
is evident even in *Imagined Communities*, which reduces the imagination
that precedes print capitalism to a single form: the vertical relationship with
divine providence represented in medieval paintings, passion plays, clerical
discourse, and so on.[23] Even as Anderson, drawing on Erich Auerbach, tries
to describe the "visual and aural" experience that precedes print technology,
he can refer only to the images and texts that mechanical reproduction itself has passed down. But there is something before such technology that

categorically cannot be represented by it: those discursive practices that understood implicitly the danger textual and philological authority have always posed to those who possess none. The point of these ephemeral practices was not to produce texts—much less leave a legal, religious, or cultural legacy—but rather to reinterpret tradition for the sake of a vanishing present. Colonial philology needed above all to undermine these acts of local appropriation—which alone have the potential to make communal life "collective" and its laws "immanent," if anything does. Whenever, like Anderson, we assume that texts articulate horizontal relationships, we play into the hands of colonial philology, confusing the artifacts of philological power with the discourse of collective life. If we recognized the extent to which world literature shares the logic of colonial law, we could begin to approach texts differently. In order to honor literature's most radical aspirations, this chapter searches, hidden within the text, for the practices literature itself served to efface.

1. The Colonial Rule of Law

During the first years of British colonial rule, the East India Company failed to balance its military expenditures and its territorial revenues, thus imperiling metropolitan finance, both public and private: whereas the British state depended on the Company's annual payment, the British aristocracy and bourgeoisie were heavily invested in Company stock. In response to this economic crisis, Parliament established a select committee to investigate East Indian affairs in 1772. Picking up on a common discourse of the period, the Company's metropolitan critics accused it of being an extension of "Asiatic" or "Oriental Despotism": supposedly like the Islamic empires that ruled the Middle East and South Asia, the Company had undermined property rights and turned land to waste.[24] One possible outcome of the select committee's hearings was the metropolitan imposition of a British legal system on the Company's territories.

In order to prevent Parliament from circumscribing Company policy in this way, Hastings elaborated a "countermodel" to the discourse of Asiatic despotism. Appealing to his connections both in the Company Court of Directors and the British state, he argued against the premise that sovereign power in India had always been founded only on its despots' "arbitrary wills" and emphasized instead that both Hinduism and Islam did in fact have written laws. Hastings wrote that the "[original inhabitants of Hindostan] have been in possession of laws which have continued unchanged, from the remotest antiquity."[25] Hence, India possessed an "ancient constitution" just as England did, and the Company was consequently obligated to align its rule with this law rather than any British system: "It would be a grievance to deprive the people of their own laws, but it would be wanton tyranny to require their obedience to others of which they are wholly ignorant, and of which they have no possible means of acquiring a knowledge."[26] Hastings attempted to prove his point—that is, Hindu and Islamic law could be viable bases for a modern state—by commissioning Company scholars to translate sastric and *shari'a* manuscripts into English. These commissions produced, respectively, Nathaniel Brassey Halhed's *A Code of Gentoo* [Hindu] *Laws, or, Ordinations of the Pundits* (1776) and Charles Hamilton's *The Hedàya, or Guide; A Commentary on the Mussulman Laws* (1791).

Hastings's "Plan for the Administration of Justice in Bengal" called on British magistrates to consult with the Islamic and Hindu jurists (*mulavi*s and *pandit*s) who were the generally acknowledged experts in their respective traditions. But this process of consultation only made both traditions appear self-contradictory and endlessly "pliable" because, to colonial observers, the *mulavi*s' and *pandit*s' opinions seemed wildly inconsistent with each other.[27] Company officials interpreted this seeming inconsistency as evidence of the native susceptibility to bribery and basic dishonesty. In his preface, Halhed commented: "In every place the immediate magistrate decided all cases according to his own religion[.] Hence terror and confusion found a way to all the people, and justice was not impartially administered."[28]

Jones devised the "obvious remedy for this evil."[29] During his final year in England—as he campaigned for and won a seat on the Company supreme court in Bengal—he published his translation of a twelfth-century treatise on Islamic inheritance law to general acclaim and sent copies to Benjamin Franklin as well as Edmund Burke and other British legislators involved in East Indian affairs.[30] Jones intended *The Mahomedan Law of Succession to the Property of Intestates* (1782) both to showcase his unique qualifications to serve on the high court and to help the East India Company implement the 1781 Judicature Act. In the preface, he wrote: "Perpetual references to native lawyers must always be inconvenient and precarious;

[even] if they be neither influenced nor ignorant, the court will not in truth *bear and determine* the cause, but merely pronounce judgment on the report of other men."[31] He insisted, therefore, that colonial administrators themselves acquire "knowledge of *Mahomedan* jurisprudence and consequently of the languages used by *Mahomedan* writers"; refer to "their books of allowed authority"; and consequently keep "a check over the native counsellors."[32] Colonial textual authority was, in other words, Jones's remedy for the evil of native clerical authority. As he told Cornwallis, the governor-general of India would need to codify Islamic and Hindu law, as Justinian had codified Roman law: "If we had a complete Digest of Hindu and Mohammedan laws, after the model of Justinian's inestimable Pandects, [we] should never perhaps, be led astray by the Pandits or Maulavi's, who would hardly venture to impose on us, when their impositions might so easily be detected."[33]

Jones arrived in India amid another parliamentary investigation into East Indian affairs, occasioned, again, by both colonial and metropolitan financial crises. Almost as soon as he was settled, he wrote "Best Practicable System of Judicature" (1784), which called for "*Digests of Hindú* and *Mahomedan* law[s] reposited in the treasuries of [the Company's civil courts]."[34] Whereas Hastings had originally invoked written law to forestall parliamentary supervision, Jones actually made it the foundation of colonial authority: legal adjudication would, in principle, be based henceforth not on personal discretion but rather on codified texts. Jones's "System" severed tradition from the local authority of native jurists and linked it instead to the intertwined and universal authority of writing and the state, which alone could preserve native laws "inviolate."[35] Jones began thus to transform both the material and epistemic bases of South Asian tradition.

But he added one final step. His plan initially called for "*Mulavis* and *Pundits*" to compile the Arabic and Sanskrit manuscripts on which the English codes would be based.[36] Such a process of compilation—already used for Halhed's *Code* and Hamilton's *Hedàya*—would have involved native scholars translating original source manuscripts into Persian and Company scholars retranslating the Persian versions into English (since only one knew Sanskrit and few, if any, knew Arabic). Eventually, though, Jones rejected this approach, observing in regard to Halhed's translation that, though Halhed "had performed his part with fidelity," the native

scholar had omitted "many essential passages" and added his own "from a
vain idea of elucidating or improving the text."[37] Jones decided, therefore,
to use his own Arabic and nascent Sanskrit skills to supervise the compilation of the source texts and then edit and translate them alone: "Sanscrit
and Arabic will enable me to [procure] an accurate digest of Hindu and
Mohammedan laws [by] which both justice and policy require [the natives]
be governed."[38] As he unfolded his plan to the secretary of Britain's India
Board, Jones explained: "[Parliament] wisely gave their Indian subjects the
benefit of their own beloved and revered laws; but the difficulty is to ef-
fectuate the intention of the Legislature without *a complete check* on the
native Interpreters of the several Codes. Never imagine, that I have an un-
reasonable prejudice against the Natives, but I must declare what I know to
be true."[39] Cornwallis quickly approved Jones's plan to produce "complete
digest[s] of Hindu and Mussulman law" and thus give the Company "total
control" over legal administration.[40] Jones's translation of a twelfth-century
Hanafi treatise on Islamic inheritance law—*Al Sirájiyyah: or, The Mohammedan Law of Inheritance* (1792)—would become the basis of all subsequent
Muslim property law in South Asia. After he obtained sufficient mastery of
Sanskrit, Jones translated the most authoritative Dharmaśāstra—*The Laws
of Manu* (*Institutes of Hindu Law; or, The Ordinances of Menu* [1794])—and
also supervised the compilation and began the translation of *Al Sirájiyyah*'s
sastric analog: *A Digest of Hindu Law on Contracts and Successions* (1797),
completed by H. T. Colebrooke after Jones's untimely death.

With Jones's codifications, therefore, a new philological approach to Arabic
and Sanskrit became the key to Islam and Hinduism and hence to the colonial
rule of law. And if the new philology was the necessary precondition for colonial rule of law, the rule of law had become equally fundamental to colonial
legitimacy. The parliamentary investigations into East Indian affairs, culminating in the Hastings impeachment (1786–94), had, as mentioned, identified
Company rule with Asiatic despotism. In order to distinguish its sovereignty
from despotic power, the Company claimed that its juridical order substituted "the rule of law" for "the rule of men."[41] In other words, whereas both
European (e.g., the Spanish and Portuguese crowns) and Oriental (e.g., the
Ottoman, Safavid, and Mughal courts) empires operated on an *ancien régime*
model, where rights were distributed differentially based on an individual's so-

cial status, the Company claimed that its new order would treat all natives as equal under the law. As the binary opposition "rule of men"/"rule of law" suggests, the latter is supposedly based not on discretionary power but rather on textual authority. Jones repeatedly emphasized this point during his colonial career. In his first address to the Calcutta Grand Jury, he explained: "It is the duty of a judge to pronounce his decisions, not simply according to his own opinion of justice and right, but according to prescribed rules. [It] is the judgement of the law, not his own, which he delivers"; "legislative provisions have not the individual for their object, but the species"; "let us be satisfied [with the] law [and] not call for equity in its popular sense, which differs in different men, and must at best be dark and uncertain."[42] In one of the notebooks he used while hearing cases on the supreme court, Jones scribbled: "When a principle of law is certain, we have nothing to do with its consequences."[43]

In each of these comments, Jones invoked what John Brewer and John Styles have called an eighteenth-century British "shibboleth": the rule of law was thought to be the "birthright" of the British, who were governed not by sovereign caprice but rather by "a set of prescriptions."[44] In fact, legal scholars such as Muhammad Zaman, Radhika Singha, and Wael Hallaq have argued that British legal practice was no more prescriptive or consistent than *shari'a*, since both were based, in effect, on customary law.[45] Even after the Company codified *shari'a* in India, it still sometimes distributed rights differentially, entrenching customary distinctions in regions such as the Panjab, for example, rather than eradicating them.[46] But even if absent, the rule of law would nonetheless become a powerful discourse, not just for the colonial state in South Asia but equally for the postcolonial regimes that would succeed it. As we shall see, this discourse has led Muslims and Hindus alike to align their own religious beliefs with civil codes.

When explaining the reasons Jones originally called for codification, Jones specialists have taken his rule-of-law rhetoric at its word, describing his codes as if they were disinterested. According to Michael Franklin, for example, Jones learned Sanskrit in order to deal with frequent perjury, fraudulent affidavits, and "unscrupulous pundits who make Hindu law ('at reasonable rates, when they cannot find it ready made')."[47] Yet codification hardly created incorruptible magistrates. Instead, it enabled British administrators to appropriate the native clerisy's juridical authority. The *Hedàya, Al Siràjiyyah, Institutes of Hindu*

Law, and *A Digest of Hindu Law* were, in this regard, part of the same project as Jones's *Grammar of the Persian Language*. Jones's relentless effort to deauthorize native clerics—however bribable they may or may not have been—in his letters to MPs, the Board of Control, and the governor-general reflected one side of the contest between colonial and precolonial forms of philological power and must be understood in this light. Colonial rule is, by definition, the effort to eliminate competing forms of social authority; we need to view philology and codification as its first scholarly weapons. The fact that the figure who is often given credit for founding the new philology in post-Enlightenment Europe also designed the rule of law in colonial India is not a mere coincidence: it marks the emergence of a new philologico-political formation.

2. *The Imperial Institution of* Shari'a

In diametric opposition to the East India Company, precolonial sovereigns rarely intervened in *shari'a*'s operation, though they often patronized the keepers of the tradition.[48] The Mughal Empire's own legal institutions had force for the gentry and urban merchants but not for other communities, which remained legally autonomous. The Mughals were concerned neither to administer these communities' laws nor to make its own laws superior to theirs. They did not, in other words, conflate sovereign power with juridical authority as such. Because jurists during the Mughal period practiced jurisprudence "without official sanction," they were able to keep their practice, per Scott Kugle, largely "outside the sphere of political control."[49] Soon after the Company conquered Bengal, one of its officers condemned such autonomy:

> Justice is suffered to be greatly perverted by [those] who, from their inherent art or abilities, substitute their own decisions where government have [*sic*] established no legal judges[.] Every Mahommedan, who can mutter over the Coran, raises himself to a judge, without either licence or appointment.[50]

Hastings reiterated this condemnation—and effectively outlawed jurisprudence outside the purview of the state—as soon as he became governor of Bengal:

> It has been too much the Practice in this Country, for Individuals to exercise a Judicial Authority over their Debtors[,] a direct Infringement of the Pre-

rogative and Powers of the regular Government[.] Publications shall therefore be made, forbidding the Exercise of all such Authority, and directing all
Persons to prefer their Suits to the established Court.[51]

In response to the "staggering variety" of native rulings, the Company
would gradually standardize the law and concentrate juridical authority in its
own institutions. It removed certain *shari'a* scholars (e.g., *qazi*s) from their
place within native society and assimilated them instead to state bureaucracies,
where its codes constrained their decisions. Scholars who were not made part
of the colonial state (e.g., *mufti*s) lost their social authority. The Company used
philological authority in this way to wrest *shari'a* from local communities, to
make it a department of the state, and thus to become the ultimate arbiter of
traditional practice on a vast array of topics, a function previously dispersed
widely across society. We need to keep in mind that such a complete identification of justice and the state, which we now take for granted, had not previously
existed—neither in precolonial South Asia nor even in premodern Europe.

The Company needed, unlike the Mughal Empire, to control the law
because its economic system depended—to a much greater extent than the
tributary economies that preceded it—on the transformation of local traditions. Company rule began with a single administrative function: the
collection of property rent. The Company's overriding concern was consequently to maximize rent, needed to pay for both Britain's exponentially
rising military debts and the dividends owed to metropolitan investors. But
as British finance became deeply entangled in the colonial conquest economy, the Company's own military debts only spiraled further out of control.
The Company compensated by expropriating agricultural production to a degree unparalleled on the subcontinent.

It gradually eliminated noncommercial relationships, including gift
economies (whereby sovereigns redistributed the rent they took from their
subjects) and usufruct (whereby peasants claimed free access to the earth's
resources). Land that had been possessed in common and could not be appropriated under any circumstances was ascribed to a newly created class of
private property owners. If they failed to meet the state's tax demands, their
land could be taken from them and auctioned to the highest bidder.[52] The
Company eventually surveyed, measured, and clearly demarcated every piece

of agricultural property, assigned it a cash value, and referred it to a single owner whose right to the land was considered real only because the colonial state had certified it. In this way, the Company delegitimized the customary rights of low-caste and outcaste groups. The only form of property the Company officially recognized was exclusive possession, a right of which women were systematically bereft because they were thought to lack the social power necessary to ensure the flow of rent from tenant farmers to colonial coffers. Only by eliminating all competing claims to the products of agricultural labor could the Company achieve the levels of extraction demanded by metropolitan finance. The Company in this way abruptly and violently enacted an epochal transformation, effectively turning the earth into liquid capital, a massive act of territorial recoding.

According to Carl Schmitt, the modern state was able to "bracket war"—thereby making itself the vessel of progress and civilization—precisely because it subordinated all legal jurisdictions to its own.[53] Henceforth, armed conflict inside Europe was bound by the principles of just war. Only actions outside the "lines of amity," where European states conquered native peoples with impunity, were not bound by these principles.[54] But Western European states were able to subordinate all other jurisdictions to their own and consequently bracket war only because they militarized themselves to a historically unprecedented degree. They paid for this militarization, in large part, with revenue from their colonies. The rise of the state within Europe led, as a consequence, to the reorientation of land outside Europe. From the perspective of the peripheries, the rule of law appears less to bracket war than to make the economy of war limitless, substituting it for all prior forms of habitation.

The Company's legal codes participated in this process by purging native traditions of hereditary customs, thus providing modern forms of ownership and exchange with the apparent sanction of tradition.[55] Jones's introduction to *Al Sirájiyyah*, for example, insisted that the Islamic legal canon established *"an absolute right of ownership, right of possession, and power of alienation"*: "nothing can be more certain, than that land, rents, and *goods* are, in the language of all *Mohammedan* lawyers, *property alike alienable and inheritable"*; "no *Muselman* prince, in any age or country, would have harboured a thought of controverting these [legal texts]."[56] But though the colonial codes were supposed to translate archaic texts, they contained passages about property absent from the originals. Even when the codes were based on source material, Jones and his colleagues fixed words whose meanings had been historically fluid, attaching them to completely alien concepts from eighteenth-century political economy and jurisprudence. For example, Jones and Colebrooke's *Digest of Hindu Law* translated Sanskrit terms for inheritance as "ownership," or an exclusive right of possession.[57] They turned terms for the division of land (*vibhāga* and *dāyabhāga*) into the "alienation" of property, thereby sanctioning land markets and state expropriation. And they rendered the term for the resolution of a dispute (*vyavahārapada*) as "legal title," thereby implying that such resolutions gained their legitimacy only from law. The earliest colonial codes were, in short, little more than treatises on property, as their titular emphases on "succession," "inheritance," and "contracts" suggest, the Islamic and Hindu "traditions" they passed down products of an effort to commercialize land wherever possible.

Ultimately, the Company's decision to institute the rule of law—or, in other words, to subsume justice completely within the state—had much less to do with clerical corruption than with its own military-financial logic.[58] In fact, notwithstanding the claims of Jones's own biographers that his jurisprudence was disinterested, Jones himself identified the interests behind the colonial rule of law. He wrote to the prime minister in 1785: "A *good system of laws*, a just *administration* of them, and a *long peace*, will render this country a source of infinite advantage to Great Britain."[59] Almost a decade later, he concluded the preface to one of his codes: "[These laws] are actually revered [by] nations of great importance to the political and commercial interests of *Europe*, and particularly by many millions [of] subjects, whose well directed industry would add largely to the wealth of *Britain*."[60] Once the Company codified *shari'a* and the Dharmaśāstra, its management of property seemed to be founded, if not on the consent of the governed, on a higher truth: their own authoritative texts. Its unmediated invocation of these texts enabled it to deauthorize all precolonial juridical and philological practices at once; colonial codification was thus, as mentioned, the counterhegemonic move par excellence. Suddenly, the Mughal order became foreign ("Turko-Persian") and Company institutions, remarkably, "native."

In his masterwork, *Economy and Society*, Max Weber created a typology of legal orders that affirmed Jones's initial evaluation of Islamic legal practices as "unsystematic, inconsistent and mostly arbitrary," depending as they did on the "undisciplined and uncontrollable legal interpretation of the [*mulavi*s]."⁶¹ Just as Weber's evaluation of Islamic legal traditions followed in the tracks of earlier Orientalists, twentieth-century European scholars have followed Weber in considering Islamic law "atomized"—despite its evident resemblance, at least before the advent of colonial rule, to British common law. The negative estimation of *shari'a* that has defined its Western reception from Jones until the present is, in large part, the consequence of viewing it through a completely alien prism that inevitably distorts its own history. This prism, the codification of law, makes the triangulation of canonical texts, juridical authority, and sovereign power appear natural. It makes all other legal systems seem illegitimate.

In fact, legal historians such as Singha, Upendra Baxi, and Lauren Benton have argued, in contrast to Schmitt, that it was in the colonies, not Western Europe, that the modern state form—that is, a secular institution that subordinates all preexisting legal orders to its own—first emerged.⁶² One could note, in support of this argument, that the first modern codes of law were produced in the colonies, not Europe. At a time when European states each still comprised various, overlapping systems of law, the East India Company had already imposed a single, overarching legal system upon its colonial territories: decades before the Napoleonic Code was instituted, Hastings had already commissioned Halhed's *Code* of Hindu law and Hamilton's *Hedàya*. Hence, when Jones recognized the inadequacy of these works, he could pattern his own codes not on any modern European model but only on Roman law.

As the Company established its courts and colleges (Calcutta Madrassa [est. 1781] and Fort William College [est. 1800] in Bengal; East India Company College [est. 1806] in Haileybury, Hertfordshire), the identification of *shari'a* with a codified or textualized law became a tenet of colonial knowledge.⁶³ Well into the late nineteenth century, legal education was thought to be more sophisticated at these colonial colleges, which taught the rules of "universal jurisprudence," than at Oxford and Cambridge, which largely avoided legal theory. As Eric Stokes and others have demonstrated, nineteenth-century British legal reformers took their cue from British India, where reform-minded liberals had already enacted their principles without the resistance of representative bodies.⁶⁴ In fact, colonial India became a model of centralized power for European statesmen in general, as they reacted to late eighteenth- and nineteenth-century revolutionary movements. In all these ways, the historical record suggests that as it standardized law, centralized legal authority, and transformed tradition philologically, the East India Company did not follow in the wake of European development but served as its vanguard.

3. Shari'a *from Colonialism to Islamism*

In late eighteenth-century colonial India, a European empire attempted, in sum, to rule conquered populations by their laws for the first time. This effort led to the earliest codes of modern law and, arguably, to a more complete incorporation of law into the state than had ever been attempted before. To the extent that this characteristic distinguishes the modern state, colonial India served as one of its prototypes. Mamdani has argued, accordingly, that it was with Company rule that "the definition and management of difference" first became "the essence of governance."[65] In his account, colonial law in particular was the "central" institution for the original definition and management of "cultural difference," which would become, in turn, the centerpiece of "modern statecraft," and, consequently, the "holy cow" of the social sciences—the fundamental category, in other words, of both representative democracy and academic discourse.[66] "The language of pluralism and difference is born," Mamdani observes, "in and of the colonial experience."[67] Whereas all prior European empires had attempted to "eradicate difference" through policies of cultural assimilation, Company rule "involved a shift in language, from that of exclusion (civilized, not civilized) to one of inclusion (cultural difference)."[68]

Mamdani dates this transformation to the nineteenth century, mistakenly grouping eighteenth-century colonial India with all "previous empires."[69] In fact, eighteenth-century Company rule was concerned, fundamentally, to "shape," not "eradicate," difference.[70] If we overlook this fact, we will misunderstand precisely how colonial law first managed cultural difference. If, as Mamdani claims, colonial law made non-European traditions suddenly univocal, unchanging, and hence knowable, it did so by reducing them to print. Jones and other Company Orientalists claimed, for example, that because Indian laws were essentially religious, they must be defined by ancient texts, not contemporary practice: he described the manuscripts from which the Company would draw its prospective legal codes as "Six or Seven Law

Books believed to be divine."[71] Their divine authority enabled the Company to deem any social customs or interpretive practices that deviated from its codes to be corrupt.

Jones put this strategy into practice even before he codified the law: "Pure Integrity is hardly to be found among the Pandits and Maulavis, few of whom give opinions without culpable bias, if the parties can [bribe] them. I therefore always make them produce original texts, and see them in their own Books; for I have greatly improved my stock of Arabick [and] have applied myself for a twelve month so diligently to Sanscrit that I can correct or verify any Translation."[72] Jones's demand that native clerics be faithful to the letter of the law—or rather to his own reconstruction of its meaning—could serve as a synecdoche for the colonial rule of law in general: it replaced native juridical practices with European legal principles wherever possible and eliminated the former wherever it was not. For example, in regard to *shari'a*, Jones and his contemporaries called the Qur'ān, the hadith, and a few archaic manuscripts the "sources" of Islamic law.[73] Particular eighth- and ninth-century legal scholars became "authorities," the "counterparts" of Coke, Littleton, and Blackstone. Their treatises were considered "legal textbooks," their opinions binding "precedents." In this way, the Company ascribed to its own Islamic—and subsequently Hindu—codes universal authority over all members of the faith.

"Colonial administrators may never have changed Islamic legal arrangements quite so profoundly," Michael Anderson has commented, "as when they were trying to preserve them."[74] Colonial law made *shari'a* "something it had never been: a fixed body of immutable rules beyond the realm of interpretation and judicial discretion."[75] It purported, in this way, to define the essence of Islam and *shari'a*, of Hinduism and the Dharmaśāstra, and, even more fundamentally, of Muslims and Hindus as distinct peoples. Legal codes became a primary medium of historical knowledge about colonized populations, not only for European scholars but even for those populations themselves. As a consequence, Muslims and Hindus came to see each other as separate "nations"; to identify their respective laws with codified texts; and to insist that law be administered only by a sovereign state. Colonial law thus led to the logical—or we could say philological—necessity of partition two centuries later.

In fact, the new philology controlled colonialism long after it ceased to be the cutting edge of European knowledge. Mamdani has followed Nicholas Dirks in arguing that "anthropology supplanted [philology] as the principal colonial modality of knowledge and rule" during the late nineteenth century.[76] Their primary example is the preeminent late nineteenth-century British imperial intellectual, Sir Henry Maine, who insisted that colonial administrators base their policies no longer on Orientalist texts but instead on the ethnographic observation of everyday life. Yet Maine's premises—which would be woven into the colonial civil service curriculum from Africa to Malaya—accorded with Jones's: Indian society was essentially stationary; the colonial state must therefore prevent social change. In fact, notwithstanding Mamdani's and Dirks's claims, Maine's "ethnographic" vision of Indian society—which presupposed that "the primitive Aryan groups[,] institutions, [and] ideas [were] arrested in India at an early stage of development"—was shaped, both ideologically and methodologically, by philology.[77] Maine himself acknowledged his theory's philological provenance, insisting on the value of "Historical [and] Comparative Method," which reveals that "a large part of ancient Europe survives in India."[78] Hence, regardless of whether colonial rule chose to codify archaic manuscripts or, instead, social customs, it ended up only reinforcing colonial law's *textual* authority.

The history of late eighteenth- and nineteenth-century colonial India would be repeated in Southeast Asia, the Middle East, and Africa. In each case, precolonial society had been characterized by "legal pluralism"—or, in other words, the coexistence of different, overlapping, relatively autonomous jurisdictions, none of which was sovereign over the others.[79] In each case, colonial rule replaced this traditional pluralism with a single, overarching legal system, which subordinated all preexisting arrangements to its own. For example, in British Africa, though the tradition was oral rather than scribal, the colonial operation was similar: in the words of John Comaroff, "vernacular dispute-settlement institutions, their jurisdictions and mandates severely restricted, were everywhere formally, sometimes forcibly, incorporated into the colonial state at the lowest levels of its hierarchy of courts and tribunals; furthermore, local cultural practices deemed 'primitive' or 'dangerous' were statutorily criminalized."[80] Colonial law thus reconstructed traditional authority in the process of producing historical knowledge about countless races and ethnicities. And in each case, even after the colony in question gained independence, it reformed but did not undo the colonial legal system.

Colonial law eventually became an almost universal language: it was not only the medium through which the colonized were obligated to address their colonizers if they wanted justice but also one framework by which European thought made non-European worlds legible.[81] For example, though they were largely philological constructs, the colonial translations of *al-Hidāyah* and *al-Sirājiyyah* became original source material both for the rule of law and for the Orientalist study of Islamic society. In fact, even before they began to be used by colonial courts, these codes established "the fundamental [premise] of all classical Orientalism": that is, "a proper knowledge [of the Orient] could not be had without a detailed study of the classical legal texts."[82] It is no coincidence that Christiaan Snouck Hurgronje—alongside Maine, the major nineteenth-century theorist of colonial law—helped codify *shari'a* in French North Africa and the Dutch East Indies *before* he founded the discipline of Islamic philology in Europe.

The colonial insistence on legally binding texts would have wide-ranging consequences. On one hand, it lies at the roots of the Western prejudice against Islam as intrinsically conservative, not to say medieval, incapable of transformation from within. On the other, the codification of *shari'a* played an essential role in the production of Islamic fundamentalism, which gained ground only after the advent of colonial law. In South Asia, scriptural fundamentalism—that is, the belief that religious truth derives solely from the Qur'ān, the hadith, and *shari'a* texts—was the direct product of colonial law, which linked clerical authority to the mastery of textual knowledge: Jones's demand that the high court *mulavi*s always "produce original texts" first established this connection.[83] Though the Muslim clerisy ('*ulamā*')— beholden to the hermeneutic techniques of the legal school in which they were trained—were conservative by nature, colonial law turned their conservatism away from traditional interpretive practices toward canonical texts. Hence, when the Company's legal system transformed the nature of the '*ulamā*''s authority, it stripped them of the power that had previously defined their professional identity: the interpretation of *shari'a*. In fact, it was no longer Muslim jurists trained in *shari'a* but rather British judges lacking in any such training who now controlled Islamic law.

By 1864, *mulavi*s (and *pandit*s) had been eliminated from colonial courts altogether.[84] In response to the absence of Muslim judges in the adjudication of *shari'a*, a situation the *'ulamā'* considered insufferable, they insisted that the faithful strictly adhere to the letter of law. In the Islamic seminary Darul Uloom Deoband (est. 1867)—where a widely influential anticolonial Islamist movement began—scriptural fundamentalism became an official *Islamic* dogma. In this way, the *'ulamā'* perversely and unwittingly identified *shari'a* with a doctrine—textual literalism—with which they themselves had been inculcated only during the previous century of colonial rule. Colonial law had reduced their authority to a literalist understanding of canonical texts and, after this transformation, completely taken even this authority away from them. In order to defend what they had come to identify as the very source of their authority, the *'ulamā'* reflexively insisted on literalism even more stridently than the colonial state had. Islamic fundamentalism is colonial philology's offspring turned, ironically, against colonial rule—the conservatism of the clerisy intensified beyond all recognition by logic of the modern state.

During the late nineteenth century, scriptural fundamentalism quickly spread, along with colonial law, from urban centers to every sector and region of Islamic society.[85] Eventually, the call for Islamic states founded on fixed legal codes—which was intended to defend traditional ways of life against colonial modernity—would become pervasive across the Islamic world. Hence, it was not merely secular statesmen such as Nehru who failed to distinguish between the British construction of "ancient Indian law" and Indian traditions themselves.[86] Orthodox believers have protested public policies in the name of their private orthodoxies, which both Muslim and Hindu communalists treat as the "sole pillar of their community."[87] But private law is, in fact, no less a colonial construct than public law. *Shari'a* became a rigid orthodoxy rather than an interpretive process only after colonial codification had brought this process largely to an end. Even anticolonial Muslim nationalists such as Muhammad Iqbal and Maulana Maududi, who attempted to oppose the Deobandi program and revive precolonial religious and legal traditions, could imagine this revival occurring only within the framework and under the purview of the state. For them, as for us, the equation of *shari'a* and codified law—justice and the state—was beyond question.

Colonial law's philological mindset has thus outlived the colonial era. In fact, it has managed to become neocolonialism's most spectacular adversary and alternative. Deobandi fundamentalists would open thousands of madrasas and mosques, first in South Asia, subsequently in Afghanistan, South Africa, and the West. The origins of the Taliban are conventionally located in Deoband. Its global ambassador, Rahmatullah Hashemi, told interlocutors at Berkeley: "Every [member of the Taliban] is a Deobandi."[88] But colonial law survives not only in Islamism but in religious fundamentalisms of every stripe, which have inherited their basic ideological premises, unwittingly, from European philology. First, the pure form of the colonized's traditions exist in an archaic past preserved now only in the sacred texts. Second, the emancipation of the colonized requires the seizure of state power and the realignment of sovereign law with the historically correct interpretation of those texts. If "these two propositions constitute the basic platform of every political fundamentalism in the colonial and the postcolonial world," Mamdani has argued, "colonial powers were the first political fundamentalists of the modern period."[89]

Ironically, though, the massive epistemic rupture colonial law produced within non-European traditions has rarely featured in discussions of colonial culture, Said's *Orientalism* not excepted.[90] Said claimed that colonial law had "symbolic significance" for "the history of Orientalism."[91] This comment betrays his failure to recognize colonial law's *material* significance for Orientalism: it was colonial law that first textualized non-European traditions, thus turning them into objects of scholarly knowledge. Said could not recognize this rupture because he remained within the philological mindset, presupposing the adequacy of texts to traditions. Said's oversight in this regard is not his alone but shared across the humanities. Whenever we assume that we can know cultures—and by extension cultural difference—by means of texts, we extend colonial law's textual attitude. We overlook the part of every tradition that rejected textual authority.

4. Shari'a *from the* Qur'ān *to Colonialism*

In fact, precolonial *shari'a*, by definition, could not be textualized. In its only occurrence within the Qur'ān, the word *shari'a* denotes the broad moral path God has provided for the welfare of people (*tahqiq masalih al-'ibad*) in this life and their resurrection in the afterlife.[92] Like the Jewish *halakha*, *shariʿa* was supposed, therefore, to guide practically every aspect of the believer's life, private as well as public. Like *halakha* again, *shariʿa* was thought to have been conveyed from God to humanity by means of a limited discursive corpus: the Qurʾān, the hadith, and the first Muslims' reported conduct (*sunna*). No less than the Torah, this limited corpus depended on an endless exegetical tradition that explained the source texts' relevance to each new generation's moral dilemmas. The tradition turned on the practice of *fiqh* (commonly called Islamic jurisprudence), which was designed to make *shariʿa*'s divine wisdom humanly accessible, to whatever extent possible. *Fiqh* manuals such as *al-Hidāyah* and *al-Sirājiyyah* were, therefore, fundamental to traditional understandings of *shariʿa*. But when the Company treated them as codes, it forced them into a role they had never played before. These works' overarching premise had been that the ontological distinction between divine wisdom (*shariʿa*), on one hand, and human interpretation (*fiqh*), on the other, entailed that the former could never be contained by any manmade text, much less codified.

Hence, in diametric opposition to the legal codes that would eventually reach every region of the Muslim world, *fiqh* manuals were, in Brinkley Messick's words, "open" texts.[93] They were designed not to define *shariʿa* but, on the contrary, to provide new possibilities for its interpretation. For example, the *fiqh* manuals the Company codified were compilations of fatwas. But before colonial rule, the pronouncement of a fatwa was absolutely not intended, as we now almost universally assume, to enforce a doctrinal truth or produce a binding precedent. Its aim was instead to rethink the legal implications of the Qurʾān, the hadith, and/or the *sunna* and thus break new ground in the understanding of *shariʿa*. In other words, rather than dictating the law to future jurists, fatwas offered them novel hermeneutic and argumentative methods to relate the source texts to their own time and place.

Fiqh manuals not only kept these texts open to interpretation but were also always open to elaboration themselves.[94] They were composed in a form that in fact demanded further commentary. Designed for the pedagogic ritual of recitation, repetition, and memorization, these manuals were necessarily compact and elliptical, omitting not only the connections between their statements but even basic explanations of their dense arguments. Hence, as a commentary repeated a given manual verbatim, it would literally open the text in order to insert elided connections and relevant explanations. Without such commentary, the manuals would have been barely legible and, for all practical purposes, useless. But as a commentary elucidated its precursor, it also replaced obsolete rulings with new interpretations or, conversely, reactivated marginalized rulings that survived within its author's memory. As a consequence of the commentaries, there is practically no topic on which the science of *fiqh* has not generated, according to Khaled Abou El Fadl, "a large number of divergent opinions and conflicting determinations."[95] Given this state of affairs, the Company's attempt to reduce *shari'a*—which could be made to say almost anything—to a closed system of law appears particularly absurd, albeit necessary for its subsumption by the state.

The written tradition of *shari'a* developed by means of the text-expansion relationship at every point in its history.[96] For example, the Qur'ān was the first source text; the hadith and the *sunna* the first expansions. Subsequently, the Qur'ān, the hadith, and the *sunna* effectively constituted the source text, the science of *fiqh* its expansion. As this science developed, the relationship resurfaced within *fiqh* itself, with the works of legal-school founders becoming source texts and manuals such as *al-Hidāyah* and *al-Sirājiyyah* expansions. Some of the commentaries these manuals inspired subsequently rose to the level of source texts in their own right and were expanded in turn. Of course, every textual tradition—after as well as before print technology and the new philology—involves the critical expansion of a textual canon. But in precolonial *shari'a*, as perhaps in other ancient commentarial cultures, the critical practice refused to invest power in the text per se and, as we shall see, often left the textual domain altogether. Understanding this tradition's attitude toward texts will help us unthink the new philology's ideology of the text.

Though the word *qur'ān* is conventionally translated as "the reading," a more precise translation would be, as mentioned, "the recitation," from the verb *qara'a*, "to recite." The Qur'ān is supposed to be God's "spoken word," given first to a prophet said to have been illiterate, who consequently recited it to others.[97] Hence, though the Qur'ān is indeed a text, it was nonetheless not originally a written one like the Old and New Testaments. Ideally, Muslims absorbed the Qur'ān by means of memorization and transmitted it by means of recitation, as Muhammad originally had—hence, the still-common practices of Muslims "by hearting" the whole Qur'ān and chanting prescribed passages during many Islamic rituals. Hence also the practice, within the Islamic legal schools, of transmitting *fiqh* by means not of reading and writing but rather of recitation and memorization: the teacher would repeatedly recite a fragment of a *fiqh* manual until the students memorized it and then move on until the students memorized the whole text. Just as the Qur'ān's written form was, in principle, secondary to its recitation, written copies of *fiqh* manuals were merely by-products of this pedagogic process. Their presence was not necessary in either the madrasa or the court because the authoritative version of the manual was already present within the cleric's memory.

Precolonial *shari'a* invested authority, therefore, not in the text's written but rather in its embodied form. The authoritative text lay within those jurists who had memorized it, who alone were licensed to recite it within Islam's legal schools, and who consequently transmitted both the text and its correct interpretation directly to the next generation of licensed jurists.[98] Owing to this genealogy of transmission, the *fiqh* manual—to an even greater extent than the Qur'ān—was literally embodied. On one hand, the privileging of embodied texts gave *fiqh* scholars monopoly possession not just of interpretive power but even of the texts themselves. But, on the other, such embodied texts also checked the concentration of philological power in subtle but profound ways.

Scholars of *shari'a* have argued that, in contrast to colonial legal codes, *fiqh* manuals presumed to define not Islamic law as such but only the historically and geographically specific principles of the author's legal school.[99] In fact, though, the point of the *fiqh* manual was even more particular than that: it was less to textualize principles, however specific, than to enable its author to make his whole life one model of the path. As scholars of medieval Islam have exhaustively detailed, jurists were treated not just as "arbiters" but more importantly as "exemplars" of *shari'a*.[100] Their public comportment was "more carefully observed and copied," according to Megan Reid, than anyone else's: "there was no difference" between their personal conduct and their juridical principles.[101] According to Michael Chamberlain, "the shaykh was as much a model of bodily norms as he was a carrier of truths."[102]

However strange such a scholarly occupation may appear to us, it reflects a concept of *shari'a* not as a definite system of law but rather as an ultimately indefinable way of life. Even when written, a given *shari'a* text pointed not to abstract truths but to the jurist's lived practice. It was "suffused," according to Messick, with his "human presence" (*haiba*): in the "old texts," writing was "a nonarbitrary mark of the person."[103] Such texts could, as a consequence, not easily be abstracted from the particularities of a given life, acquire their own objective existence, or legitimize institutional or sovereign power. *Fiqh* constituted a paradoxical form of philology, one that depended on written texts but remained alert to the perils of textual authority.[104]

In fact, *fiqh* was linked, at one extreme, to a form of life that rejected philological power altogether. According to the biographies of famous jurists from the *fiqh* canon's formative period, many were honored as much for their withdrawal from the world of learning as for their participation in it.[105] Such jurists might, for example, remain in their homes during the day in order to avoid human contact, visit only abandoned mosques at night, or take ascetic rituals (fasting, poverty, bodily mortification, etc.) to their physical limits. As these rituals illustrate, following *shari'a* was associated less with the possession of scriptural knowledge than with the practice of "bodily devotion" (*ta'abbud*). Hence, even more starkly, these jurists would periodically trade their scholarly lives within the urban network of madrasas, mosques, and courts for a radically different existence among the lawless holy men (*muwallahun*) who inhabited mountain and desert retreats—or in the case of Yusuf al-Qamini (d. 1259), a hospital refuse heap. Urban jurists came to be seen, remarkably, as even better examples of world renunciation than the *muwallahun* during this period.

But the former's understanding of *shari'a* depended, nonetheless, on the latter's antinomian practices. Even as the *muwallahun*'s transgressive behavior mocked the *'ulamā*'s hegemony, it was intended not to abolish *shari'a* but on the contrary to fulfill it. Their rejection of the *'ulamā*'s judgments on good and evil not only emphasized the ontological distinction between divine wisdom and human interpretation—demonstrating that God, not law, was sovereign—but also suggested precisely where the discrepancy between the two lay. Not coincidentally, then, despite acts that were normatively unacceptable, the *muwallahun* were revered by the illiterate and members of the *'ulamā* alike. Whenever the *muwallahun* shattered social norms, they revealed the divine path hidden by human law.

If jurists modeled their understanding of the *shari'a* on the *muwallahun*'s heterodox relationship with it, laypeople modeled their own, of course, on the jurists': medieval Muslims were indeed immersed in *shari'a*, but their engagement with the law at every level of society, across gender as well as class, was creative. Yet precisely to the extent that this ceaselessly creative tradition opposed philological power, it cannot be recovered philologically (for example, the discursive practices of the *muhallawun*, who did not themselves write, no longer survive).

In sum, the precolonial tradition demonstrates that if *shari'a* was ever a collective (or "immanent") practice, it was so by virtue less of the production of texts than of their constant appropriation. Such appropriation is in fact the essence of *shari'a* as an ethical path each person must discover for him- or herself. *Shari'a* is ideally embodied, not written, because in the human realm it can take only particular, not universal, forms. "According to classical legal reasoning," Abou El Fadl has observed, "no one jurist, institution, or juristic tradition [has] an exclusive claim over the divine truth, and hence, the state does not have the authority to recognize [one] to the exclusion of all others."[106] Any text that might potentially circumscribe *shari'a* must, therefore, be reopened, reinterpreted, mocked, transgressed, and so on. The rulings that pertained to relations between people (as opposed to ritual relations with God) could not be abstracted from the particular cases because, furthermore, no sovereign entity possessed the power to enforce such universal laws.[107]

Colonial rule overturned this state of affairs—and, along with it, traditional concepts of what constituted a text, a legal opinion, and a collective practice.[108] Enacting a prototypically modern episteme, the East India Company turned *fiqh* manuals into printed texts, located all juridical authority within these texts, and equated them with the principles of Islamic life. However logical this approach appears to us now, its effect—if not its conscious aim—was to dismantle the textually sophisticated tradition of *shari'a* as it had been practiced for centuries. Colonial law thus revealed its raison d'être: not just to establish private property or any particular mode of production but also to concentrate juridical power within the state. This history belies the still-widespread premise that written texts alone contain a society's collective principles. It suggests that this premise began its life as the ideology of the modern state.

By replacing embodied texts with codified ones, the Company turned *shari'a*, in any case, into one more species of state law: what counted as licit or illicit ceased to exist only on a case-by-case basis and acquired the a priori reality of statutory law.[109] The Company effectively codified *shari'a*, we should note, as soon as it translated *al-Hidāyah* and *al-Sirājiyyah* into English. The moment it did so, it severed these texts from the Arabic commentarial tradition, which had kept such manuals open. In fact, Jones made sure that wherever *al-Sirājiyyah* was open, his translation would provide closure instead. In the Persian translation of *al-Sirājiyyah* Hastings had commissioned from a *mulavi*, Jones found Siraj al-Din's manual "so intermixed" with the *mulavi*'s own commentary, together totaling more than six hundred pages, that, he complained, "it is often impossible to separate what is fixed law from what is merely [the *mulavi*'s] own opinion."[110] Jones's criticism here of the *mulavi*'s commentarial insertions repeated his previously cited criticism of the *pandit*'s insertions into the *sastra*s Halhed had translated. Jones's translation broke off *al-Sirājiyyah* from the *mulavi*'s commentary and then reduced what remained to a mere fifty pages, "omitting all the minute criticism, various readings, [and] subtil controversies with the arguments on both sides."[111] Jones himself added his own "commentary" to his abridged translation of *al-Sirājiyyah*—though, tellingly, not within the original text, in order to reopen it, but rather at its end, in order to close it once and for all. The commentary to end all commentary, it thus encapsulates the textual transformation of precolonial *shari'a* into colonial law. Precolonial *shari'a* depended, in fact, much less on the manuals the Company codified than on the commentaries that made them pertinent to the present; the former remained meaningful only by virtue of their symbiosis and physical integration with the latter. In themselves, *al-Hidāyah* and *al-Sirājiyyah* did not possess the historical importance the Company claimed.

When it codified these compilations of fatwas, it effectively foreclosed the practice. Whereas fatwas had enabled judges to interpret *shari'a* in historically unprecedented ways, the Company's Muslim judges had no choice but to apply its legal codes. Perversely, though, the Company nonetheless preserved the term: it called those judges' rulings "fatwas," even though they merely rehearsed colonial statutes.[112] Whenever those judges pronounced a fatwa in its traditional form, the Company overturned their rulings on the premise that *shari'a* prohibited new interpretations. The Company was responsible, in this way, for pioneering the fatwa in the sense we now understand the term: a legally binding judgment on the guilt or innocence of an individual based on a literal reading of the law. In a manner emblematic of colonial philology, the Company turned the fatwa's significance upside down: where the fatwa had been one source of *shari'a*'s sophisticated capacity for historical adaptation, it became the symbol of *shari'a*'s supposed stasis instead.

The fatwa had been the primary expression of *ijtihad* ("independent reasoning"), the analytic process by which qualified jurists made decisions that did not adhere to any existing school or ruling. To the extent that *fiqh* was "a field of debate and dissent" that "evolved in the context of changing social circumstances," as Talal Asad has argued, *ijtihad* was its essence.[113] The Company entrenched its policy of prohibiting new interpretations by claiming, incorrectly, that Islam had closed the gates of *ijtihad* centuries ago. In its place, the Company imposed the alternative doctrine of *taqlid*, which bound jurists to school authority.

But even here colonial policies effaced and overwrote *shari'a* practices. Before colonial rule, the point of *taqlid* was not to eliminate jurists' autonomy but, on the contrary, to prevent sovereign power from intervening in the juridical sphere. Only after the Company had incorporated *shari'a* into the state could it make *taqlid* a sovereign policy. During the late nineteenth and early twentieth centuries, Islamic nationalists across the colonial world called for the gates of *ijtihad* to be opened again. This nationalist vision was founded—ironically, if typically—on a colonial fallacy: in this case, that Islam had enforced *taqlid* since the tenth, eleventh, or twelfth century. Regardless, Islamic nationalism would ultimately suffer a different fate: the colonial codification of *shari'a* led naturally to postcolonial Islamic states founded on written constitutions.

Company scholars selected two manuscripts to stand for *shari'a* as such, despite their realization that many others had informed the tradition in South Asia. *Al-Hidāyah* and *al-Sirājiyyah* acquired "almost exclusive authority" in colonial courts—the latter becoming the basis of all Islamic property law, as Jones had intended.[114] They remained authoritative throughout the nineteenth century, during which time only one other work was added to the canon of Anglo-Islamic law.[115] These codes enabled the Company to deauthorize not only all the *shari'a* texts its scholars had not translated but also, even more importantly, all constructions of *shari'a* besides its own. Only after the Company separated orthodox *shari'a* from the pedagogic, hermeneutic, and ritual practices I have described above could it appear backward and benighted, incapable of modernization from within. Colonial philology thus arrested the very history it claimed to know.

At the same time, it hurtled *shari'a* into another history. Codification was supposed to replace the socially embedded authority of the clerics with the suprasocial authority of the state.[116] Instead, it started a conflict that, far from being concluded within the colonial period proper, has become only more intractable over time. The *'ulamā'*'s capacity to mobilize popular resistance proved even more threatening to postcolonial governments than it had been to their colonial predecessors. From the Maghreb to Southeast Asia, these governments attempted, as a consequence, either to subordinate clerical organizations or to exclude them from politics altogether—thus turning the postcolonial polity into a mirror image of colonial rule. In response, disenfranchised but now politically astute clerics have created an endless series of Islamist networks, parties, and paramilitary organizations, most hoping to found an orthodox national or transnational state. The colonial attempt to collapse the political and juridical spheres is, in other words, one precondition of the now four-decades-long dialectic of state and nonstate (i.e., "terrorist") violence. Only after colonial administrators took control of *shari'a* did its previous guardians try to take over states.

More to the point of my argument, once *shari'a* was co-opted by colonial philology and modern sovereignty, the part of the tradition on which I have focused here and which rejected textual authority, singular orthodoxies, and the fusing of sacred and secular power, became marginal, if not altogether invisible. Like Christian pastoral power, *shari'a* metamorphosed from the ethical practice of individuals and communities into the biopolitical strategy of sovereign entities.[117] Whenever a tradition mutates from the first to the second, its texts must undergo a corresponding transmutation: from particular/ephemeral to universal/permanent; from embodied/open to printed/standardized. The raison d'être of "the text" as we know and fetishize it now was to foreclose tradition as it had operated before.

In that tradition, *shari'a* works were appropriated, fleetingly, in ways textual scholarship can now barely grasp—opened up by new generations, reinterpreted in local contexts, consciously violated by those who considered the law itself to be illicit. Perhaps Western-educated scholars are still too blinded by the ideology—not to say fundamentalism—of the text to see the relationship between textuality and collectivity implicit in such acts of textual appropriation. But others recall a different time. The revolutions that swept across the Arab world from the end of 2010 invoked a vision of *shari'a* that, in stark contrast to Islamization campaigns, actually harked back to precolonial traditions. Even as they justified their political demands in terms of *shari'a*, the jurists who participated in these revolutions not only did not call for the imposition of "*shari'a* law" but in fact refused to identify *shari'a* with any system of positive law at all. For example, many of the clerics from Al-Azhar Mosque and University (est. 972 A.D., arguably the most respected center of *fiqh* in the world today) participated in the January–February 2011 demonstrations that overthrew the Mubarak regime. According to the proclamation of the Al-Azhar scholars, whereas dictatorship produces "social alienation," *shari'a* presupposes a fundamentally "collective or communal ethos."[118] This proclamation (*Wathiqat al-Azhar*) insisted that *shari'a* considers *democracy*, not positive law, to be the foundation of legitimate sovereignty and that it sanctions *any* legal system that supports democracy. Such a modern reinterpretation of *shari'a* as the police state's antithesis points not only to the democratization of *fiqh* but, more importantly, to a reconsideration of the constitutional principles that now underpin "democracy" itself.

5. State Models and War Machines I:
The Mu'allaqāt, 1782 A.D.

On one level, the politics behind the two works Jones translated from Arabic in 1782—when the first British Empire, oriented around the American colonies, began its transformation into the second, oriented around East India Company territory—appear to contradict each other. *The Mohamedan Law* explicitly supported British colonial rule in India: it aligned *shari'a* with a modern property regime. In contrast, *The Moallakát* implicitly supported the American Revolution: it aligned nomadism with the struggle *against* imperial power. Jones's support for the American (and later the French) revolutionaries, universal male suffrage, and abolitionism placed him, famously, on the Whig party's far left wing.[119] He published *The Moal-*

lakát—with its repeated expression of the nomad's violent contempt for rulers—near the war's end in order to rebuke British imperial overreach and to encourage anticolonial insurgency against it. Jones introduced one of the poems within the collection in precisely this way: "The king of HIRA, who, like other tyrants, [left] *all nations free but his own*, had attempted to enslave the powerful tribe of TAGLEB, [but these] warlike possessors of the deserts [openly] disclaimed his authority, and employed their principal leader and poet to send him defiance, and magnify their own independent spirit."[120] According to Jones, the Arab "*Nomades* have never been wholly subdued by any [other] nation" and, as a consequence, still enjoy "liberty."[121] Even when they exist on the margins of states or empires, they "only keep up a show of allegiance to the sultan, and act, on every important occasion, in open defiance of his power."[122]

On a deeper level, though, the two works were part of a single philological project. Jones intended the concept of literature implicit in *The Moallakát*—like the concept of property rights articulated by *The Mahomedan Law*—to model the proper constitution of a state. For him, Bedouin poetry reflected—more clearly than even Hafiz's *Dīvān*—the true source of all poetic language, that is, the expression of violent passion: the nomads "pour out" their poems "extempore, professing a contempt for the stately pillars, and solemn buildings of the cities."[123] But *The Moallakát* joined Jones's concept of poetry as the expression of violent passion to another concept that would become even more seminal for Romanticism: ancient literature is "the voice of a people still in its infancy."[124] As the previously cited quotation from Wellek attests, this concept made "literature" the immanent language of a "nation," that is, a people who possess the capacity and therefore the right to be sovereign.[125]

The Moallakát is linked, via this definition of literature, to three poems Jones wrote at the same time, each of which would circulate for many decades among English radicals: "Ad Libertatem Carmen" (1780), a loose translation of William Collins's "Ode to Liberty" in support of the American revolutionaries; "An Ode in Imitation of Alcaeus" (1781), an original composition sent by Jones to Joseph Priestley and Benjamin Franklin that would be published by the Society for Constitutional Information in 1787; and "An Ode in Imitation of Callistratus" (1782), which Jones patterned on the Greek poet's praise of tyrannicide.[126] The "Ode in Imitation of Alcaeus" foregrounds the question of the state's proper foundation:

> What constitutes a State?
>
> . . .
>
> Not cities proud with spires and turrets crown'd;
>
> . . .
>
> Not starr'd and spangled courts,
>
> . . .
>
> No:— MEN, high-minded MEN,
>
> . . .
>
> Men, who their *duties* know,
> But know their *rights*, and, knowing, dare maintain,
> Prevent the long-aim'd blow,
> And crush the tyrant while they rend the chain:
> *These* constitute a State,
> And sov'reign LAW, *that state's collected will.*[127]

In this poem, the British constitute a nation only to the extent that they preserve the will to war against autocratic power. And only to the extent, in turn, that this ancient will pervades their body politic can it constitute a "state" in the proper sense of the word. Here, the ancient practice of the war machine—whose origins lie, according to Georges Dumézil, Pierre Clastres, Gilles Deleuze, and Félix Guattari, in a primordial opposition to the state's emergence—becomes, paradoxically, the foundation of the republican state, that is, one that replaces tyranny with popular participation.[128] The "Ode in Imitation of Alcaeus" thus delineates the larger political vision within which Jones's embrace of nomadism took place: Bedouin poetry was important to Jones precisely to the extent that its violent opposition to every principle of rule outside itself expressed the republic's—or, in other words, constituent power's—essence.

Hence, if *The Mahomedan Law* and *The Moallakát* have diametrically opposed attitudes toward colonial rule, they nonetheless share a single purpose: to evoke a people whose opposition to autocratic power displays the prerequisites of immanent sovereignty and hence legitimate statehood. The nomad's war against oligarchy recurs in the civil defense of private property, though at a more advanced stage of social development. According to Jones, *shari'a* identifies "freedom" with "the civil existence and life of a man" and hence with "his right of property": "subjects without property" are "mere slaves without civil life."[129] But as the publication of both *The Moallakát* and *The Mahomedan Law* attest, a people's right to be sovereign must be produced philologically, in the reconstruction of their literary and legal traditions. After the new philology, languages and texts must, therefore, contain *historical* knowledge about *national* peoples, thus documenting the shifting fortunes of popular sovereignty.

This requirement has less, however, to do with democratization than with centralization, with sovereign and scholarly institutions that sought authority over culturally heterogeneous populations. "The people" is a reification "reinvented," according to Jacques Rancière, by "philologists, antiquarians and archaeologists" partly to oppose *ancien régime* politics.[130] According to this reification, "poetry did not [originally] exist as a separate activity" but was instead woven into "the fabric of collective life."[131] Like the bardic, the Bedouin became one sign of this lost paradise, which Romantic nationalism mourned and dreamed of restoring. For many decades after *The Moallakát*'s original publication, pre-Islamic poetry was understood in these terms, whether by early nineteenth-century intellectuals such as Goethe or late nineteenth-century Arabists such as Ignác Goldziher and Wilhelm Ahlwardt, who claimed in *Über Poesie und Poetik der Araber* that the Arab love of poetry constitutes "the very character of the nation."[132] Arabia thus became "the land of poets and singers."[133] Whether they studied literature in nationalist or in comparatist terms, nineteenth-century philologists took an interest in pre-Islamic Arabic poetry only to the extent that it remained tied to this reification, the people in its infancy. Almost a century after Jones called on the British nation to mimic the Bedouin war machine, the Semitic philologist Theodor Nöldeke reiterated this call in the context of the Franco-Prussian War: "This manly disposition, which expresses itself throughout the songs of the old desert nomads, can also serve us as examples. Especially now when the German nation faces the question of whether it has the mind to cleanse old shame with its blood!"[134]

But if Arabists in the late nineteenth century still understood literature in Romantic terms, as the quotations from Ahlwardt and Nöldeke attest, most of them no longer felt that pre-Islamic Arabic poetry fit the category. On one hand, rather than creative, this poetry was captive to predetermined themes and forms. On the other, it was irredeemably "atomized," like Islamic law—unable to think collectively. Revising his earlier positive valuation, Nöldeke eventually described Arabic poetry in the same terms in which Weber described *shari'a*: though pre-Islamic poetry remained the vessel of the Arab people, both poetry and people were now understood to be static and hence fundamentally underdeveloped.[135]

When the late nineteenth-century study of pre-Islamic poetry aspired to be more than a method for establishing historically authentic texts, it became part, along with the study of *shari'a*, of a broader, anthropological approach to "the Arab mind." A leading philologist of the period, Julius Wellhausen, announced: "The interest which we take in the old songs of the Bedouins is not poetic but linguistic and historical."[136] Hence, even as Western philology turned its evaluation of the *Mu'allaqāt* inside out in the century after Jones's translation, it never surrendered its commitment to the aesthetic values and historical approach Jones had helped establish. Late eighteenth- and early nineteenth-century philologists claimed that the pre-Islamic poetry tapped directly into the very source of poetic language and, consequently, gave voice to the people. Late nineteenth-century philologists believed that it lacked all artistic value because it was historically arrested. In either case, European philology conceived of "art" as an expressive practice untouched by—and diametrically opposed to—philological power.

No such practice exists, of course: philological power necessarily shapes both the production of all hegemonic art and the history of its transmission. But, like every other field of literary studies, recent scholarship on pre-Islamic poetry continues to see its task as the production of historical knowledge about a people and tradition, rather than as the investigation of its own philo-logical presuppositions. In fact, even as early twentieth-century comparatism chose the path of critics devoted to humanistic values over that of philologists committed strictly to the scientific study of language, it did not question the basic philological axiom that printed texts provide historical knowledge.[137] Decades later, counterhistoricist schools such as poststructuralism ended up serving only as brief, albeit resonant, interludes between different historicist movements. Hence, even when contemporary Arabists such as Jaroslav Stetkevych or Suzanne Pinckney Stetkevych leave more conservative approaches behind and masterfully analyze pre-Islamic poetry as the expression of symbolic archetypes or, alternatively, as "a total social phenomena," they still align the text with a collective consciousness—not philological power.[138]

In fact, though, the printed texts we now call the *Mu'allaqāt* constitutively misrepresent the aesthetic phenomenon they name—and by extension the culture from which they are said to descend—because these poems did not originally take textual form. Many scholars have, of course, criticized Orientalism for treating non-European societies as purely textual entities, as well as for claiming that, absent Western intervention, these societies would not have developed historically. But these criticisms nonetheless leave unscathed the axiom that texts provide historical knowledge—precisely the premise that has made non-European legal and literary traditions appear historically arrested in the first place.

The alternative to the new-philological position is to disavow this premise altogether. Archaeological approaches are concerned less to reconstruct history than to become conscious of their own limits and, by extension, the epistemic principles and discursive practices that have been marginalized along the way. It is not now possible for the study of literature simply to transcend the colonial reconstruction of tradition or, to paraphrase Aamir Mufti, be produced from a position uncontaminated by it: comparatism as we now know it would not exist without colonial philology.[139] Hence, if literary studies is to be "postcolonial," it must be so in the sense not of having moved beyond this particular history once and for all but, on the contrary, of being condemned to grapple with it indefinitely. It could begin to do so by ceasing to confound philological artifacts with immanent practices. It would need instead to treat every text any tradition has passed down to us as the site of conflict between different forms of philological power and, ultimately, between those who possessed such power and those who did not. These conflicts are the ones most immediately responsible for the production and dissemination of any canonical work of literature. As Michel de Certeau argued in *The Writing of History*, an archaeological approach must use the study of texts neither to transcend nor to resuscitate the past but, on the contrary, to recognize its stubborn and invisible persistence in contemporary methods.[140] The task is, in other words, not to turn history into an object but rather to objectify our own scholarly premises instead, in order to recognize how tradition has become reified and hence naturalized therein.

6. State Models and War Machines II: *The* Muʿallaqāt, *550 A.D.*

The originally unwritten *Muʿallaqāt* comprises seven separate poems composed by seven different authors, each of whom was a member of a sixth-century Bedouin tribe. These tribes existed between Byzantine and Persian Empires and their Arab client states, all of whom wanted to incorporate—or at least circumscribe the movement of—the tribes, in order to stop their raids on desert trade routes.[141] In response, the poems insist, above all, on the Bedouins' refusal to subject themselves to any empire. Here is the conclusion to the *muʿallaqah* translated as "The Regicide," by 'Amr, who himself reputedly killed a king:

> When kings deal with their peoples unjustly
> we refuse to allow injustice among us.
> We are called oppressors; we never oppressed yet,
> but shortly we shall be starting oppression!
> When any boy of ours reaches his weaning
> the tyrants fall down before him prostrating.[142]

It is in the refusal of any external authority that Jones discerned an affinity between the explicitly antistatist *Muʿallaqāt* and American republican politics. In his view, these poems articulated the consciousness that precedes the rise of writing and the state. In fact, though, they go much further, expressing not just the tribe's rejection of transcendent sovereignty but the nomad's disavowal of human settlement altogether. After Jones, Arabists have insisted that the *Muʿallaqāt* constitutes a fundamentally different relationship between language and history—or, even more profoundly, the experience of time as such.

Each of the seven *muʿallaqah* begins with a memory of settlement only to break with this experience and cancel it out. They follow the classical Arabic form of the *qaṣīdah*, opening with the poet's return to an encampment in which he had had a sexual encounter but which has since been abandoned. In this opening motif (the *aṭlāl*, from *al-wuqūf ʿalá al-aṭlāl*, "stopping at the ruins"), the poet literally reads the traces of the abandoned desert encampment.[143] Take for example the first lines of Labid ibn Rabia's *muʿallaqah*, called

"The Centenarian": "The abodes are desolate, halting-place and encampment too[,]/[naked] shows their trace,/rubbed smooth, like letterings long since scored on a stony slab"; "Then the torrents washed the dusty ruins, until they seem/like scrolls of writing[.]/So I stood and questioned that site; yet how should we question rocks/set immovable, whose speech is nothing significant?/All is naked now, where once the people were all forgathered."[144] Here, as at the beginning of each *mu'allaqah*, the deserted encampment becomes an inscription, "like lettering long since scored on a stony slab," whose significance the poet must glean: "I stood and questioned that site." Yet here inscription does not preserve or consolidate memory but in diametric opposition dissolves into the "trace" of irretrievably lost worlds: "naked shows their trace,/rubbed smooth." The deserted encampment thus represents experience not in its content but rather in its loss; this image, paradoxically, represents loss. One could claim that, like Hafiz's work, each *mu'allaqah* is designed, therefore, to make the world fade away. The deserted encampment's meaning is always the same: whatever people make is essentially temporary; any attempt to achieve immortality or permanence ends in failure; built environments become wild again; only the wild—and the devastation of human life—is everlasting.

Within the *Mu'allaqāt*, all sign systems must, therefore, symbolize human mortality: ruins become a metaphor for poetry itself.[145] Each *mu'allaqah* expresses a historical vision in which the tragedy of historical transformation is not mitigated by reference to progress in any sense. Every poem within the *Mu'allaqāt* begins with a loss that is never—within Hegel's terms—negated or sublated. Loss is not the precondition of a higher stage: its consciousness is in fact the highest stage. The poem merely forestalls the past's total obliteration: "Yet the true and only cure of my grief is tears outpoured:/what is there left to lean on where the trace is obliterated?"[146] Memory likewise preserves nothing but the experience of loss. The act of reading that initiates the poem constitutes the form of consciousness that distinguishes what it means to be human, one who is separated from nature by his or her mortality and from the animal by an awareness thereof: it is the human alone who *knows* the experience of mortality.

If in the *aṭlāl* and *nasīb* (or the memory of lost love) section of the classical *qaṣīdah* the poet reads the traces of the deserted encampment in order to experience the transience of all human building, in the section that follows (the *raḥīl*) the poet crosses the desert, at the risk of his life, in order to incorporate this experience of transience into his own being.[147] See, for example, the *muʿallaqah* of Tarafa: "When grief assails me, straightaway I ride it off / mounted on my swift, lean-flanked camel, night and day racing."[148] Whereas states and empires presume to confer some measure of their own immortality on their subjects, any antistatist society must, in diametric opposition, celebrate and indeed court death, as the *qaṣīdah* does not only in the desert-crossing but also in the paean to warfare with which it often concludes. Every act of departure and abandonment becomes an opportunity to take the experience of death into oneself, to accept mobility and mortality as the conditions of human life and hence to free oneself from one's fear of death, a freedom that any attachment to the state's quasi-permanence forecloses. The journey enacts, in Suzanne Stetkevych's words, "the failure of the polity, the destruction of the social order, and the dispersal or scattering of its members."[149] Hence, it also symbolizes the poet's willingness to break any social relationship or convention that binds him. In Arberry's literal translation, Labid proclaims, "I / am skilled to knot the bonds of friendship, and break them too[.] / I am quick to be gone from places when they're unpleasing to me"; in O'Grady's free translation, Labid is "glad to void void places."[150] If the *Muʿallaqāt* lies at the origins of a tradition, the *qaṣīdah*, that would not only dominate Arabic poetry but also shape Hebrew, Kurdish, Persian, Turkish, Hausa, and Urdu verse well into the twentieth century, it nonetheless insists that the past should have no hold on the present. In this regard also, it appears to be aligned with constituent power.

Yet, by its conclusion, every *muʿallaqah* culminates in an affirmation of value, whether the poet's skill, the tribe's ethos, or some countervailing ethic, normally involving violence and/or hedonism. Take Tarafa, for example, again:

Unceasingly I tippled the wine and took my joy,
unceasingly I sold and squandered my hoard and patrimony
till all my family deserted me, every one of them[.]
. . .

So now then, you who revile me because I attend the wars
and partake in all pleasures, can you keep me alive forever?
If you can't avert from me the fate that surely awaits me
then pray leave me to hasten it on with what money I've got.[151]

Most commonly, the poet chooses to rejoin the tribe in the *qaṣīdah*'s third and final section, which often takes the form of the *fakhr* (the poet's praise of himself or his tribe). But the very form of the *qaṣīdah*—which always radiates out from *aṭlāl*'s initial separation of language from stable denotation—insinuates that the experience of transience that begins the poem imbues and destabilizes the values that conclude it. In other words, because the poet has chosen freely to reenter the tribe, he possesses the same power to withdraw once again whenever it becomes unjust. Labid observes that "the best knotters of friendship sever the bond at need" and hence enjoins his listeners to "bestow your gifts in plenty on him who entreats you fair; / you can always break, when his love falters and swerves away."[152] Each *muʿallaqah* implies, in short, that the tribe constitutes an immanent community, founded on the absolute freedom, mobility, and contingency of the desert, recognizing no law outside the will of its members.

Hence, contemporary Arabists read in the *Muʿallaqāt* the spirit of the Jahiliyyah, the time of "ignorance" before Islam, which left no written record but poetry. M. M. Badawi, for example, has called pre-Islamic poetry "the product of a tribal desert society with its own ethos" and a "re-enactment of the common values of the tribe[,] enabling the tribe to face with greater fortitude the forces of death in a hostile world."[153] Mohammed Bamyeh has likewise inferred from the *Muʿallaqāt* "the desert's inhospitability to any other life than one of permanent wandering" and, hence, "an altogether different arrangement of the world," where spatial and temporal indeterminacy "posed little problem."[154] The *Muʿallaqāt* articulates the Bedouin's belief in "the normatively tragic meaning of existence," whose only recompense is poetry.[155] Bamyeh reiterates the centuries-old claim that, in the Jahiliyyah, "the only form of communication worthy of immortalizing, the only records worthy of any effort at preservation were seen by contemporaries themselves to consist of nothing other than poetry."[156]

But these scholars have inherited their premises about the organic relationship of the *qaṣīdah* to Bedouin life from, ironically, an Abbasid philological establishment that had itself appropriated the *qaṣīdah* for distinctly ideological purposes, to sing the praise of the Prophet and, above all, the Caliphate. In fact, the *Muʿallaqāt* was itself not written down until the Abbasid Caliphate, when it was "codified and institutionalized as one of the twin foundations," along with the Qur'ān, of Arabic literary culture.[157] It was furthermore composed, in its written form, in the Qurayshi Arabic of the Qur'ān, not in the earlier dialects of the pre-Islamic Bedouin. In other words, the *Mu'allaqāt* we have inherited descends to us not from the desert but from Islamic cities and empires. We are left, effectively, with no written records from the Jahiliyyah. The figure of the intrinsically poetic Bedouin reflects not the immanent principles of nomadic life but rather the ideology of medieval Arab scholars.

Even the almost universal premise that nomadic life is exterior to urbanization and state formation should be reconsidered. Sixth-century Arab nomads were, on the contrary, integral elements of peninsular commerce and politics, which was intimately connected, in turn, to both the Byzantine and Sassanid Empires that bordered the peninsula. In fact, the Bedouin often served as conduits from one to the other. Some settled temporarily on the edges of a city; others established permanent roots therein. As Wael Hallaq has observed, "no clear lines [can] be drawn between the two."[158]

The Bedouin performed poetic recitations such as the *Mu'allaqāt*, furthermore, at the precise interface of nomadic, mercantile, and agrarian cultures—at the market in al-Ḥīrah, the capital of the Arab Lakhmid kingdom, and at trade fairs in 'Ukāẓ, near Mecca, which was a merchant republic as well as a pilgrimage site and literary center.[159] Hence, the *mu'allaqah* were performed before sovereigns, and though some of them do defy monarchs, as Jones emphasized, other pre-Islamic *qaṣīdah*s in fact swear oaths of fealty. In either case, though, such poems are the expression less of nomadic consciousness than of the formal relationships that obtained between Bedouin chiefs and these various polities, "the cutting and binding of ties of allegiance" with various sovereigns.[160] The performance of a *mu'allaqah* was therefore, like every other form of ritual exchange, a "formal pretence and social deception": they simultaneously express the tribal aristocracy's explicit hostility to, and ritualize its complicity with, sovereign power.[161] The pre-Islamic *qaṣīdah* has been passed down to us precisely because it was a ceremonial form; it must be understood, during Jahiliyyah no less than after the rise of Islam, as the instrument of philologico-sovereign power.

Yet the supposedly immanent language that each *mu'allaqah* evokes may exist elsewhere within Bedouin culture—not in these poems composed by members of the political elite but rather in a discursive practice that has always shielded itself from them. The everyday poetic performances of Bed-ouin women and youth purposefully avoid transcription and, on a deeper level, simply cannot be transcribed. As Lila Abu-Lughod's ethnographic research has demonstrated, the purpose of these performances is, in part, to convey "non-virtuous" sentiments, that is, to articulate emotions that defy masculin-ity, masculine authority, and the tribal code of honor.[162] These include, in particular, desire outside the confines of marriage, affective dependence on those who are absent, and a sense of the self's essential vulnerability. It is no coincidence, then, that the tribal leadership reflexively denigrates this poetic form (*ghinnāwa*, or "little song") or, furthermore, that male anthropologists have failed to take it seriously as well. And precisely because they dare to question the authority of the tribal leaders, *ghinnāwa*s are never intended for them or any public audience but only for one's intimates in private: the aes-thetic experience of the *ghinnāwa* vanishes as quickly as the recitation itself.

Though Bedouin women have sometimes allowed anthropologists to record the tribe's collection of *ghinnāwa*s, the genre nonetheless remains completely beyond the grasp of textual understanding. A given *ghinnāwa* performance cites and, often, creatively reconstellates images, lines, and poems from the tribe's repertoire, in order to articulate personal feel-ings about interpersonal relationships within the tribe.[163] The meaning of a recitation—in itself extremely condensed, necessarily vague, and often conventional—derives therefore not from the semiosis of Arabic in general or even of this genre of Arabic poetry in particular but rather from the poet's allusion to the specific poems the tribe knows and the precise circumstances of its members. For these reasons and others, the emotional effect (and in-deed, practical efficacy) of these recitations—which frequently both move their auditors to tears and inspire them to act—depends on a social context that cannot be reconstructed philologically. It will be invisible not just to literary scholars who study only printed texts but even to ethnographers who, lacking access to private exchanges, focus only on public life. The philologi-cal condemnation of Arabic poetry as formulaic, atomized, and historically arrested—like the historical stereotype of *shari'a* as static—completely ig-nores such contexts. The even older philological praise of Arabic civilization as particularly poetic—even to the extent that it is true—is equally devoid of substance for the same reason.

In the *aṭlāl*, *nasīb*, and *raḥīl* sections of the *qaṣīdah*, poetic language is supposed to become unbound first from human settlement, then from the tribe, and ultimately from stable denotation altogether. Liberated in each of these ways, the poet's language can instead become immanent to his individual experience and, once he rejoins the tribe at poem's end, to its collective life. The language of the *qaṣīdah* is thus itself the performative realization of the poet's and the tribe's independence. In fact, though, each *muʿallaqah* served to articulate and perhaps inculcate the tribal code of honor (*sharaf*), whose social function was, in turn, to legitimate tribal relations of inequality, dependence, and control, particularly between men and women.[164] Within the terms of this code, men must present themselves as powerful, self-willed, and self-controlled (as in fact every author does well before each *muʿallaqah*'s conclusion), their only sentiments anger, vengefulness, and an overarching indifference toward their own fate. But for women and youth, those whom the tribe renders dependent, the honor code produces an irresolvable contradiction: if they commit themselves to it, as tribal belonging demands, they will subscribe to ethical ideals from which they are, constitutively and paradoxically, excluded.

The *ghinnāwa* responds precisely to this contradiction by turning the honor code upside down. It cites themes—namely, abandonment, absence, emptiness, and grief—that are as old as the *Muʿallaqāt*, that in fact serve as the starting point of each *muʿallaqah* and hence of the tradition as a whole.[165] But the *ghinnāwa*, unlike the official tradition, refuses to suggest that one can ever transcend the paradigmatically nomadic (and human) experience of distance, separation, loss, and longing. In diametric opposition to the emphatically autonomous and self-disciplined subjectivity of the *Muʿallaqāt*, the *ghinnāwa* never ceases to be haunted and destabilized by the experience of unrequitable and hence immodest desire.

In the *ghinnāwa*, authorship is unimportant, proper names absent, pronouns always plural, and gender usually unmarked. These conventions make the poem's author, auditors, and subject indistinct and ensure, furthermore, that only they will ever know the poem's referents.[166] To the extent that the *ghinnāwa* expresses the very desires tribal belonging forbids and makes such prohibited desires the basis of a self-organizing community, this genre, in contrast to any elite poetic tradition, constitutes a truly immanent and collective practice. Whereas pre-Islamic ceremonial poems such as the

Mu'allaqāt could be performed only by a select few, the *ghinnāwa* is open to everyone—or at least all those excluded from the political elite. And whereas the *Mu'allaqāt* explicitly rejects sovereign power, only the *ghinnāwa* actually resists such power: it voices the suffering produced by those who are sovereign *within* the tribe; aligns itself only with the values they proscribe; makes no normative claims; and is, in fact, even more fugitive than the always particular experiences it names. In short, every *mu'allaqah* begins by invoking a language that leaves no mark on the historical record and by aligning itself with this language. Yet such languages belong not to the *Mu'allaqāt* proper but rather to poetry that appropriates its themes for nonsovereign ends. Women's everyday poetic performance is thus the discursive practice on which the *Mu'allaqāt*'s deep meaning actually depends.

The problem with the centuries-old premise—from the Abbasids to contemporary Arabists and beyond—that the *Mu'allaqāt* reflects the immanent principles of Bedouin life is that the production of texts cannot constitute a truly immanent practice. As the *ghinnāwa* as well as precolonial *shari'a* attest, only their appropriation can. The *Mu'allaqāt*, like the Company's codes, was an attempt to define, once and for all, the rules of collective life. It was, in other words, a transcendent, not immanent, practice. The philological revolution only reinforced such practices: after it, printed texts became the primary medium through which democratic collectivities were imagined, whether on the plane of law or literature, the statesman or the scholar. Our failure to recognize the fundamental distinction between the sovereign production and the nonsovereign appropriation of textual authority is one index of how completely the modern disciplines of law and literature now limit our understanding.

This failure recurs, needless to say, in fields far from philology, even in what we take to be the most radical forms of philosophy. In the *Handbook of Inaesthetics*, Alain Badiou uses Labid's *mu'allaqah* to exemplify a discursive practice that makes truth "immanent" to individual and collective experience.[167] In response to the dead ends of liberal democracy and the Communist Party, both of which make truth transcendent, Badiou asks "thought" to "take a step back" toward "the desert," the "bare place," and "the void" of the "pre-Islamic ode," so that "truth" may become, once again, "immanent and terrestrial."[168] His term "the void" refers, in the context of the *mu'allaqah*, to the abandoned desert encampment with which every *qaṣīdah* begins. But it is also intended to connect this poetic motif to the concept of truth that distinguishes Badiou's philosophy, which emphasizes the constitutive importance of that which does not now count and has therefore been rendered "void." Take, for example, the undocumented workers (*sans-papiers*) on whose behalf Badiou's Organisation politique advocated: the state depends on their labor but refuses to count them as members of the polity; it discounts their work by calling them "illegal aliens." As Badiou's *Ethics* explains, the state is, in fact, that which by definition miscounts labor in order to expropriate its product.[169] In any case, though, a radical politics—or, more precisely, the only praxis that rises to the level of "politics" for Badiou—fights for some reality that does not now count, something beyond the existing limits of representation, some "void," as its truth.

When the *qaṣīdah* stops at ruins and then makes this experience of emptiness its own foundation (or abyss), it is, Badiou implies, doing precisely that. In fact, he identifies the *aṭlāl* with his own concept of truth: "Truth always begins by naming the void, by voicing the poem of the abandoned place"; "there is no possible truth save under the condition of crossing the place of truth, conceived here as a null, absented, and deserted place."[170] The *mu'allaqah* does even more: it attempts "to sustain the ordeal of the empty place and of dispossession to its conclusion."[171] The poem never forgets, in other words, that "dispossession"—history's inevitable erasure of every nonsovereign form of life—characterizes the human condition. To the extent that the *mu'allaqah* sides with what has been erased from the historical record, it makes truth immanent rather than transcendent: "The great strength of this poem lies in rigorously maintaining a principle of immanence."[172]

Badiou thus illustrates this chapter's overarching thesis: as a consequence of the philological revolution, we identify immanent truths with printed texts. He claims, in fact, that his philosophy "assumes the poem as one of its conditions."[173] Yet the historical function of elite poetry such as the *Mu'allaqāt* was to articulate and inculcate the tribe's sovereign honor code; it was much less "the poem of the abandoned place" than the official ideology of the tribe. Badiou himself intuits the disjunction between immanent practices and written poetry:

> The poem, forever inscribed and lying stellar upon the page, is [persistence's] exemplary guardian. But are there not other arts devoting themselves to the

fugacity of the event, to its allusive disappearance, to what is *unfixed* in the becoming of the true[?] Arts of mobility and of the "just once"? What are we to say of dance[,] cinema[,] theater[,] of which one day—the actors vanished, the sets burned, the director omitted—nothing will remain[?] Is philosophy as comfortable with these arts of public passage[?][174]

But even here Badiou fails to recognize that poetry itself often resists inscription in order precisely to keep faith with the "fugacity" and "disappearance" of "the event." Whereas the *Mu'allaqāt*'s motifs of stopping at the ruins and crossing the desert are, in fact, precisely what philological power has passed down as Bedouin life's historical truth, the everyday poetry of women and youth submits exactly to the evanescence that Badiou's radical politics simultaneously desire and fear.

Like the arts Badiou describes above, the politics he advocates must always be ready to dissolve its structure the moment it solidifies. As his *Metapolitics* observes, "A genuinely political organization, or a collective system of conditions for bringing politics into being, is the least bound place of all."[175] But such an immanent politics will remain unrealized as long as we are unable to discern the discursive practice on which it depends: not the production of texts but the effort instead to escape textual authority. How rigorous—or radical—can any philosophy that fails to make this basic distinction actually be? This failure—far from Badiou's alone—reflects how profoundly the philological revolution reshaped the text's social role. The principles we now imagine are "immanent" to a given people, period, or place appear so only after philology's grand colonial design—to substitute eternally fixed texts for always evolving practices—has long been complete.

Conclusion

I have used Badiou's reading of the *Mu'allaqāt* to illustrate this chapter's argument about the relationship of texts and immanent principles in the context of literature. I turn, finally, to the ongoing debate about the colonial "invention of tradition" in order to illustrate this chapter's parallel argument in regard to law. Whereas the volume edited by Eric Hobsbawm and Terrence Ranger that initiated the debate claims that colonial law calcified previously pliable customs, British imperial historians such as C. A. Bayly have insisted that colonial law, far from a British invention, emerged directly from *pre*colonial history.[176] In a deeply erudite reconsideration of colonialism's preconditions, he argued that colonial policy was "effective mainly where it went with the grain of indigenous social change."[177] But despite its many nuances, Bayly's argument for the continuity of precolonial legal traditions and colonial legal codes misses the fundamental distinction between the two: the sudden shift from manuscript to print society, which undermined the forms of textual appropriation that had obtained before colonial rule. Hence, from his perspective, precolonial no less than colonial law comprises normative texts and settled orthodoxies. For Bayly and those who accept his argument, the difference between tradition transmitted via manuscripts that differ across space and time and legal codes that standardize such manuscripts becomes historically insignificant, if not invisible. Somehow the same "native" tradition, albeit inflected by British jurisprudence, is responsible for colonial rule.

Drawing on Bayly, Rosalind O'Hanlon and David Washbrook have emphasized that the Company's late eighteenth-century codes were the "jointly authored products" of colonial "officials" and their clerical "informants."[178] In fact, O'Hanlon and Washbrook make the continuity even deeper, arguing, contra Cohn, that "individualism," "contract," "private property rights," and "commercial rationality" were not introduced by colonial law and Company rule but rather by precolonial economies.[179] When one overlooks such forms of collaboration and continuity, one "underplay[s] [India's] own capacity for agency": the Company "did not abruptly introduce new processes of rule [but] inherited most of its servants, some at least of its purposes, and almost all of its early instruments for penetrating rural societies from [precolonial] states."[180]

This line of argument has recently become as influential as the invention-of-tradition paradigm. New versions of it reach far beyond Oxbridge historiography, now often passing for postcolonial studies itself. Typically taking issue with Said's *Orientalism*, such scholarship claims, perversely, to "recover" native "agency" by describing its role in the *creation* of colonial culture. This scholarship thus depoliticizes the very category of agency (and postcolonial studies along with it). In order to reduce native agency to colonial complicity, such scholarship must overlook the fact that the forms of state-controlled and standardized textual authority demanded by colonial rule had never existed in native society before.

Yet we all—Oxbridge, Marxist, and postcolonial scholars alike—exist on this side of the philological divide. Hence, even when we accept that colonial rule fundamentally transformed native traditions, we will apprehend that transformation only with the greatest difficulty. No less than Bayly, O'Hanlon, and Washbrook, we will confuse normative texts and philological formations, on one hand, with native traditions and precolonial society as such, on the other. We will lose access, in the process, not just to the full range of discursive practices that preceded the philological revolution but, more importantly, to those who lacked sovereign and philological power even before the advent of colonial rule. For example, while Ronald Inden's *Imagining India* argues that Orientalist knowledge displaced "the agency of Indians," it implies that this agency (the "capacity of Indians to make their world") belongs only to those who controlled precolonial "Indian economic and political institutions"—in the case of the medieval period on which he focuses, to "kings," "courts," "states," and "imperial formations."[181] In her study of the transition from precolonial tradition to colonial law, Nandini Bhattacharyya-Panda explicitly follows Inden in this regard: the transformation she describes is from "traditional normative texts," a "vast *written* tradition," to "colonial legal codes"—in, other words, from one form of philological power to another.[182]

We need to finally recognize that, in the spheres of law and literature, the appropriation of otherwise authoritative texts by willfully nonsovereign formations is the *pre-* and *anti*colonial practice par excellence. Only this discursive practice truly articulates an agency from below, one that does not seek to colonize others in turn. Hence, the conflict between the fleeting appropriation of textual authority, on one hand, and the philological revolution, on the other, is the paradigmatic colonial encounter we have so far failed to name. Until we do, every new vision of postcolonial democracy will metamorphose into yet another colonial ruse in the end.

THE ORIGINARY

The Dharma *and* Śakuntalā, *1794 A.D.–1400 B.C.*

Introduction

I now bring this archaeology of the philological revolution to its conclusion, turning to the innovation whose consequences were the most far-reaching. The idea of Indo-European civilization, first hypothesized by William Jones in 1786, triggered a feverish quest throughout the following century to reconstruct humanity's prehistorical language and thus return to a period otherwise "lost in the darkness of time."[1] The hypothetical language we call Proto-Indo-European took the place, within the philological imagination, of the divine tongue spoken from Eden's creation to Babel's destruction.[2] Indeed, if Proto-Indo-European was even older than Hebrew, its recovery promised European intellectuals almost everything the discovery of the Edenic-Babelic tongue had and more. Poets and philosophers assumed it would contain the trace of humanity's original consciousness, the spiritual union with both the earth and the cosmos that was supposed to be prior and perhaps antithetical to the whole trajectory of European civilization. On a more scientific plane, philologists assumed this protolanguage would disclose the *ur*-form and hence structural unity of the otherwise diverse forms of speech, religion, and culture that had descended from it.

But if, in these ways, the concept of Proto-Indo-European merely refined the age-old paradigm of the divine language, it also placed this paradigm within historical time, thus exploding the singularity of the divine language

and the unity of language in general. It replaced both with irreducibly different language families, each possessing its own origins and history, analogous
to the mutually incomprehensible languages with which God punished
humanity after Babel. The sudden fragmentation of the previously discrete
phenomenon of language into incommensurable and infinitely complex
histories produced two, dialectically opposed, intellectual movements. On
one hand, European scholars of a cosmopolitan bent devoted their careers
to non-European languages and literatures, Indic ones first of all, because
they wanted to understand humanity's cultural development in a truly in-
tegrated fashion for the first time.[3] In the process, they precipitated the era
of European intellectual history Raymond Schwab would call "the Oriental Renaissance." On the other hand, nationalists in India as well as Europe
appropriated the arguments of Indo-European philologists for antithetical
ends. For them, the philological reconstruction of Proto-Indo-European
revealed the *exclusive* essence, identity, and continuity of the Aryan race
throughout its history, whether they considered its most evolved form Hindu
or Germanic. Proto-Indo-European was, in this sense, even more fundamental to both Hindutva fascism and National Socialism than any subsequent
theory of homeland, biology, or blood.

On an even deeper level, though, the idea of Indo-European civilization
transformed the concept of origin itself. Before the late eighteenth century,
European scholars typically treated language as the reflection of an a priori
reality, some origin outside itself, whether divine providence, the laws of
nature and/or reason, or human sensation and passion. But after the Indo-
European hypothesis divided the phenomenon of language into countless,
different histories, the goal of philological inquiry ceased to be understanding the general origin of language as such and became instead studying the
particular evolution of each language in itself.[4] Simply put, every language
suddenly became an origin itself: its evolution disclosed the development
of the nation, tradition, or civilization that belonged to it. Indo-European
root words—the Indo-European people's earliest concepts, reconstructed
from the analysis of written languages—enabled philologists to return to
human prehistory.[5] From there, they used comparative method to track
the migrations of peoples around the world through countless generations,
establishing "connections across vast expanses of time and space."[6] Root

words also enabled them to trace the institutional genealogy of civilized life. For example, Émile Benveniste's *Indo-European Language and Society* famously glossed, in successive chapters, "Economy," "Kinship," "Social Status," "Royalty," "Religion," and so on from their Indo-European roots: "law" comes from *dhē-* ("to bring into existence"), *med-* ("measure" or "moderation"), *bhā-* ("to speak [with a divine voice]"), *kens-* ("to affirm a truth with authority"), and so on.[7] But Proto-Indo-European was merely the first, most widely accepted, and most intensely studied of the many protolanguages historical linguistics would reconstruct "out of oblivion."[8] Root words provided the starting point for a complete history of civilization; they became the indispensable basis of the philological endeavor to map human development in its historical totality. From a philological perspective, no origin outside language possessed metaphysical reality; language alone enabled all human phenomena to be understood empirically, with previously unimaginable historical detail and depth.

The humanities have of course long since abandoned the racist overtones the concept of Indo-European civilization acquired during the course of the nineteenth century. But they have never ceased being shaped by the relationship this concept presupposes between the roots and evolution of languages, on one hand, and the origins and development of culture, on the other. The originary nature of language is, along with its literary dimension and its immanent quality, one source of the aura that has attached to textual study since the late eighteenth century. Even our most sophisticated theorists, from Antonio Gramsci through Clifford Geertz to Ranajit Guha and beyond, have treated language as the originary element of social life. Gramsci considered language "the spontaneous act of a peculiar inner life, springing out in the only form that is suited to it."[9] Paying particular attention to Indian history, Geertz considered language a "primordial" constituent of identity, affect, and social affiliation.[10] Guha likewise identified the beginnings of an "Indian"—or native language—historiography of India not with any explicit anticolonialism but rather with the writer's "primordial" connection to his or her "mother" tongue.[11] Hence, not just for literary studies or the humanities in general but across the qualitative social sciences as well, the premise that languages are originary has become fundamental. If we can know ourselves in an a posteriori way only by studying language, then language's originary

nature becomes, ironically, the last a priori truth, too axiomatic for our mode
of inquiry to be made an object of critical scrutiny itself. We have, in short,
moved beyond Aryan race theory but not the philological model on which
it was built.

In fact, this model—which, starting from originary concepts, creates
complex genealogies of peoples, traditions, and institutions—still lies at the
foundation of the humanities. This chapter calls this model into question
by studying its colonial history and logic. From the late eighteenth century forward, the reconstruction of Indo-European civilization's linguistic
origins enabled the colonial state in British India to claim possession of
"transregional" and "metahistorical" knowledge about—and hence continuity
with—the colonized's religious and national identities.[12] As Michel Foucault observed, origins always presume to exist outside history, "immobile
forms that precede the external world of accident," the "exact essence" of the
civilization or tradition, its "purest possibilities."[13] But rather than originary,
"prehistorical" languages are, in fact, at least doubly contaminated by history, "restored" by philologists living in one historical moment analyzing
written records from other moments. Whenever we treat these languages as
originary, we blind ourselves to such forms of contamination, the historical
conflicts that produce every "origin." And when we confuse the linguistic
roots philology has itself reconstructed with languages that precede history,
we merely imprison ourselves within the history of philology. If we hope even
to glimpse the prehistorical languages for which the new philology seeks—
those alone that would enable us to perceive both the history of civilization in
its totality and a consciousness exterior to this history—we will need another
approach. We will need to look, beneath our Indo-European origins, for a
form of life philological methods cannot even access, much less comprehend.

The previous chapter studied the beginning of legal codification in India,
focusing on Anglo-Islamic law. This chapter continues with the same subject
but shifts the focus to Anglo-Hindu law instead. The first authoritative work
in this field—*Institutes of Hindu Law; or, The Ordinances of Menu* (1794)—was
William Jones's translation of the oldest canonical Dharmaśāstra text, popularly known as the *Laws of Manu*.[14] A second codification that Jones began

before his untimely death in 1796—*A Digest of Hindu Law on Contracts and Successions* (1797)—followed soon after.[15]

To codify the Dharmaśāstra, Jones needed first to master Sanskrit, an exceptionally difficult language of which he had no knowledge before arriving in Bengal. He managed to do so, somehow, in just two years (1785–87), despite the fact that he could find the time to study Sanskrit—and, subsequently, to read, edit, and translate the Dharmaśāstras—only in the interstices of his official labor as an East India Company supreme court judge.[16] His explanation, in both private correspondence and public addresses, of his decision to undertake these seemingly impossible tasks—to master Sanskrit and translate Dharmaśāstra texts in his spare time—reiterated the justification for his plan to codify *sharīʿa*. According to Jones, the native clerics who possessed juridical authority and on whom Company magistrates relied could not be trusted to administer the law impartially: "I could not with an easy conscience concur in a decision, merely on the written opinion of native lawyers, in any cause in which they could have the remotest interest in misleading the court."[17] In actuality, though, Jones's codification of the Dharmaśāstra, as of *sharīʿa*, was designed to transfer authority over legal tradition from the native clerisy to the colonial state. Jones's Hindu legal codes would eventually form one foundation of the colonial *and* postcolonial Hindu civil code: they helped establish both modern law and a modern understanding of law in India.[18]

But Jones's incidental decision to study Sanskrit would have effects far beyond the legal domain. This course of study led him, first of all, to formulate the Indo-European hypothesis (1786), conventionally considered his single greatest contribution to the philological revolution. The Indo-European hypothesis undercut the claim of Hebrew—or indeed of any historically attested language—to be original and therefore divine. In the process, it forced philologists to surrender any lingering hope that the genealogy of language could be understood in unilinear form (starting from a single origin, undergoing simple degeneration, culminating in the historically corrupt languages spoken in the present). The genealogy of language revealed itself to be multilinear instead, with diverse origins following different trajectories, each constituting a "history" in the modern sense, that is, a temporal unfolding of previously unimagined granular complexity. The suggestion that Sanskrit

might be older than Hebrew furthermore enabled poets and philosophers
to give historical priority to a different kind of sacred consciousness, one
whose origin and development occurred outside Greco-Roman as well as
Judeo-Christian civilization and hence that could potentially challenge every
European aesthetic and ethical paradigm.

But the effort to master this language also led Jones to study, translate,
and publish ancient works of Sanskrit literature—above all, the dramatic
masterpiece popularly known as *Śakuntalā* (1789), as well as the Bhakti-era
long poem *Gita Govinda* (1792)—even before his edition of *Manu* was complete.[19] Along with Charles Wilkins's versions of the *Bhagvad Gita* (1785)
and *Hitopadeśa* (1787), the only previous works translated from Sanskrit into
English, Jones's *Sacontalá* first disclosed to Western intellectuals an otherwise
inaccessible ancient literature.[20] Inaugurating the idea of Indo-European
civilization, Jones's essays on this language and his translation of its literary
and legal texts stoked Western scholarly interest in ancient India and laid
the groundwork for Indo-European philology. In fact, even more than the
works we have studied in the previous two chapters, they inspired the Oriental Renaissance. Jones's versions of *Śakuntalā* and, later, *Manu* astonished
Romantic-era writers, who imagined these works transported them back to
the linguistic origins of the people subsequently called "Indo-European."
Herder, Friedrich Schlegel, and Goethe, among many others, each found in
Śakuntalā a consciousness that considered the earth sacred and experienced
infinitude within material experience. Their reading of *Śakuntalā* expressed
a nascent desire to restore the time before not only Judeo-Christian and
Greco-Roman history but even the ecological violence of history as such.
One could argue that such a desire has never ceased to haunt the humanities,
which pursue it still in archaic and Eastern traditions, in supposedly primordial texts and languages older than history itself. In any case, fantasies of the
time before history would lead nineteenth-century philologists to seek the
universal mythology behind all religions, which they believed would revitalize Western culture.

In response to philology's trajectory from Jones's hypothesis forward,
this chapter offers an archaeology of Proto-Indo-European. Its aim in this
regard is not, of course, to produce a complete history of civilization but,
on the contrary, to understand what such histories constitutively exclude. It

excavates, in particular, the three-thousand-year-old history of *dharma* (from the Sanskrit root *dhṛ*, "give foundation to"), a word that, however ultimately untranslatable, now denotes the original law. This term, like every other Sanskrit concept considered originary, is instead the product of various philological formations, from the Vedic and dharmasastric traditions to colonial and postcolonial law. From its earliest texts, the *dharma* has been identified with nonviolence (*ahiṃsā*) and ecology, the prescription that one must protect the earth. In diametric opposition, an archaeological approach reveals that ecological sensitivity belongs only to forms of life that textual culture attempted to destroy. The *dharma* texts were, for example, deeply implicated in Indo-European violence: that is, the burning of the forests, the dispossession and displacement of its inhabitants, and the erasure of their way of life. Supposedly originary texts such as *Manu* and *Śakuntalā* that evoke the code of nonviolence expropriated it, therefore, from those who preceded and those who opposed this epoch-making change. Those who were truly exterior to civilization—that is, who refused to play *any* part in it—would not have left records behind. To imagine their consciousness—which refused to take part in civilization—we will need first to retrace philology's millennia-long unfolding.

In other words, like the preceding chapters, this one practices a critical method whose intent is, ultimately, to recognize the forms of life philology itself has excluded. This method thus turns philological research against its own history. In the manner of the prototypical philological quest, we will return to the origins of Indo-European civilization. But we will find there not the key to total historical knowledge but, on the contrary, relics that remain outside philological understanding. An archaeological approach does not care to advance the cause of literary history. Its aim is rather to throw the violence of this civilization-founding craft into relief.

1. From the Indo-European Hypothesis to Hindu Nationalism: The Laws of Manu, 1794 A.D.

Before the late eighteenth century, as mentioned, the orthodox view held language's origin to be divine. In contrast, the cutting edge of philosophical speculation—represented in the work of Turgot, Condillac, and Monboddo, among others—understood language in terms of sense perception instead.[21]

From this perspective, every language is reducible to the interaction of two ultimately invariable entities, mind and nature. Articulating precisely the same material reality, different languages can, therefore, be exchanged for each other without semantic loss. But from the late 1750s to the early 1770s, the Berlin Academy initiated a series of formal debates on these theories, the most famous contribution being Herder's *Treatise on the Origin of Language* (1772), which shifted the ground of debate from language's metaphysical origin—whether divine, rational, or natural—to its historical evolution.

These debates form one precondition of Jones's pioneering argument that, in the study of language, "philosophical" (i.e., a priori) methods must give way to "historical" (i.e., a posteriori) approaches.[22] Jones called on scholars, in other words, to treat language not as the *reflection* of "transcendental" truths but, in diametric opposition, as the *basis* of empirical knowledge.[23] At a time when archaeological techniques had yet to be discovered, the study of language was, in Jones's view, the primary means to an understanding of humanity's historical development: "How little soever I may value mere *philology*, considered apart from the knowledge to which it leads, yet I shall ever set a high price on those branches of learning, which make us acquainted with the human species in all its varieties."[24]

Jones's philological research had begun to model the historical approach to language and literature that would become the sine qua non of the new philology even before he started to study Sanskrit, as we have observed in the previous two chapters. But only after the Indo-European hypothesis definitively replaced the divine language with irreducibly different language families did humanistic study acquire a strictly historicist foundation and philology become an independent discipline.[25] Nineteenth-century comparative philologists and historical linguists imagined that if they could delineate the development of each language and language family from its origins, they would produce a complete outline of human history. As they created ostensibly rigorous divisions between different language families— and, by extension, national peoples—they systematized the techniques of comparative method. The echoes of Jones's new project for philology could thus be heard throughout the following century: in Max Müller's words, "the object and aim of philology, in the highest sense, is [to] learn what man is, by learning what man has been."[26]

In his "Anniversary Discourses" before the Asiatick Society in Calcutta, Jones claimed that the filiation between the Indo-European languages was demonstrated by their verb "roots" (as well as "the *forms of grammar*"), and he adduced cognate words from the different languages as further evidence of their common derivation.[27] Jones's emphasis on root words and comparative grammar in his formulation of the Indo-European hypothesis prefigured the dominant tendencies of nineteenth-century philology and linguistics, which focused on the internal development of language to the exclusion of its social and material contexts. In fact, using metaphors first found in Herder, philologists from the Schlegels and Humboldt to Grimm and Schleicher explicitly described languages (no less than "nations" and "races") as natural organisms, each possessing a "life of its own."[28] The point of this metaphor was to imply that languages contain the "seeds of their own evolution," conform without exception to regular laws, and are, as a consequence, amenable to scientific analysis.[29]

Jones's concept of the root word suggested another principle that would become seminal for nineteenth-century philology: the origin of a language, tradition, or civilization holds the key to its development.[30] Jones designed his discourses to trace "the origin and progress" of Asia's "five principal nations"—Hindus, Arabs, Persians, Turks, and Chinese—and, in regard to the first of these, claimed he had extended his inquiry "upwards, as high as possible, to the earliest authentick records of the human species."[31] In this way, he prefigured the German Romantics, who also "undertook to trace everything back to its origins": "In the convenient vocabulary of short German particles[,] 'Ur' was the key to 'sym,'" that is, the origin ties everything together.[32]

By the 1830s, the study of the protolanguage in the work of Franz Bopp and Eugène Burnouf began to fulfill the agenda Jones had originally set forth: Proto-Indo-European became the object of linguistic science rather than the expression of a merely mystical desire for the universal religion.[33] In the wake of the Indo-European hypothesis and Jones's "Discourses," nineteenth-century philology presupposed not simply that the past produces the present but rather that the origin effectively determines everything that succeeds it. The new philology's premise was that once one has recovered the origin of an object, one can explain its subsequent history by specifying its "principles of change."[34] Philologists became obsessed, as a consequence, not just with humanity's earliest records but also with the languages that came even before. They needed only to deduce, from a given language's supposedly original texts, its prehistorical roots and to specify its subsequent laws of development to possess total historical knowledge—not only of the tradition in question but also of the "people," "nation," or "race" to whom it belonged. Even though history was infinitely heterogeneous, such original texts coupled with proper critical methods were thought to make every past available.

One could argue, then, that Jones and the scholars who followed in his wake used philology not to think history for the first time but rather to escape it once again. Even after philology disentangled itself from theology, it accorded epistemic privilege to the putative origin of the object under study. Both "historically and historiographically," the origin became "the master moment."[35] This privilege attests to the obduracy of philology's theological habits of mind, to its belief that, because our linguistic origins precede history, they possess the singular power to shape it. As Foucault observed, "the origin always precedes the Fall. It comes before the body, before the world and time; it is associated with the Gods, and its story is always sung as a theogony."[36]

Jones's presentation of *Manu* exemplifies Foucault's point—and the new-philological concept of the originary text—precisely. As previously mentioned, *Manu* had long been considered the original Dharmaśāstra. But Jones's translation, which first disclosed the dharmasastric tradition to European scholars, presented *Manu* not merely in this way but as the very origin of Indian religion as such. In fact, he made *Manu*'s originary function even more fundamental. Jones linked the origin of Indian religion—by virtue of the deep linguistic connections the Indo-European hypothesis had uncovered—to the origins of European civilization as well. Jones assumed *Manu*—which he dated to 1300–900 B.C.—to be a millennium older than it actually was, claiming, incorrectly, that it was "one of oldest compositions" extant anywhere in the world.[37] He suggested that his translation of *Manu* had therefore made the origin of non-Hebraic law available to Europe once more: "If Minos, the son of Jupiter[,] was really the same person as Menu, the son of Brahma, we have the good fortune to restore, by means of *Indian* literature, the most celebrated system of heathen jurisprudence."[38] Jones furthermore offered his reconstruction of root words as evidence that

Manu contained the trace of the original law: "We cannot but admit that Minos and Mneues [Egypt's 'first lawgiver'] have only *Greek* terminations, but that the crude noun is composed of the same radical letters in *Greek* and *Sanskrit*"; "the name of Menu is clearly derived (like *menes*, *mens*, and *mind*) from the root *men*, to *understand*."[39] Neither European nor Indian scholars would ever overturn the priority Jones accorded *Manu* within the history of Indian law.[40]

In fact, nineteenth-century Europeans treated *Manu* as the single most important text for an understanding of India's ancient past.[41] And, as a consequence of Jones's pioneering research, European intellectuals came to believe that ancient Indian texts—whether *Manu* or the significantly older Vedas (1700–500 B.C.)—contained the traces of an undocumented culture that encompassed both South Asia and Europe and would shed light on the deep structure of European civilization. From its very origins, Indology appeared to be the key that would unlock Europe's secret history. In Müller's view, "no one [interested in] the historical growth of human speech, [in] the first germs of the language, the religion, the mythology of our forefathers, [or, even more fundamentally, in] the wisdom of Him who is not the God of the Jews only [could afford to ignore] the language and literature of ancient India."[42] A half century later, another prominent Sanskritist, Moriz Winternitz, observed: "If we wish [to] understand the beginnings of our own culture, we must go to India, where the oldest literature of an Indo-European people is preserved. . . . We can safely say that the oldest monument of the literature of the Indians is at the same time the oldest monument of Indo-European literature which we possess."[43]

The fact that Müller adverts to the divine, just as Winternitz emphasizes the "beginnings" of culture, attests to nineteenth-century philology's belief that the origin exists outside history—and, as a consequence of that fact, determines and limits everything that follows. The search for the divine language had thus metamorphosed seamlessly into the reconstruction of humanity's Indo-European roots. During the course of the nineteenth-century, this quest focused for a time on ancient India's "classical age," to which both *Manu* and *Śakuntalā* belonged. Jones's reconstruction of "original" texts and rigorously language-based approach to historical study thus formed the building blocks of comparative philology, which would become the nineteenth century's "master-science of the human mind"—or, in Ernest Renan's words, "la science historique de l'esprit humain."[44]

Because the Indo-European hypothesis precipitated the search for each nation's linguistic roots, the route from it to European fascism was not very long.[45] At least since Herder's *Treatise*, philologists had considered language an entity that continuously evolves but nonetheless contains within itself the vestiges of early humanity and the *Volk*.[46] By the early nineteenth century, the model of a master civilization migrating from its homeland across the world, sharing in common a conquering ethos expressed in its root words and syntactic structures, had already begun to emerge. Racism presupposes, of course, the idea that every people possesses a "primordial" element that, by virtue of its originary position, cannot be changed: before the development of biology and anthropology, this element could reside only in the prehistorical roots of language. Racism naturally follows, in other words, from the new-philological premise that root words lie at the origins of history and culture; the modern category of race began with the idea of protolanguages and the supposed derivation from them of language families, religions, nations, and laws.

This "master-science of the human mind" satisfied the demand not just of European philologists but also of colonial administrators for total epistemic authority. British colonial rule used supposedly originary works (*Manu* and the other *dharma* texts as well) and the equally originary concepts (caste above all) articulated therein to define the transhistorical and supraterritorial bases of "Indian civilization."[47] Indeed, these texts and concepts enabled the British Empire to turn the subcontinent's widely disparate cultures into a single, coherent, continuous "civilization" for the first time. While colonial scholars obviously did not invent the concept of caste (i.e., *varna*), they were responsible for making its explanatory value for "Hindu" society axiomatic: as Nicholas Dirks has observed, "*varna* came both to signify all [hierarchical] relations and to explain them in some ultimate sense."[48] Hence, while the two sides in the famous nineteenth-century debate over the foundation of colonial rule—Anglicists such as James Mill on one hand, Orientalists such as Horace Hayman Wilson on the other—held diametrically opposed attitudes toward the value of caste, both drew their understanding of this originary practice from the same originary text, the *Laws of Manu*.[49] Colonial rule thus bequeathed to the philological revolution not just the methods and materials that made it possible but even the sociopolitical imperatives—that is, the necessity of governing difference on its own terms—that made its knowledge essential.

But the idea of originary texts—and of caste as an originary concept—managed to outlive colonial rule. Even those such as Gandhi who sought a third path between Orientalism and Anglicism (or, subsequently, between Hindu fundamentalism and liberal reform) nonetheless tended to insist on the primordial place of caste, *Manu*, and the Vedas in Indian civilization.[50] As late as the 1970s, Ronald Inden and McKim Marriott—leading Indologists from the University of Chicago who aspired to develop a "comprehensive theory" of Indian society and its "conceptual underpinnings"—would return once again to originary texts and hence to caste: they argued that "Vedic thought" provided the "basis for formulating Indian unity and for understanding much of South Asian history and ethnography consistently."[51] Even as they hoped to escape Western social scientific categories and inhabit "Indian" concepts instead, they depended on historiographical principles originally invented by colonial philology and immediately co-opted by Hindu nationalism. Its founding figures—Dayananda Saraswati (1824–83), Bal Gangadhar Tilak (1856–1920), Aurobindo Ghose (1872–1950), Vinayak Damodar Savarkar (1883–1966)—each imagined Indian civilization (and the Aryan race) to be unified and ennobled by a *dharma* that, originating in the oldest books humanity possesses (the Vedas), had been passed down across countless generations.[52] From the perspective of Hindu nationalism, the return of Hindus to their rightfully sovereign position depends on a revival of this knowledge: they constitute a race, after all, only by virtue of this common linguistic and textual origin. If the various movements, parties, and paramilitary organizations grouped around the rhetoric of the Hindu *rashtra* (nation) and Hindutva (Hindu-ness) claim the Vedas and the Dharmaśāstra as "our history books," thus blurring the distinction between scripture and historiography, they are merely the progeny of the colonial premise that the protolanguage, reconstructed from the oldest texts, determines everything that follows it.[53]

Geertz called the belief that one's native language is primordial to one's identity "linguism" and devoted particular attention to its analysis in India, where, he claimed, "for some yet to be adequately explained reasons," this phenomenon "is particularly intense."[54] The reason is, in fact, simple: from its very first decades, the colonial state had insisted that not just the historical truth but even the racial essence of every colonial subject within India lay in one language or another. Hence, the premise that language is primordial became even more fundamental to the colonial administration of India than it had been to nation-state formation in Europe. Decades before India was granted independence, the Congress Party would make the division of post-colonial India into language-based states one plank of its electoral platform; in the decades immediately after independence, twenty-one such states would be called into existence, in line with popular demands. The modern state thus created the native's supposedly "nonmodern" attachment to his or her particular language: linguism lies, as Sheldon Pollock has argued, "at the very heart" of the colonial project.[55] The attitudes of "language purity, exclusivity, and singularity" evident in India today are, as he has emphasized, "of entirely recent stamp and largely exogenous origin" (as, needless to say, was their enforcement by sovereign power)—facts that both colonial philologists and Hindu nationalists needed to overlook.[56]

2. The Idea of Indo-European Civilization: Śakuntalā, 1789 A.D.

Ernest Gellner and Benedict Anderson have both argued, as mentioned, that the modern nation's invention depends on standardized languages.[57] Only literature written in such languages could serve, for example, the nationalist struggle against colonialism. Aamir Mufti has contended, in the same vein, that Orientalism first presented South Asian literary traditions in national or, in other words, communal (either exclusively Hindu or exclusively Muslim) terms.[58] Though unquestionably true and important, such arguments cannot fully capture the epistemic transformation colonial philology wrought in the study of language and literature. As a consequence of the philological approach pioneered by Jones, classical literary texts, and *Śakuntalā primus inter pares*, were thought to articulate not just national or communal traditions but, much more fundamentally, the origins and unity of Indian civilization. Their literary power and prestige lay precisely here.

In fact, Jones went to such extraordinary trouble, given his already overwhelming professional obligations, to translate Sanskrit literature precisely because he believed it possessed this power.[59] In the preface to his translation, Jones claimed that *Śakuntalā* had been composed five hundred years earlier than it actually had been, during the "first century before Christ[,] when the Britons were as unlettered and unpolished as the [monkey] army of Hanuma[n]," in a court that "was equal in brilliance [to] that of any monarch in any age or country."[60] *Śakuntalā* formed part of a theatrical tradition that, Jones insisted, was "immemorially" old and could "fill as many volumes" as the drama of any European tradition.[61] This play was in particular one of "the most universally esteemed" works of Indian drama and "one of the greatest curiosities that the literature of Asia has yet brought to light."[62] Jones thus built on Indian philological traditions more than a millennium old, which had treated *Śakuntalā* as *the* embodiment of the dramatic rules set forth in the *Nāṭya Śāstra*, the authoritative text within the sastric tradition for the performing arts.[63] But he also turned these traditions in an altogether different direction: *Śakuntalā* became not merely the expression of normative aesthetic principles but suddenly the very apex of Hindu civilization.[64]

Jones's presentation of *Śakuntalā* and its author Kālidāsa—whom he called "the Shakespeare of India"—participated in the Romantic redefinition of "literature," which referred no longer, as it had during the Enlightenment, inclusively to all the written texts of a specific language or period but instead exclusively to those aesthetic writings that constituted "the deepest and most valued 'expression' of the spirit of a race, people, society, or nation, or of a national character."[65] Hence, Jones could claim that *Śakuntalā* was "a mos[t] authentick picture of old Hindû manners."[66] It is within this new concept of literature that *Śakuntalā*, the single most celebrated translation from colonial India, would become paradigmatic for British scholars and East India Company officials, for European philologists, poets, and philosophers, and for Hindu nationalists alike.[67]

Jones's *Sacontalá* would be reprinted three times in England by 1796 and five times by 1807.[68] In the 1817 edition of *The History of British India*, James Mill famously adduced it as evidence of Hindu civilization's moral degeneracy.[69] At mid-century, Monier Monier-Williams—a Bombay Presidency surveyor-general's son who taught at the East India Company College before becoming Boden Chair of Sanskrit at Oxford—claimed that *Śakuntalā* was a "key to 'Hindu' culture."[70] Like Mill, he took for granted Jones's claim that ancient Indian texts such as *Śakuntalā* telescope Hindu civilization: "To the antiquity of [Hindú plays] is add[ed] their value as representations of the early condition of Hindú society—which, notwithstanding the lapse of two thousand years, has in many particulars obeyed the law of unchangeableness, ever stamped on the manners and customs of the East"; "[the British public] ought surely be conversant with the most popular of Indian dramas, in which the customs of the Hindús, their opinions, prejudices, and fables, their religious rites, daily occupations and amusements, are reflected as in a mirror."[71] He retranslated *Śakuntalā* in 1853 on the premise that its study would be essential both for the Company to know its subjects and for educated Indians to know themselves. He subsequently created the Oxford Indian Institute to train students for the Indian civil service and repeated his claims about *Śakuntalā's* epistemic value for colonial administrators at century's end.[72] In the 1920s, A. B. Keith—Jones's twentieth-century legal and Orientalist counterpart, a widely published scholar in the field of imperial law as well as Regius Professor of Sanksrit at Edinburgh—once again rehearsed Jones's civilizational claims, arguing that Kālidāsa had provided "the permanent master paradigm of Indian poetry, across most languages, regions, and historical situations on the subcontinent as a whole."[73] More recently, an American Sanskritist, editor of the *Journal of the American Oriental Society*, declared *Śakuntalā* "the validating aesthetic creation of a civilization," a text that does not merely provide "evidence about culture" but that "defines [the] outlook and internal relationship of a civilization."[74]

Jones's *Sacontalá* was retranslated into German in 1791, French in 1803, Italian in 1815, and, according to Barbara Stoler Miller, "every European language" eventually.[75] Almost as soon as its first retranslation, *Śakuntalā* had become even more foundational for European Romanticism than it would subsequently be for colonial Orientalism. Herder, Goethe, Forster, the Schlegels, and Humboldt all claimed their interest in Sanskrit began with their reading of *Śakuntalā*, their "first link with the authentic India."[76] Assuming that *Śakuntalā* was even older than Jones had imagined, these writers identified the play with ancient Indic wisdom. In his private correspondence, Herder invoked the Romantic concept of literature when he explained *Śakuntalā's* significance: "It is [in ancient poetry that] the mind and character of a nation is best brought to life before us, and I gladly admit, that I have received a truer and more real notion of the manner of thinking among the ancient Indians from this one Śakuntala, than from all their [religious scriptures]."[77] Like Herder, due in part to his influence, Friedrich Schlegel, Schelling, and Novalis each believed that ancient Indian poetry contained traces of the "universal revelation" that lies at the origin of all religion—that constitutes, in other words, "humanity's original religion."[78] Schlegel claimed that India was "truly the source of all language, all thought, and the dreams of the human spirit"; it was the "origin" of "everything, without exception."[79] The invocations of *Śakuntalā* across nineteenth-century European literary culture and of the "universal religion" it supposedly articulated are far too numerous to be recounted here. Suffice it to say that Schwab renamed Romanticism's first decades the "*Shakuntala* Era," as mentioned.[80]

For the Romantics, *Śakuntalā* represented a time "beyond history," when human consciousness still considered nature animate.[81] In regard to the play, Herder wrote, "Here plants, trees, and the entire creation speak and feel."[82] Like Herder and Heine, Goethe would write a poem in praise of *Śakuntalā*'s ecological sensibility. According to his cryptic (often-quoted but rarely glossed) quatrain: "If you want the blossoms of Spring and the fruits of the later year,/If you want what excites and delights, if you want what satisfies and nourishes,/If you want Heaven, Earth in one name to grasp/I name you, Sakuntala, and thus everything is said."[83] In private correspondence almost four decades later, Goethe would himself interpret his poem: "Only now do I grasp the extravagant impression that this work excited in me. Here the poet appears to us in his highest role, as a representative of the natural state[:] at the same time however he remains lord and master of his creation; he can dare common and ridiculous opposites which nevertheless must be considered as necessary links in the whole organism."[84] In the view of Goethe and his contemporaries, *Śakuntalā* combined a primordial sensuality (the "blossoms of Spring," "what excites and delights," "the Earth," "the natural state") with a refined understanding ("the fruits of the later year," "what satisfies and nourishes," "Heaven," creative "master[y]"). They considered the play a model of (Romantic) literature by virtue of this combination: *Śakuntalā* effectively contained within itself both the origins and ends of civilization.[85] In the conventional binaries used to describe the Romantic movement, *Śakuntalā* unified "mythology" and "poetry" or, alternatively, "religion" and "art": on one hand, a language that recalls a moment before history, when the earth was still sacred; on the other, an aesthetic practice that would make this moment the basis of an advanced culture, law, and politics.[86] After reading *Śakuntalā*, Schlegel believed his quest "for the universal and infinite," on which he hoped to found Romantic poetry, had finally come to an end: ancient India, which possessed "the highest Romanticism," was their source.[87]

In precisely the same vein, Jones claimed that "a spirit of sublime devotion, of benevolence to mankind, and of amiable tenderness to all sentient creatures, pervades [*The Laws of Manu*; but it also] sounds like the language of legislation, and extorts a respectful awe."[88] After Jones's translation, *Manu*'s supposed constellation of sacred consciousness, ecological sensibility, and legal sophistication would fascinate countless Romantic writers, including Blake, Coleridge, Shelley, and Emerson; Herder, Goethe, Fichte, Schelling, Novalis, the Schlegels, and Grimm; Maistre, Lamennais, Constant, and Michelet.[89] They hoped that such Indic constellations—which they imagined captured a time earlier than either Hellenic civilization or the Hebraic revelations—would reintroduce the ancient mysteries of pagan and esoteric religions. If so, these texts would enable European scholars and poets, in effect, to synthesize the Orient and the Occident and thus renew Western religion. In the view of Friedrich Schlegel, Schiller, and Schopenhauer, the study of such texts might, in this way, reshape European history as fundamentally as the Renaissance had. By the second half of the nineteenth century, European philologists had published numerous studies on the origins of Indo-European civilization, in order to do nothing less than redefine the identity and future of the West.[90] At least in Germany, this project became scarcely distinguishable from the humanities as such.

Indo-European philology's civilizational paradigms were imported back to India by means, ironically, of translated texts such as *Manu* and *Śakuntalā*. The prestige the latter had acquired in Europe added to its authority within India: it became a work "every cultured Indian should know."[91] This authority derived, in other words, not from the work's traditional forms but rather from its new status as "literature," proof of Indian civilization's capacity to contribute to the world republic of letters.[92] But if literature expresses the spirit of a race, people, nation, or civilization, then *Śakuntalā* must contain India's

Aryan origins. By the late nineteenth century, members of the upper castes had, in fact, become obsessed with Aryanism, which enabled them to claim racial parity and even filiation with their British rulers. Hence, a prominent Indian Sanskritist, M. R. Kale, proclaimed at century's end that *Śakuntalā* enabled one to "breathe [the] purer air [and] pristine times of Aryan India."[93] As the supposed product of India's "Classical" or "Golden Age," the play was turned into a symbol of Hindutva, the supposedly proper ethos of all genuinely Indian people. It became a standard text in the study of Sanskrit, taught in schools and colleges, often performed both there and in colonial theaters at a time when the political and cultural elite were attempting to produce a unified national culture. The character of *Śakuntalā* came to embody the perfect Aryan woman (*gṛhiṇī* or *pativrata*); she is, in Tagore's words, "the model of a devoted wife."[94] Anticolonial nationalists would use precisely this ideal to defend Hindu tradition against liberal reform. Yet this ideal and their sense of the tradition alike were produced by the new-philological fetish of originary languages and texts.

In fact, though, neither a text's language nor its conceptual horizon reflect a religion, nation, or civilization per se. Texts articulate not these reified categories but rather historically particular forms of, and contests over, linguistic hegemony and philological power. The civilizational terms in which *Śakuntalā* and Sanskrit literature in general have been understood serve only to obscure literature's historical constitution in this sense. As Romila Thapar has observed, when Orientalists made Sanskritic high culture "the sole depository of tradition," they effaced divisions within Sanskrit between, for example, upper- and lower-caste (or brahmanic and popular) sources.[95] Once language and literature are reduced to the expressions of a supposedly unified civilization, they are rendered, in Simona Sawhney's words, "safely dead" for the present, cleansed of the conflicts that actually constituted them.[96] I would add that, in the production of a text, the first such conflict must be over who will possess textual authority and who will surrender or be excluded from it; it is this prior conflict that our supposedly originary languages can never comprehend. Until historical approaches to literature excavate this conflict, they will, ironically, only conceal the fundamental historical struggle that produces literary texts, the immediate interrelationship of text and "history." Put differently, we literary scholars presume to undertake historical and

political analyses of texts only after we have severed them from their proxi-
mate historical and political context.

3. The Dharma and Sacrificial Violence, 100 A.D. to 1400 B.C.

Johan Hüttner's 1797 German retranslation of Jones's *Institutes of Hindu
Law* wound its way to Nietzsche, who praised *Manu*'s supposedly capa-
cious understanding of human possibility in both the *Twilight of the Idols*
and *The Anti-Christ*.[97] The Sanskrit text had created, according to Nietzsche, a "healthier, higher, *wider* world" than the Christian scriptures did.[98] If
Judeo-Christian law reflected the slave's morality, *Manu* reflected, so Nietzsche argued, the master's. He defined master morality, of course, in terms of
the warrior-philosopher's originally life-affirming desires, which the priest-
philologists subsequently devalued in their rise to power. Hence, whereas
Judeo-Christian law is the product of "rabbinism," that is, priestly-philologi-
cal power, Nietzsche considered *Manu* "genuine philosophy," the affirmation
of desire against such power.[99] He contrasted Christianity's "*bad* purposes"—
the "negation of life, hatred of the body, the degradation and self-violation of
humans through the concept of sin"—with *Manu*'s "noble values": its intention to let "the *noble* classes, the philosophers and warriors, stand above the
crowd."[100] In fact, *Manu* was, in Nietzsche's eyes, nothing less than a manual
for the self-cultivation of masters: "To prepare a book of law in the style of
Manu means to give a people the right to become master one day, to become
perfect,—to aspire to the highest art of life."[101] But when Nietzsche conflated *Manu* with master morality, he fundamentally misunderstood the text,
which, if anything, resembles slave morality. As we shall see, *Manu* produced
a new priestly hegemony by abjuring the Vedic will to power in the name of
nonviolence and vegetarianism.

  As his interpretation of *Manu* attests, the aim of Nietzsche's archaeological method was to read against the grain of European philology and thus
break its hold on the interpretation of tradition, Eastern as well as Western.
His reading of Eastern texts tended, therefore, to serve a polemical purpose:
Nietzsche expressed his antiphilological spirit precisely in his ironic interpretation of these texts. His understanding of *Manu* (as of Hafiz) must be seen,
nonetheless, as a symptom of precisely the philological mindset he dedicated

his lifework to overturning. Like Jones and nineteenth-century philologists in general, Nietzsche wanted to believe that *Manu* expressed a form of life that was prior and hence exterior to civilizational decay. He consequently could not afford to acknowledge that *Manu*, like any traditional text, was itself the product of a philological formation: in its case, one that co-opted the antiphilological movements that had emerged in response to brahman hegemony. To realize Nietzsche's methodological ambition—that is, a dialectical response within and against the history of philology—we will need to read *Manu* differently.

Throughout its history, before as well as after colonial rule, *Manu* has in fact always served as a cornerstone for the construction of philological power. Like every other *sastra*, it was originally a "second-order"—rather than a popular—discourse. It recorded, that is, a clerical vision of what social practices should be, not those practices themselves.[102] This vision claimed and eventually acquired the status of divine knowledge; it was designed, in other words, to give jurists, priests, and scholars authority over daily life. It was *Manu* that first made brahmans sacred figures who should not be killed, expropriated, taxed, or even disobeyed by kings as well as articulating the rules of the caste system (*varnasrama-dharma*). Colonial philologists from Jones forward took *Manu*'s claims at face value: they identified it not with brahmanic authority but rather with collective life and hence made it normative for all Hindus.

But if *Manu* thus lay at the foundation of philological power in colonial Bengal as it had, almost two millennia before, in ancient India, its form had changed completely in its transit from one context to the other. Before colonial rule, philological power was exercised not by an impersonal state bureaucracy governing millions of subjects but rather by a priestly caste whose authority obtained only in local and regional settings. Hence, like the *shari'a* manuals discussed in the previous chapter, *Manu*'s ancient function was not to codify the law but instead to train the clerics who controlled it.[103] In this setting, again like *shari'a* manuals, if *Manu* was present as a written text at all, it was intended only to aid the process of oral transmission: its verse form—characterized by repetitions meant to facilitate memorization and hence precise reproduction—attests to this fact. *Manu*'s largely oral existence reflected, akin to the suspicion of textual authority within *shari'a*, the brahmanic tradition's explicit hostility to the graphic reproduction of sacred texts such as the

Dharmaśāstra and long before it, the Vedas. As a text, *Manu* had no juridical authority at all; its importance lay in its pedagogic role within the subject-formation of the scholar-priests who possessed actual authority over the law.

Like *shari'a* manuals once more, *Manu* had rarely been cited during judicial proceedings before colonial rule: jurists were more likely to rely on treatises (*nibandhas*) and commentaries (*ṭīkās*) on the Dharmaśāstra, other Dharmaśāstra texts or altogether different traditions (Bhakti devotional movements, Tantric cults, and so on) than they were to invoke *Manu*.[104] The Dharmaśāstra comprised ethical principles open to reinterpretation and historical adaptation, not state-mandated, -enforced, and -adjudicated rules: its precolonial form was designed to help jurists transform the tradition in line with the particular circumstances in which they found themselves. In fact, as the product of scribal cultures, *Manu* named less a single text than a general category containing innumerable regional and historical variations, countless manuscripts written in nine different scripts, spread across South Asia. Such self-divided scribal works are amenable to hieratic control but resist sovereign appropriation.

The East India Company claim that it would replace the rule of men with the rule of law and thus emancipate natives from the immemorial despotism under which they had suffered was crystallized in the very form of the transition from brahmanic to British power. The Company's first attempt to create a Hindu legal code in 1776 was based not on a written text but, ironically, on the oral Sanskrit performance of a single brahman pundit.[105] In the decades that followed, the colonial legal codes' historical authenticity would be founded instead on the new philology's historical authority. Yet even philologically reconstructed codes such as Jones's *Institutes of Hindu Law* did not correspond to any precolonial manuscript; they were instead composite creations. In other words, colonial philology restored something that had, in fact, never existed.[106] More importantly, when Jones transferred juridical authority from countless brahman priests to a single printed text, he raised philological power to a historically unprecedented level of abstraction. As Wendy Doniger has observed, British colonial rule replaced a "multiplicity of legal voices" and "centuries of case law" with "a single voice, that of Jones's *Manu*."[107]

But if, unlike Jones's *Manu*, the precolonial version had never been a single written, much less codified, text, the latter was, no less than the former, an attempt to expunge the traditions that preceded it. In other words, whereas both European philology and Hindu nationalism considered *Manu* originary, we need to understand it instead as an appropriation of even earlier discursive practices. Though the oldest Dharmaśāstra, *Manu* is far from the origin of Indian law. In fact, the roots of the very word *dharma* predate *Manu* by more than a millennium.

Dharma developed from *dhárman*, a new word—and an embryonic concept—in the *Rgveda*.[108] This word derives, in turn, from the Sanskrit √*dhr*, meaning "uphold or support": the *dhárman* is he who provides a foundation; he is the "foundation giver." The construction of the *Rgveda* canon from the fourteenth to the twelfth century B.C. accompanied the establishment of the Vedic world's first "supertribe" (the Kurus) and hence its first proto-state. With the Kurus, Vedic chieftains started to become kings, the rulers of expansive, centralized, and indeed imperial societies. Whereas *raja* originally referred merely to the chieftain who leads the tribe into battle in order to pillage others or who presides over it in times of peace, the later books of the *Rgveda*, composed when the Kurus were establishing the first Vedic state, redescribe the raja as the *dhárman*, aligning him no longer with Indra, the god of war, but instead with Varuna, the god of empires. Hence, though the *dharma* in *Manu* and after is aligned with the doctrine of nonviolence, its etymon is deeply implicated in the Indic origins of political and ecological violence.

The Vedas were in fact premised on a vision of both secular and sacred existence as a hierarchy of violence—in Sanksrit, *himsā*. But this word—the root of *ahimsā* or "nonviolence"—refers not merely to violence but more precisely to the desire to inflict injury.[109] From the perspective of the Vedas, this desire is the basis of all social and natural orders. Hence, the Vedas celebrate the act of violence: it is always better to be the eater than the eaten, the ruler than the ruled. The Vedas in fact articulate the theory and practice of violence's highest form, the priestly fire sacrifice (*yajna*), which fed the divine desire for violence; their authority was tied precisely to this practice. When performed properly, the fire sacrifice possessed the power to transform the cosmic order itself; sacrificial violence was thought to be parallel to—but even more powerful than—sociopolitical violence. It consequently conferred social supremacy on its brahman practitioners, who alone knew how to pronounce the sounds and were authorized to recite the mantras contained in the Vedas; brahman priests possessed a monopoly on sacrificial violence. Because they did, their power reached beyond the gods: "the gods control the world; *mantras* control the gods and the Brahmans control the *mantras*."[110] The authority this violence conferred on brahmans would subsequently descend to other brahmanic texts, including the Dharmaśāstras.

Though the fire sacrifice's explicit purpose was to consecrate upper-caste ambitions, it also effected a much broader—indeed epochal—transformation. This ritual typically occurred on the frontiers of agricultural or pastoral land. The fire, which sometimes burned for days or even continuously, consumed both wood and animal fat in vast quantities.[111] The resulting large-scale deforestation extended civilization (i.e., royal domains) into territories that lacked sovereign entities. In the *Mahābhārata*, for example, the burning of the entire Khandava forest—and every creature that inhabits it—to sate the fire god Agni is a precondition for the construction of the ancient Indian dynastic capital Indraprastha (supposedly on the site where Delhi now sits).[112] According to D. D. Kosambi, the conquest, clearing, and agrarian settlement of tribal forests—not political conflict between dynasties—was the driving force behind ancient Indian history.[113] In any case, though, the fire sacrifice's supreme violence lay precisely in its capacity to clear the forests. Like the term *dhárman*, the fire sacrifice sanctified territorial expansion and hence the emergence of sovereign power. In fact, rajas donated tax-free sacred groves (*āśrama*s and *agrahara*s) to brahmans at the edge of their own territories, where the priests' sacrificial rites would simultaneously bring the king merit and clear the forest for settlement and agricultural production. *Śakuntalā*'s opening acts are set in one such grove, where Śakuntalā was born and raised; the play's final act is set in another. We will, as a consequence, not be able to read *Śakuntalā*—or any *dharma* text—antiphilologically without this understanding: the burning of the forests, expropriation of its tribal inhabitants, and destruction of their way of life silently precedes the *dharma*, its originary claims, and its subsequent dissemination.

Ironically, the first attested use of the word *dharma* expresses exactly this awareness. It belonged to the *śramaṇa*s, homeless monks (*parivrajaka*) who renounced the world and retreated to the forests during the sixth century B.C., Buddhism becoming the most influential part of what had originally been a much broader social revolution. The *śramaṇa* movements offered an alternate path to liberation, founded on nonviolence and vegetarianism, which, in the śramaṇas' hands, were originally a reaction against the Vedic tradition that one must kill to eat.[114] Their practice of ahiṃsā was opposed to a particular form of violence, as their name attests: śramaṇa was the antithesis of brāhmaṇa. Hence, the śramaṇas opposed sacrificial violence in particular. They disavowed each of the civilization-founding acts contained within the fire sacrifice: deforestation, animal slaughter, and exhaustive resource use. Whereas the Vedic root of the word dharma aligned kings with the imperial god, the śramaṇas co-opted this root to create an explicitly nonviolent and nonsovereign, but no less sacred, philosophy. When they withdrew from their settled, and sometimes upper-caste, lives to the forests, they reverted, in part, to the way of life Vedic political violence had targeted. The śramaṇas' conservation practices in regard to specific plant and animal species were based on and contained the trace of the forest-dweller's ethos and knowledge. The śramaṇa movements recognized that the philological formation ruling their world—founded on the authority of the Vedic mantras, brahman control of the sacred texts and rituals, and the royal conquest of territory—had effaced other possible origins. This recognition is encoded within the very concepts of ahiṃsā and dharma, even if both now conceal the resistance to philological power that originally inspired them.

In fact, this resistance was effaced almost immediately: the śramaṇa revolution soon became the foundation of a new hegemony. Śramaṇa opposition to the priest-warrior (or brahman-kṣatriya) alliance appealed to the merchant classes that had emerged with the growth of agricultural surpluses. Just as the brahman āśramas and agrahāras were the vanguard of agricultural expansion, Buddhist (and Jain) monasteries became essential nodes in the development of trade routes.[115] As Buddhist monks acquired their own political patrons, they began to undercut the brahmans' privileged access to political power. The authority previously ascribed to sacrificial violence was now transferred to the Buddha's word (buddhavacana), which became, ironically, the new basis of textual authority within another, increasingly hegemonic, tradition.

As he created the largest empire South Asia has yet seen, Aśoka Maurya (304–232 B.C.) made the Buddha's dharma an imperial ideology.[116] He could do so, of course, only because of a millennium-long process of pushing agricultural society into tribal forests, begun by the fire sacrifice but extended in a much more systematic way by the Maurya Empire itself. Aśoka's "edicts on *dharma*" (in Prakrit, *dhammalipi*)—part of a decades-long *dharma* campaign he waged across his empire to implement his own version of the *dharma*—further institutionalized the *śramaṇa* revolution. Aśoka organized the *dharma* into a set of rules and defined which texts contained the true *dharma* (*saddhamma*) and which ones did not. He created a *dharma* bureaucracy with both central and provincial officials (*dharma* "superintendents" and "controllers"), who where responsible for instilling the *dharma* in all people, regardless of caste. Aśoka thus turned the *śramaṇas*' inclusive spiritual practices into an imperial strategy. His intention—as he claimed in the Kalinga Rock Edict after his armies had, according to his own estimate, enslaved 150,000 Kalinga *adivasi*s and killed 100,000 more—was to conquer henceforth by the *dharma*, not by violence. But his *dharma* was nonetheless conquest, if by another name.

The earliest brahman texts focused on *dharma*, the Dharmasutras, were written, very roughly, at the same time.[117] The concept of *dharma* that still obtains today—that is, the essential, transhistorical, and universal truth of the religious tradition, whether Buddhist or brahman—appeared at this time as well. Responding to the threat the *śramaṇa*s and, even more powerfully, the Maurya Empire posed to brahman authority, the *dharma* texts, including *Manu*, appropriated the sramanic ideal of renunciation and made it the supposed basis of brahmans' caste superiority and social power. With these texts, the brahman suddenly became the one who is most capable of self-control and self-denial and who is, as a consequence, the most pure. *Manu* reasserted brahman authority, furthermore, by redescribing the practice of fire sacrifice—at a time when animal offerings had generally been prohibited—as the highest form of *ahiṃsā*, an association that, however fundamentally inaccurate, still defines the general perception of the brahman tradition from the Vedas forward. In these ways, *Manu* was able to achieve a remarkable dialectical reversal: the *dharma* of nonviolence and vegetarianism—designed to oppose territorial conquest, the caste system, and priestly power—ended up merely reinforcing each of these interrelated institutions again.

European philologists and Hindu nationalists alike took *Manu* as the origin of an overarching pan-Indian—or even Proto-Indo-European—civilization. But far from originary, *Manu* was—like the Vedic mantras,

Aśoka's imperial *dharma*, and the Dharmasutras before it or Anglo-Hindu law much later—an attempt to expropriate language's constituent power from widely dispersed individuals and communities. The tradition humanities scholars inherit always comprises, by definition, systems of discursive domination such as these—layer upon historical layer, sedimented on top of each other—as the foundation of our own thought. No wonder that despite our best intentions, we mistake the artifacts of more or less successful hegemonies for the culture of a people, period, or religion in general.

To read antiphilologically, we would need no longer to presuppose the adequacy of language or literature to history but instead to investigate what linguistic and literary histories constitutively exclude. For example, we identify the evolution of the word *dharma* with the history of Indic and/or Indo-European civilization. In fact, though, the Vedic roots of the word—which glorify sovereign violence—absent precisely those who inhabited the forests before they were burned, cleared, and settled. The dharmasastric meaning of the word—which promotes, dialectically, the ideology of nonviolence—appropriates, in particular, the sramanic endeavor to reinhabit the forest-dweller's form of life. In either case, the lives of those—*adivasi*s and world-renouncers—who were not concerned to leave textual inscriptions precede the philological origin. Their discursive practices, so literally fundamental to Indo-European civilization, can neither be recovered philologically nor comprehended by any possible history of the people or period. Yet to read antiphilologically, truly to think archaeologically, we would need to orient our inquiry precisely toward that which remains outside recorded history. Such unhistorical practices are the material preconditions, furthermore, of every *dharma* text, as the analysis of *Śakuntalā* that follows is designed to demonstrate.

4. The Sovereign and the Earth: Śakuntalā, 415 A.D. to 400 B.C.

The previous section analyzed *Manu* antiphilologically, as the expression, in other words, not of a people, religion, civilization, and so on, but rather of conflicts between different philological formations. *Śakuntalā* is equally amenable to this archaeological approach. Though European philologists, philosophers, and poets identified Śakuntalā and the sacred grove in which she was raised with a nonviolent and ecologically sensitive consciousness, the play itself alludes to the forms of life the sacred grove—the vehicle of Indo-European violence—destroyed. Precisely where the Romantic generation imagined an originary language, *Śakuntalā* draws attention to what exists outside and comes before the origin. It exemplifies the uncanny capacity of texts to exceed the limits of supposedly originary languages. One could argue that *Śakuntalā's* brilliance is precisely its self-consciousness in this regard.

In fact, to an even greater extent than *Manu*, *Śakuntalā* is a palimpsest of the different historical strata that constituted Indo-European expansion. The story of Śakuntalā dates to at least 900 B.C., when it was mentioned in a Vedic-era text; its most significant version before Kālidāsa's dramatic adaptation occurs in the *Mahābhārata*, whose origins may lie in the earliest Vedic period, its standard version likely written sometime after 400 B.C.[118] The Śakuntalā narrative is thought to have originally existed, therefore, in the form of bardic recitations before tribal clansmen. But the play was not composed until the reign of Chandragupta II (ca. 375–415 A.D.) of the Gupta Empire, during a period when deforestation, the subordination of *adivasi* societies, and the caste system had already become highly evolved. Hence, between the origins of *Śakuntalā's* epic form and its dramatic adaptation lie the origins of Indian agrarianism and territorial expansion, state-formation and imperial development, and urbanization and social stratification. The play stages these historical transformations, retelling an episode from a tribal genre during the early history of dynastic states in India, turning the genealogy of the clan into an apparent apology for the court.

Kālidāsa was, in fact, a court poet and *Śakuntalā* a court performance under the empire's royal patronage.[119] By the time the play was performed, the Guptas had completed the conquest of Central and North India—a vast, multilingual area—and had formed the largest Indian empire since the Mauryas. In order to receive brahman legitimation for their power, the Guptas made Sanskrit the language of the court (a conscious archaism, since kings then spoke demotic languages) and Sanskritized popular traditions, making what had been oral textual. It is by virtue of this archaism that colonial philologists could call Chandragupta II's reign the "Golden Age" of Indian civilization, the epithet by which it is still known.

Scholars such as Thapar have identified *Śakuntalā* with the ideology of the brahman-*kṣatriya* alliance during the Gupta dynasty.[120] On even more than a cursory reading, *Śakuntalā*'s plot would appear to confirm this interpretation. The story concerns the relationship of Śakuntalā, who inhabits the edge of royal territory along with brahman ascetics, to the *kṣatriya* king Dusyanta, who resides in the opulent urban court of the Puru dynasty. When he enters the grove on a hunting expedition in the play's first scene and discovers Śakuntalā, they immediately desire each other. With her guardian away from the grove on a pilgrimage, Dusyanta takes his privilege as a *kṣatriya* to wed Śakuntalā in a *gandharva* marriage, which occurs on the basis of mutual desire and needs no social sanction: it is realized simply by the act of sexual intercourse itself. Before he returns from the sacred grove to the court, Dusyanta gives Śakuntalā a royal ring with his name inscribed on it, telling her that he will return to her within a span of days corresponding to the number of letters in his name.

But after Dusyanta leaves, a sage angered by Śakuntalā's failure to wait upon him makes Dusyanta forget her; only the ring can reactivate Dusyanta's memory. Months later, pregnant with Dusyanta's child, Śakuntalā departs for his court, where she is subsequently humiliated by his refusal to believe her story and the discovery that she has lost his ring en route. When her brahman companions abandon her to a life of servility in the court, she is seized by a ray of light and disappears.

The ring, eventually recovered, is brought to Dusyanta, enabling him to overcome his amnesia. Realizing what he has lost, he falls into depression before being summoned to fight demons besieging the god Indra. After he defeats them, Dusyanta is taken to a celestial sacred grove, where he encounters a boy wrestling with a lion cub, whom he recognizes to be his own son borne by Śakuntalā. This boy, Sarvadamana, will grow up to become Bharata, the legendary emperor from whom India (or Bharat) takes its name. Dusyanta is reunited with Śakuntalā, and the family returns to his urban palace, concluding the play.

Though Thapar does not make this point, *Śakuntalā* is, transparently, an allegory of early Indo-European sovereignty's relationship to the earth. Within this allegory, Śakuntalā of course embodies the earth, as both British and German Orientalists immediately discerned. For example, she communicates with animals, trees, and flowers, and is repeatedly described in terms of nature—even as the "rich earth" in which Dusyanta has implanted his "seed" and the "harvest" he owns.[121] And Dusyanta becomes not merely a particular king but the figure of sovereignty as such. Like the hunting expedition that opens the play, Dusyanta's seduction of Śakuntalā thus represents the sovereign taking possession of the earth. Hence, when Dusyanta disavows the *ghandarva* marriage, he effectively turns their sexual intercourse into rape: the play in fact compares the act to theft.[122] The *Mahābhārata* had gone further: there, Dusyanta is not cursed with amnesia but explicitly lies about the marriage. His intercourse with Śakuntalā thus extends the exceptional cruelty of his hunting expedition, in which he massacres animals without number and ravages the forest.[123] In the play as well as in the epic, when Dusyanta disavows his union with Śakuntalā, the implicit relationship of sovereign power to the earth becomes one of pure violence, conquest, and self-aggrandizement. If *Śakuntalā* apologizes for *kṣatriya* power, it does not do so, then, in any simple way.

The identification of Śakuntalā with the earth in both epic and drama occurred during periods when royal territory was expanding, when questions of succession depended in turn on the control of female sexuality, and hence when the ownership of territory was closely bound to the ownership of women's bodies.[124] The marriage of the sovereign to the earth in *Śakuntalā* alludes, therefore, to the links between kingship, ownership, and marriage that shaped the *dharma* texts. No longer a Vedic-era chieftain who redistributes his wealth to the tribe, Kālidāsa's Dusyanta has become instead the classic emperor of a tax-gathering state. South Asian polities of this period had already begun to tax both privately held and state-controlled property and create elaborate revenue, military, and police apparatuses. The Vidusaka (or court jester) alludes to this fact when he reminds a hesitant Dusyanta that an emperor does not need permission to enter the sacred grove but can "just walk in and order them to give up a sixth of their wild rice tax."[125]

To resolve its internal contradictions, the play must reunite sovereign power with the earth in a nonexpropriative form by its conclusion. The sovereign must relate to the earth in terms of protection (a concept the play echoes throughout), not mastery. Hence, from their very first words, the play's brahman characters attempt to place limits on sovereign violence, their sacrifices within the sacred grove dictating the channels in which desire is allowed to flow. Only after Dusyanta submits to their authority in this regard do they bless him with the promise of a son who will become world ruler.[126] When Dusyanta discovers the infant Sarvadamana ("world-tamer") wrestling with a lion cub near the play's end, he instructs him to be gentle "towards all living things."[127] Like the classic *dharma* texts, *Śakuntalā* emphasizes both the intrinsic tension between rulers and priests and their possible unification if the former embrace the *dharma* of nonviolence. The play's close, like its opening, presents the vision of a state founded on precisely the kind of brahman-*kṣatriya* alliance that characterized the Gupta Empire, with a brahman instructing Dusyanta to "Honour the gods in full measure / With holy rites and all due offerings" and Dusyanta pledging that he will "strive" toward such a state.[128]

But though *Śakuntalā* clearly stages the historical emergence of sovereign power, I would argue against any reading that reduces the play to any apology therefor. Such readings understand the work—and ancient literature more broadly—as the expression of philological power alone, when it necessarily expresses much more. In the ancient as in the modern world, unwritten traditions constituted a much greater part of the culture than lettered traditions.[129] Sanskrit literature had little choice but to build on traditions that did not possess philological power; Sanskrit drama was, in particular, a stylization of prior folk performance conventions. When we imagine that such texts are capable of thinking only in line with philological power, we displace onto the text a limit that is in fact our own. To push against this limit, we would need to trace the practices philology has effaced—in other words, to recognize the effects of philological power but not to reduce language, literature, and history to them.

We could note, in this regard, that *Śakuntalā* subtly represents the opposition between lettered and unwritten traditions. The play is not itself confined to Sanskrit but instead multilingual, comprising also various Prakrits (or vernacular languages): the former is spoken by those who exercise sovereign or hieratic power; the latter by those who do not, namely, women, the lower castes, and the jester.[130] Remarkably, the play makes clear that only the latter, those without authority, are to be trusted. Not coincidentally, *Śakuntalā* was performed by people from the lowest ranks of the Gupta Empire's strictly stratified society; like their Roman counterparts, the actresses were, for example, often courtesans. Hence, if unwritten traditions return with a vengeance in *Śakuntalā*, the reason might lie less in authorial intention than in the lost cultures that actually constituted the play. In any case, though, contrary to Thapar's claims, *Śakuntalā* does not mirror brahman-*kṣatriya* discourse; read antiphilologically, it calls this discourse into question.

For example, *Śakuntalā* refers to the brahman hermits who reside in the sacred grove as "withered," the implication being that if the earth depended only on their mantras, sacrifices, and asceticism, it would become barren in their hands.[131] This association is, presumably, one reason the union of Dusyanta and Śakuntalā takes the form of a *ghandarva*, rather than a brahman, marriage. At the same time, though, the *ghandarva* marriage is, as mentioned, practically indistinguishable from rape. In fact, rape—or, more precisely, *rākṣasa*, the violent abduction of a woman—was itself a sanctioned form of *kṣatriya* marriage. Because it was done secretly, in the absence of marriage rites or witnesses, realized only by the act of intercourse itself, a *gandharva* marriage was susceptible to *kṣatriya* duplicity. In all the versions of the Śakuntalā narrative and all similar narratives wherein a *gandharva* marriage occurs, the "fundamental problem" is, as Uma Chakravarti has observed, that "the King can lie."[132] In the *Mahābhārata*, Śakuntalā tells Dusyanta that his lie about their marriage will shatter his head "into a thousand pieces": in ancient Indian literature, this curse was meant to expose lies surrounding rape.[133] In the play, when Dusyanta rejects her, Śakuntalā claims that though sovereign speech is treated as always unimpeachable and the speech of "immodest" women as always unreliable, the reverse is closer to the truth.[134] In short, the play purposefully uses Prakrits to ironize the supposedly originary power of Sanskrit speech, whether in the form of the brahman's Vedic chants or the *kṣatriya's ghandarva* vows, sacrificial or sovereign violence.

Notwithstanding the whole history of Indo-European philology, Sanskrit is, in fact, in no sense originary for Indian, much less Indo-European, civilization. Sanskrit cannot be given priority within either civilizational construct nor can it be made adequate to their origins. The very meaning of the word *Sanskrit* (*saṃskṛta*) is "refined," "perfected," and hence "artificial."[135] Contrary to the false philological premise that Indian vernaculars derive from Sanskrit, the name of the language itself indicates that it did not precede but rather followed the Prakrits (*prakṛta*, "original, natural, normal," from *prakṛti*, "making or placing before or at first, the original or natural form or condition of anything"). As elite speech, Sanskrit was merely the language that was recorded, preserved, and passed down. Anyone who knew Sanskrit would of necessity have also known at least one other language: Sanskrit was never an everyday language and was furthermore not generally spoken by women, children, or members of the lower castes. As a consequence of its speakers' multilingualism, Sanskrit was itself in constant communication with popular traditions.

But Indo-European philologists have tended to describe the origins of Indic civilization in terms of Sanskrit alone. They have reduced a language family, multiple civilizations, and, in principle, history as such to the idiom of power. As a consequence, when they use their own reconstructions of Proto-Indo-European concepts to define what was prior and hence exterior to the West's subsequent historical trajectory, their definitions of the "outside" emerge invariably from within philological power. Take, for example, the twentieth century's most influential Indo-European theorist, Georges Dumézil, who considered the brahman-*kṣatriya* alliance even more fundamental to Indo-European civilization than Thapar subsequently would. Claiming he had returned to "the earliest documents" and studied cognates across languages, Dumézil argued that a bipartite conception of sovereignty comprising the king (*raj* or, in Rome, *rex*) who makes war and the priest (*brahman* or *flamen*) who refuses even to look upon it characterized the originary form of Indo-European political power.[136] To become sovereign, to form a state, the warrior requires a priest who will legitimize the exercise of despotic power, making it appear no longer to encroach on the prerogatives of the deity. The brahman's or *flamen*'s ritual sacrifices make a compact between god and man, implying that the king will protect, rather than violate, the earth. These blood sacrifices also inscribe an ethical code on people's bodies: desire becomes "the property of the sovereign, even though he be the death instinct itself," and people become, in turn, "obedient of their own accord" to a warlord who has gained power over them.[137] Hence, the chief's war-making, originally the tribe's collective practice, is now free to lay the foundations of a transcendent state: the priest helps the warlord escape, we could say, Agamemnon's fate.

If the warrior/priest dichotomy defines the conceptual limit of Indo-European sovereignty, it must also define, if only negatively, what lies outside this limit. Hence, in Dumézil's account, there is a third principle that comes before both warrior and priest. The *gandharva* are bands of centaur-like nomads who represent unrestrained desire (in the mythic literature, they "kidnap," "ravish," and "fertilize" women) and who cannot be assimilated into society, sovereignty, or the state.[138] This Dionysiac principle is, unlike the state, productive: only the *gandharva*, not the priest or the king, can make the earth fertile. According to custom, even after the establishment of states, the *gandharva* would throw all restraint aside one day each year, purify the earth, and make it fruitful: the "miracle" of "restoring fecundity" is "the great feat performed by the men-animals."[139] And indeed, in *Śakuntalā*, Duṣyanta effectively becomes a *gandharva* at the moment of conception. The *gandharva* create because they are excessive; *flamines* and brahmans sacrifice because they are merely "correct": "The Gandharva are so free in their pursuit of sensual pleasure that the summary union of a man and woman is termed 'a Gandharva marriage'"; in contrast, brahmans are "austere" and "passionless," brahman marriages "the most solemn and ritualistic of all."[140]

Dumézil's "trifunctional hypothesis" about Proto-Indo-European society would have ramifications far beyond Indo-European philology, influencing not only Benveniste but also Mircea Eliade, Claude Lévi-Strauss, Marshall Sahlins, and Jean-Pierre Vernant, among many others.[141] It even shapes Gilles Deleuze and Félix Guattari's "Treatise on Nomadology," which begins with Dumézil's bipartite concept of Indo-European sovereignty but focuses on his third principle in order to understand what remains outside. The treatise's first axiom observes that state formation and political thought have immemorially revolved around two essential poles, the mysterious power of the king and the articulable law of the priest.[142] But the axiom's point is to identify that which is "exterior to the State apparatus," namely, the "war machine," whose exteriority they deduce in part from Dumézil's description of the *gandharva*, anciently linked to the warrior castes.[143] "In every respect, the war machine is," Deleuze and Guattari insist, "of another species, another nature, another origin than the State apparatus[,] outside its sovereignty and prior to its law: it comes from elsewhere[,] the pack, an irruption of the ephemeral and the power of metamorphosis."[144] The "Treatise on Nomadology" attempts to extricate the originary creativity of the war machine from its subsequent appropriation by the state and to let this creativity drive cultural production—or, in other words, to "place thought in an immediate relation with the outside," to "make thought a war machine."[145]

Like their valorization of the nomad, Deleuze and Guattari's dependence on Dumézil reflects their endeavor to imagine the desire that precedes the origins of civilization. Yet Dumézil's reconstruction of this desire ends up only imprisoning the "Treatise on Nomadology" within the history of philology. Deleuze and Guattari's mistake is to assume that comparative philology can reveal what precedes sovereign power, as if what has been recorded and transmitted were not always already contaminated by such power. *Śakuntalā* suggests, in diametric opposition, that the figure of the *gandharva* is merely the rhetorical disguise of sovereign violence. The effort to oppose the whole history of European sovereignty by reference to a prehistory reconstructed by European philology itself is, we should note, the strategy of Hindu nationalism as well, precisely the strategy I have targeted throughout this book.

Śakuntalā suggests a different strategy. Precisely where European intellectuals imagined an originary consciousness, *Śakuntalā* also alludes to the form of life that came before this origin. In other words, even as the play's sacred groves appear to be the privileged site of the *dharma* and nonviolence, the play insinuates that the very creation and preservation of these sacred groves presupposes the eradication of those who had previously inhabited the forests. It registers the fact that sacred groves were both the site and the product of the very sacrifices that dispossessed forest-dwellers when it refers to the "smoke" of the "Sacred Fire" that "dim[s] the soft sheen of tender leafbuds."[146] Even more to the point, Dusyanta defends Śakuntalā's sacred grove from the attack of Rākṣasas at the end of act 2 and Piśācas at the end of act 3.[147] Both these mythic demons have been traced to ancient *adivasi* tribes; the former were known in the myths for disrupting the fire ceremony. And the *āśrama* in which Śakuntalā and Dusyanta rediscover each other is located within the realm of the Kimpuruṣa, one of the *adivasi* tribes conquered in the *Mahābhārata*.[148] Hence, when the play reunites the sovereign and the earth at its conclusion, its image of the earth, embodied by the sacred groves and Śakuntalā, both effaces and contains the trace of the *adivasi*s. Perhaps on its deepest level, the sovereign forgetting of the earth thematizes this effacement—for if the code of nonviolence properly belongs to anyone, it is neither sovereigns nor priests but rather only those who preceded and/or opposed the destruction of the forests.

They would have had to refrain from the prototypically human endeavor to master and remake nature. They would have refused, in other words, to prioritize the growth of human life over the protection of life per se and, in this way, resisted Indo-European expansion in particular and environmental destruction in general. Of course, those who preceded or truly opposed civilization would have also, by definition, left few artifacts, textual or otherwise: take, for example, the *śramaṇa*s, who did not write, or the forest-dwellers on whom the *śramaṇa*s patterned their lives. In other words, their perspectives are not commensurable with those of any textual culture; the form of life antithetical to the destruction of the forests could not, by definition, be recorded and consequently exists outside textuality, history, or any origin we could ever know. When *Śakuntalā* names the Rākṣasas, Piśācas, and Kimpuruṣa, it bears, accordingly, only the *trace* of languages that preceded Indo-European expansion. It alludes to another form of life but makes no claim to represent it. *Śakuntalā* here dramatizes the relationship between the philological origin (in this case, the Vedic ritual of fire sacrifice) and the alternative practice (in this case, the forest-dweller's relationship to the earth) rendered unintelligible by this "origin." The play thus arrives at an absolutely crucial aporia—the theoretical impossibility of comprehending a truly ecological or nonviolent consciousness—that has too often been overlooked, not just by Indo-European philologists of the nineteenth and twentieth centuries but also by the global discourse around environmentalism and indigeneity still today.

In India as in the West, environmentalists have projected onto the "aborigine" or "indigene" values that articulate their own intellectual positions instead.[149] They have argued, for example, that *adivasi*s intrinsically possess ecological wisdom, egalitarian societies, and economic practices based on "reciprocity and subsistence" rather than "competition and accumulation." But when environmentally minded scholars—or, for that matter, heterodox historians such as Thapar—invoke a binary opposition between Indo-European civilization on one hand and the *adivasi* (from Sanskrit: *ādi* "earliest" + *vāsi* "inhabitant") on the other, they risk turning the latter into a reified origin as well. The very concept of indigeneity inscribes a claim, of course, about the earth's "original" identity. Hence, in the words of the *adivasi* Narmada activist Khajan: "God made the earth and the forest; then He made us, adivasis, to live upon the earth[.] We are born of the earth[.] We live in the forest and we keep it alive. Governments and politicians

come and go but we have never changed; we have been here from the beginning."[150] The primordial claims made on behalf of the *adivasi*—a term that
is itself a late colonial invention—possess, naturally, little historical validity.
Ancient *adivasi* tribes themselves conquered and expropriated others' territory and have been intimately intertwined with the Hindu communities that
surrounded them for millennia. These days, the Hindutva movement increasingly assimilates *adivasi*s in order to appropriate their claim to indigeneity
and justify violence against supposed "foreigners" such as India's Muslims.

My point is not to deny the history of the violence to which *adivasi*s have
been and continue to be subjected but rather to emphasize that such general
categories can neither name nor comprehend forms of life exterior or antithetical to this history. We cannot allow such categories to become, in other
words, placeholders for the different relationship to the earth and territorial
expansion that has opposed and consequently been targeted by such violence.
Nor can we can use them to identify the form of life marginalized by the
production of Sanskrit texts such as *Śakuntalā* or *Manu*. However seductive
they may be, historical stereotypes such as the *adivasi* only foreclose the difficult, indeed necessarily endless, effort to imagine a consciousness antithetical
to territorial conquest.

To imagine such a consciousness now, we would have no choice but to
retrace, stage by stage, our own philological formation. Take, for example,
sacred groves, which not only survive in India today but are still believed by
anthropologists and historians to be the sites of a prehistoric, nonviolent, and
ecologically sensitive form of life; the common practice within them is to
prohibit the removal of plants, the hunting of wild animals, the pasturing of
domestic animals, the construction of homes, the felling of trees, and so on.[151]
The anthropological study of sacred groves, which has been gaining speed
over the past few decades, is motivated by the urgent need to devise forms of
forest conservation that, unlike the Indian state's large-scale programs, will
actually work. Yet even the earliest sacred groves—coeval with Vedas circa the
middle of the second millennium B.C.—were the products of shifting culti-
vation. They already attest, in other words, to the time of civilization, when
settlers had begun to burn forests, destroy their fragile ecologies, and replace
them with agrarian economies; the original sacred groves probably had more
in common with the sacred enclosures at the boundaries of the ancient Greek

polis than they did with the forest-dweller's world. Between the sacred grove and a truly ecological sensibility, there lies, therefore, a long history of territorial conquest—and the textual tradition that accompanied it.

It was only at a relatively late phase in this history that Sanskrit literary culture began to identify the sacred with anthropomorphic deities.[152] When it built these deities the elaborate shrines their worship demanded, it circumscribed the sanctity of the forest within the sacred grove's temple. Temple-building required the forest's resources and hence the destruction of the surrounding environment. But even before the development of a mature literary tradition, when the expansion of Vedic civilization first began to destroy the forests, Sanskritization deified the general forces—above all fire (Agni)—on which deforestation depended. Before this, the object of worship appears to have been, as in early Greek and Roman religion, aniconic: for example, crude stones, termite mounds, or shrines with the simplest imaginable structure, often housing a vacant cult spot. Only if we were able to work our way back from these historical phases—and many more particular ones—could we return to the consciousness of those who perhaps revered not abstractions but rather specific trees, groves, rivers, and mountain peaks and who protected the forests from all human appropriation except what was necessary for bare survival. Such a consciousness is the implied origin and essence of all the *dharma* texts and *Śakuntalā*, the ideal of nineteenth-century Indo-European philology, the template for the modern environmental movement, and the source of the fetish-character that attaches to indigeneity still today. Yet this consciousness cannot be comprehended by any historical figure or account we could conceive. It is, rather, a set of practices too tenuous to survive the coming of philological power, something to which we as a consequence lack even indirect access, something that would bring our own form of life to crisis.

We philologists thus fruitlessly seek a form of life that was destroyed by the immemorial profession of philology itself, a profession always complicit with conquest and colonization. Until we acknowledge this legacy, we will not be able to imagine a fundamentally different relationship to linguistic and literary authority—or to sovereign violence. There is no way for us to arrive at discursive practices exterior to this history of violence without, in other words, first making the historical consequences of our own craft visible across the longest timespan possible. This is the work that the archaeology offered in this chapter and the previous two have attempted, however modestly, to begin, the aporia they have attempted to acknowledge and confront. Without such work, the ideals of the new philology (nonviolence, indigeneity, originarity), so deeply embedded in our own scholarly desires, will remain nothing more than another sovereign ideology.

Conclusion

The discovery of Proto-Indo-European both abolished and fulfilled the search for the divine tongue that preceded the Tower of Babel's destruction. But the asterisk before every Indo-European root or stem marks the fact that the more than five-thousand-year-old language to which these asterisks refer is not historically attested but instead reconstructed: our earliest written record of an Indo-European language, Hittite, comes only from the fourteenth century B.C.[153] The absence of any textual evidence for Proto-Indo-European suggests, in fact, that its speakers did not even know how to write.

The problem with the speculative reconstruction of Proto-Indo-European is obviously not the premise that prehistoric languages metamorphosed into multiple other languages over time. The mistake is, rather, the belief that a single (historically unattested) parent language could be *the* historical origin of every language subsequently grouped into its "family." The prehistoric "parent" language is, by definition, a back formation philologists have reconstructed from later writing. It is, in other words, a reflection less of prehistoric language use than of the tacit philological principle that one can use texts to reconstruct immeasurably older nontextual languages and from such reconstructions draw conclusions about the conceptual origins and development of the supposedly continuous "civilizations" they produced. The construction of language families emphasizes what is common to the languages that constitute a "family" or the various dialects and vernaculars that constitute a "language." In the process, it marginalizes the explanatory value of what is peculiar to a language and, a fortiori, to a dialect. In other words, it discounts the historical importance of local relationships, for example, the influence of *adivasi* or Dravidian languages on Indo-European languages. The genealogies of language we have inherited from the new philology militate against an understanding of languages not as the pure descendants of prior languages but rather as the self-divided products of linguistic and philological conflicts.

Similarly, the premise that a philologically reconstructed prehistory can explain, in effect, everything that follows it—or serve as the starting point for a
total knowledge of human development—overlooks the formative influence
of all those lives that existed outside the written record. Philologists have
built elaborate theories about prehistoric society, per Doniger, on a "flimsy
Indo-European linguistic scaffolding."[154]

The new philology focused on the meaning of "the text" and its supposedly
originary place within cultures, histories, and civilizations. Hence, even philologists with the extraordinary erudition of Patrick Olivelle and Alf Hiltebeitel
insist, respectively, that *Manu* and the *Mahābhārata* need to be treated as discrete, coherent texts.[155] But as *Manu* as well as *Śakuntalā* illustrates, every
language and literary tradition contains within itself countless strata in the
historical conflict between different philological formations and, ultimately,
between those who possess philological power and those who do not. If we accept the philological principle that we can use texts to draw conclusions about
the conceptual origins and development of traditions and even civilizations,
we reduce the history of language and culture to nothing more than a series of
philological constructs. We program ourselves to treat writing as adequate to
language and culture per se. But we inherit the written records on which we
base our reconstructions from past forms of philological power, whose overarching effect, if not intent, was to efface the linguistic (and hence political)
agency of others. The philological reconstruction of language's origins reduces
history to writing, willfully forgetting that what is written reflects not society
in general but rather the interests first of those who wrote and subsequently
of those who controlled writing's dissemination. The philological revolution
in this way only reinforced the erasures of every philological formation that
preceded it. Needless to say, the principles of the new philology pervade the
various forms of historical reconstruction we call the humanities today. If we
do not want to become one more link in the endless chain of philological
power, the politically urgent question becomes less the meaning of the text
than the discursive practices it has absented. Behind every supposedly originary language lies the irrecoverable, but nonetheless historically fundamental,
languages of those whom philology can neither name nor comprehend.

CONCLUSION

Genealogies of Emergency

1. The Colonial Matrix of Emergency

During the 1960s and 1970s, Marxist scholars developed theories of imperialism intended to explain the new planetary dispensation, in which European colonies had largely vanished but imperial relationships had nonetheless managed to survive.[1] These theories responded to the global division of labor between developed and underdeveloped countries by emphasizing either the operation of monopoly capital seeking markets and raw materials in the Third World (e.g., Paul Baran and Paul Sweezy, Tom Kemp, and Harry Magdoff) or, alternatively, the world-systems dependency of peripheral on metropolitan economies (e.g., Andre Gunder Frank and Samir Amin).[2] But the almost universal ascendancy of so-called flexible production and international finance capital over the last four decades appears to have made all such theories of imperialism obsolete.

In a recent study, Partha Chatterjee has argued that, in this postcolonial world, the essence of imperialism reveals itself to be neither territorial conquest nor uneven development but instead the power to decide which states have the right to be sovereign and which states must forfeit this right. "The imperial prerogative [lies]," according to Chatterjee's reformulation of Carl Schmitt's famous dictum, "in the claim to declare the colonial exception."[3] This definition, Chatterjee has claimed, "covers most examples of imperial power in the world" since the late eighteenth century.[4] Just as imperialism before decolonization did not always depend on the annexation of foreign territory, the international prohibition of such annexation has not ended imperialism, which we still see today in various forms: the external supervision of national constitutions, as in Iraq or Afghanistan; foreign interventions to fix deviations from international norms in regard to social indicators, economic measures, and, above all, human rights; the imposition of austerity policies, first in Africa and Latin America, more recently in the European peripheries; and, finally, the frequent "flashes of national emergency" visible around the world.[5] Chatterjee's definition of imperialism as the power to declare the exception emerges from a new imperial order in which the United States' and Europe's "real economic capabilities" are in decline but their military and diplomatic ambitions are not.[6]

Chatterjee is not the first political theorist to describe imperialism in terms of exception. Discussing Africa, Achille Mbembe has observed that from the very beginning of colonialism there, European states gave their merchant companies the power to create a "régime d'exception": sovereign rights belonged to the corporation alone; natives possessed none.[7] Never conceived as mature "subject[s] of law," consigned instead "to a minority without foreseeable end," they were believed to be bereft of the power to constitute a body politic by themselves.[8] The point of colonial law was consequently not to place limits on sovereign power but on the contrary to "bring [the colonized] to heel" in order to "extract" from their bodies the "maximum possible use."[9] For Mbembe, the postcolonial state's problem is, in part, that it "inherited this regime of [unconditional] impunity."[10]

I invoke Chatterjee's and Mbembe's arguments not to reduce empire to emergency but rather to think about one precise sense in which we still live in a fundamentally imperial world. In fact, if we accept their arguments, we would have to conclude that, with the proliferation of emergency decrees around the globe, imperial relationships became, paradoxically, even more pervasive after decolonization than they had been before. From this perspective, understanding emergency would be a precondition of opposing imperialism now.

The arguments of these political theorists are borne out by the work of legal historians. In the colonies, in contrast to the metropole, emergency was not external to the rule of law. As both Nasser Hussain and Bhavani Raman have demonstrated in regard to British India, emergency measures were in fact woven into the very "fabric of statutory law": from the late eighteenth century forward, "the rule of law and emergency, norm and exception, the standard and that which contravenes it, [were] powerfully and intimately connected."[11] Due to the perpetual prospect of insurrections, insurgencies, and border conflicts, extraordinary laws deriving from wartime conditions often replaced civil law even during times of peace. Considering how immediately and how frequently colonial law devolved into martial law, one might infer that colonial governments created constitutions only so they would have the power to suspend them afterwards. In any case, though, the institution of an almost continuous state of emergency enabled the colonial state, Raman has argued, to turn its sovereignty over territory into a "sovereignty over life" as such.[12] Giorgio Agamben has argued that European states treated World War I "as a laboratory for testing and honing [the] state of exception as a paradigm of government," but Hussain's and Raman's work suggests that colonial rule has precedence by more than a century in this regard.[13]

There is another, perhaps obvious, aspect of emergency that has been, I believe, deemphasized in the many discussions of it published in recent years. Modern states of emergency follow close on the heels of modern revolutions. They are, per Agamben, "a creation," ironically, "of the democratic-revolutionary tradition and not the absolutist one."[14] Though he does not himself make this point explicitly, we could consider emergency an instrument that emerges from within the revolution to turn its most radical tendencies back. When a revolutionary government suspends its own constitution, it undermines the constituent politics—that is, the popular power to form a truly egalitarian body politic—that originally precipitated the revolution and which the constitution is supposed to enshrine. Emergency decrees are, in this regard, the counterinsurgent practice par excellence. They circumscribe constituent power within the sovereign's voice, which arrogates to itself the right to suspend the normal functioning of the law and to declare univocally the extraordinary laws that will govern the polity in its place. In the state of emergency, the sovereign's decree ("decision" or "command") possesses the singular power, in fact, to define empirical reality: "sovereign is the one who decides on the exception"; only the sovereign can determine the state's very existence to be in danger.[15]

The antitheses of emergency must therefore be discursive practices that do not alienate but on the contrary reinforce people's constituent power. Protests against emergency power tend now to take place in the name of the law, whether civil rights, constitutional restraints, or international norms. But the practice for which we must search cannot lie in the rule of law. As colonial history demonstrates, modern law only leads back, inexorably, to emergency; they compose a single trajectory. Modern law is one face of the very juridical order that makes emergency possible. To resist emergency powers, we would need not to invoke legal norms but instead to retrace the history that produced both exception *and* norm. The antithesis of emergency must lie outside this history.

2. Philology—Colonial Law—Emergency

At the origin of colonial law, we will find an approach to language and texts that lies, curiously, at the origins of the modern humanities as well. The creation of Islamic and Hindu law in late eighteenth-century colonial India presupposed the principles of the new philology: all truth is historical; historical knowledge is derived from textual study; such study requires a historically specific understanding of the language being studied. These principles gave the East India Company's philologically trained scholars authority over native traditions: only their methods, not native customs, could grasp the truth of tradition. These scholars learned Persian, Arabic, and Sanskrit; recovered and reconstructed the Islamic and brahmanic legal manuscripts they claimed were authoritative; edited, translated, and published these manuscripts; and thus suddenly made textual authority the foundation of native law. The explicit intention behind the philological approach to native traditions was to undermine the discursive practices that had previously constituted those traditions, which had been centered not on sovereign texts but rather on socially dispersed clerics. Colonial philology's intention was, in other words, to incorporate the law into the state—or, we could say, to make the declaration and the suspension of law a sovereign prerogative. In the colonies, philology was, in other words, a precondition of emergency. Colonial history reveals, more broadly, that the philological principles on which the humanities are still founded were partly designed to appropriate the constituent power of precolonial practices. Colonial law merely took philology to its logical conclusion:

it marginalized the social authority of *all* precolonial discursive practices. It realized philology's capacity to continue war by other means. From this perspective, the "return to philology" for which postcolonial scholars, beginning with Edward Said, have repeatedly called in recent years would serve less to expose the culture of imperialism than unwittingly to extend it.

Our problem is precisely that we end up returning to philology even when we make every effort not to. The principle of Schmitt's philology—that is, only the conqueror's laws and traditions are legitimate—might appear to reflect his fascist predispositions alone.[16] But this principle tends to insinuate itself into the work of even the most subtle scholars, regardless of their political position. Bernard Cohn, Walter Mignolo, Talal Asad, Michel de Certeau, and Dipesh Chakrabarty have each explicitly retraced the history of colonial law or philology in order to recover the discursive practices that came before. In every case, though, the practices they have recovered are themselves moments in the genealogy of philological power. They have, in other words, each ended up following the new philology's blueprint, taking an earlier form of philological power as the way out of the political and philological impasse of the present. They dissociate discourses and texts from the specific philological formations that produced them and treat them instead as the direct reflection of a people or a period. As a consequence, though their work intends to make visible the contemporary limits of the humanities, it ultimately obscures the extent to which the proposed alternatives were themselves hegemonic forms. In other words, the discursive practices that supposedly came before European law and philology—those that would define precolonial constituent power—fall in every case squarely within the traditions of the victors

Cohn's *Colonialism and Its Forms of Knowledge* and Mignolo's *The Darker Side of the Renaissance* both argue that precolonial language was not abstracted from the material world but an intrinsic part of physical acts. Cohn drew his evidence from claims made for the documents (*farman*s and *paravana*s) issued by Mughal sovereigns, namely, that they transmitted the sovereign's very "authority" and even "substance" to the person who received the documents. He treated these claims not as what they were, the ideology of Mughal sovereign and textual power, but rather as an "Indian" theory of substantive meaning, in contradistinction to the European theory of denotative meaning.[17] He likewise considered the aura that attached to brahman chanting, its supposed power to transform the "substance" of whoever hears it, not as the ideology of brahmanic linguistic authority but again as a universal Indian view.[18]

Mignolo has understood the conflict between colonial philology and Amerindian discursive practices in terms of the same binary opposition. He has claimed that whereas alphabetic writing is disembodied, precolonial forms of representation and recording such as the Mesoamerican *amoxtli* (a "book" comprising pictographic signs) and the Peruvian *quipu* (a historical record made from knotted strings) require physical labor and are tactile experiences.[19] But the precolonial practices to which he refers belong to the court elites of the Aztec and Incan empires, not Amerindians in general. Cohn and Mignolo were of course correct to argue that colonial philology actively targeted and ultimately marginalized such elite practices. But their own seminal work is itself, ironically, trapped within the philological mindset: it treats discursive practices as expressions of collective histories, not particular forms of philological power.

The binary opposition between precolonial embodiment and postcolonial abstraction recurs in Asad's *Formations of the Secular* and de Certeau's *The Writing of History*. Asad has argued that precolonial *shari'a* was learned by means of physical training or what he has called, after Marcel Mauss, "techniques of the body."[20] According to Asad, only after the advent of colonial rule, "when the *shari'a* fails to be *embodied* in the judge," does it comprise "impersonal," "transcendent," and "sacred" rules.[21] De Certeau extended this opposition to tradition as such, arguing that, in contrast to tradition, philology from the Renaissance forward has occurred at a distance from the social body, in enclosed spaces created and protected by sovereign power.[22] Both have emphasized that tradition cannot be analyzed philologically because it existed only in the form of "embodied aptitudes" and consequently encompassed a whole way of life.[23] Yet *every* form of knowledge—modern as well as premodern, literate as well as oral—presupposes a physical infrastructure and hence embodiment of one kind or another.

Asad and de Certeau have not only reiterated this stereotype about tradition but have also both added another: tradition does not conceive past and present on a linear continuum but imagines them instead to be simultaneous and mutually constitutive. Asad has claimed: "In tradition the 'present' is always at the center[,] separated from but also included within events and epochs[;] time past authoritatively constitutes present practices."[24] Relying on Louis Dumont's anthropological research, de Certeau has claimed that historicism is "a uniquely Western trait."[25] Outside the West, "far from being an 'ob-ject' thrown behind so that an autonomous present will be possible, the past is a treasure placed in the midst of society that is its memorial, a food intended to be chewed and memorized."[26] In Indian traditions, "new forms never drive the older ones away"; in African societies, tradition is understood as a "speech" that is continuous with the present.[27] Asad and de Certeau here invoke tradition's "internal temporal structure," like its embodiment, to distinguish what precedes and therefore resists colonial reason.[28] But even if such stereotypes were historically valid and extended, furthermore, to tradition as such rather than just its clerical practices (Asad refers only to jurists, de Certeau to no one in particular), the capacity to recognize the past's continuing relevance to the present would not in any way distinguish a truly pre- or anticolonial mindset. Neither does the premise that pasts become obsolete belong only to colonial reason, as my discussions of both *shari'a* and the Dharmaśāstra before colonial rule implicitly demonstrate.

Like Asad's and de Certeau's studies, Chakrabarty's *Provincializing Europe* targets the epistemic rupture between "secular" and "religious" consciousness. But it understands this rupture in terms of a different binary opposition: precolonial languages do not rely on universal categories when they translate cultural difference but instead use "very local, particular, one-for-one exchanges."[29] Focusing on eighteenth-century Muslim proselytic texts, Chakrabarty has claimed that this "nonmodern mode of translation" takes "barter," rather than commodity exchange, as its "model."[30] Though confessing his inability to decipher the rules of this translation process, he nonetheless has chosen to privilege it, claiming it preserves "singular" experiences and thus "incorporates" what would otherwise be "untranslatable" (it is therefore closer, he claims, to "magic-realist" fiction than to social scientific prose).[31] But, in order to do so, he must overlook the fact that *every* use of language, precolonial or post-, religious or secular, necessarily depends on abstraction and, furthermore, that its abstractions will, at the same time, be irreducibly local and particular. More to the point of my argument, when

Chakrabarty privileges these precolonial texts, the philological formations that produced them fade from view. As I have suggested throughout this study, performative languages constitute their own forms of philological power no less capably than constative ones do.

Whenever, like each of these scholars, we create dichotomies between precolonial or premodern languages and our own, thus overlooking the former's constitutive exclusions, we unwittingly import these exclusions into our own perspectives. Such subconscious continuities blind us to and thus keep us imprisoned within philology's intrinsically elitist outlook—hence the almost universal, but nonetheless perverse, demand we return to philology. See, in this regard, Mignolo's claim that "a 'new philology' is of the essence to contextualize cultural objects and power relations alien to the everyday life of the scholar" and hence the "necessary approach to understanding colonial semiosis."[32] The categories scholars have employed to distinguish counter-hegemonic discursive practices—for example, embodiment, not abstraction; simultaneity, not historicism; singularity, not universalism; performativity, not denotation; and so on—are firmly rooted in the history of academic knowledge and, by extension, of philological power. They cannot be used to describe the antithesis of such power. The privilege even leftist scholars grant such categories only reflects how deeply implicated our work remains in the reproduction of this power. Needless to say, no scholar can escape such complicity, but we could at least acknowledge that our authority depends on its immemorial history.

To "decolonize" critical method, we would need to think beyond the limits of not just colonial philology but philological power as such. We would need, for example, to understand our work less as recovering supposedly lost concepts of language and literature (which always return us only to earlier forms of philological power) than as the much more demanding effort to discern what has been constitutively excluded by philology and literature throughout their histories. In any case, though, even if the theories adduced above were somehow adequate to the texts on which these scholars base their claims, these texts cannot be identified with precolonial language per se. In each case, they derive, more narrowly, from the clerical transmission of tradition, which, though it precedes colonial philology, is no less a philological formation.

In fact, V. N. Volosinov located philology's origins in the ancient priests who "decipher[ed] the mystery of the sacred words," always, as mentioned, "to some degree in a language foreign and incomprehensible to the profane."[33] These sacred, usually dead tongues circumscribed language's constituent power within a form the priest-philologists could control. According to Volosinov, the new philology still serves this ancient function. In contrast to him, we humanists today too often fail to make philological authority itself the object of critical suspicion. Philology's different phases—aligned with sovereign power's various forms—are analogous to the successive cycles of capital accumulation Giovanni Arrighi delineated in *The Long Twentieth Century*.[34] Together they constitute the *long* imperial era, literally as old as civilization itself. To oppose the global state of emergency in which we now live fundamentally, we would need a critical method designed to liberate us from this immemorial history.

3. The Real State of Emergency, the Tradition of the Oppressed, the Nameless

Jacques Rancière has retraced the concepts of politics and emergency in order to recover the practices they now obscure. According to Rancière's genealogy, politics must be understood, contra Schmitt, as a discursive practice diametrically opposed to emergency: it is the democratic demand for representation by those who now play no part in rule but who have an acknowledged right to partake in rule.[35] We should note, though, that Rancière's influential definition of politics as "the part of those who have no part," from which Slavoj Žižek draws his own, is a philological reconstruction based on an ancient Greek root word, *politēs* (citizen).[36] Rancière has inferred that "politics," strictly speaking, is the rule of the citizen. He has argued that we lose touch with the original meaning of politics whenever we identify it with either the practical exercise of power or the theoretical inquiry into the grounds of legitimate power, rather than with the paradoxical condition of being ruled but also having the right to rule.[37] Rancière has insisted therefore that democracy constituted the original "state of exception."[38] This claim both accepts Schmitt's identification of the political domain with the suspension of all laws and turns Schmitt's terms upside down. For Rancière, politics begins not with conquest but with democratic resistance; the law it suspends is the sovereign's exclusive right to rule. Politics is a praxis without law—or, in other words, "an-archy": the delegitimation of every *archē* in the sense both of the ruler and of any transcendent principle of rule.[39]

Yet in Rancière's and Žižek's scheme, political action depends, by definition, on the demand to partake in rule. It cannot accommodate the attempt, for example, to disentangle one's language, traditions, and way of life from rule, force, and the state altogether. The limitation of Rancière's and Žižek's concept of politics is predetermined by its origins, which they both have located strictly in ancient Athens, in the praxis of the elite, not to say slave-owners. In this state society, the traditions that preceded the state had lost the authority to organize life. As Jean-Pierre Vernant explained, "with the advent of [the Athenian city-state] there developed a whole system of *strictly* political institutions, modes of behavior, and thought. [There] is a striking contrast with the old mystical forms of power and social action that, together with the practices and mentality that went with them, are now replaced by the regime of the polis."[40] Political praxis—even in Rancière's fundamentally oppositional sense—was founded on this erasure. Indeed, the "old" forms of "power" and "action" are precisely what the category of politics originally effaced and still now obscures. The very term "politics"—which pertains to the state and valorizes rule—thus produces a theoretical impasse. Not surprisingly, even philosophers such as Rancière, Žižek, and Alain Badiou, who advocate the apparently most radical forms of political praxis, show little, if any, interest in the traditions that characterize nonstate societies. But to move beyond the impasse of politics today, we would need to study the practices our political institutions excluded at their very origins. Like Schmitt's thought, Rancière's disagreement with him takes place within the fold of philology. Though diametrically opposed, the positions they occupy are ringed around by the state. This criticism is no less true even for Gilles Deleuze's implicit arguments with Schmitt in both *Difference and Repetition* and *A Thousand Plateaus*, which also unfold on the terrain of—and take for granted—classical and Indo-European philology.[41]

Long before Deleuze and Rancière, Walter Benjamin's early published writings, which I have discussed in the first and second chapters of this book, also attempted to retrace the history of law and politics in order to locate a prior tradition. His final essay, "On the Concept of History," returns to this tradition and aligns it with what he referred to, strangely, as the "real state of emergency": "The tradition of the oppressed teaches us that the 'state of emergency' in which we live is not the exception but the rule. We must attain to a conception of history that accords with this insight. Then we will clearly see that it is our task to bring about a real state of emergency."[42] Benjamin's "real state of emergency" plays, I think, on the French term *état de siège fictif*, a fictitious (or political, not military) state of emergency. Napoleon created this concept with his decree that the emperor would henceforward have the right to seize emergency powers even when the state was not actually under threat.[43] Against this category of false emergencies, which would gradually subsume most emergency decrees, Benjamin insisted that we inhabit a real state of emergency at all times. But in his concept of emergency, the political order is not in danger but itself the source of danger: it threatens to extinguish "the traditions of the oppressed." Always under attack, these traditions exist in an undeclared but eternal state of emergency. If in "political" states of emergency, the sovereign attempts to suspend people's constituent power, thus turning them into the oppressed, in the real state of emergency, people must attempt, dialectically, to suspend the sovereign's expropriation of their power. They must aspire, in this way, to accord everyone constituent power again.

In other words, if the danger that produces an emergency comes not from outside the polity but from the polity itself, then the point of emergency must be not to preserve but, on the contrary, to destroy the polity, in order to defend the forms of life it endangers. Like Rancière after him, Benjamin thus both accepted Schmitt's principle that politics properly understood is not the rule of law but its suspension and turned this principle inside out.[44] In a revolutionary state of emergency, it is not the sovereign but on the contrary those opposed to sovereign power who suspend the law (and, in fact, juridical authority in general). Benjamin's real state of emergency would thus, finally, create the "anomic space for human action"—a polis paradoxically subordinate to no power, where life need not obey any law—from which both "the ancients and the moderns retreated in fright."[45] Hence, the distinguishing feature of revolutionary action here, as in Benjamin's much earlier "Critique of Violence," is not just the destruction of the existing law but the refusal to create a new one—the deposition not of a particular legal system but of the law as such.[46] An action can be considered revolutionary within Benjamin's terms only if it never aspires to become sovereign itself.

Only in this way could states of emergency be declared in the name of—and keep faith with—the oppressed. Yet in his notes toward "On the Concept of History," Benjamin referred to the "oppressed" as the "anonymous" instead: it is to their "memory" that "the historical construction is dedicated."[47] His famous thesis on the barbarism of culture ("There is no document of culture that is not at the same time a document of barbarism") repeats this substitution, linking the "spoils" of the "conquerors" to a philological artifact (*ein Dokument der Kultur*) designed to conceal "the anonymous [*namenlosen*] toil of others."[48] Revolution is thus the appropriation of emergency powers on behalf, dialectically, of those whom political states of emergency, "historicism," and culture all render anonymous. We could note here that Nietzsche's own essay-length critique of philology, "The Uses and Disadvantages of History for Life," likewise identifies "historicism" as Europe's sovereign discourse and focuses on what Nietzsche also calls the "anonymous"—or "unhistorical" forms of life—as historicism's antithesis.[49] In diametric opposition to philology, Nietzsche's archaeological method, like Benjamin's "historical materialism," is interested in the historical record not in itself but only for its exclusions. We will therefore not understand what is most radical in either of these counterhistorical methods if we reduce them to, respectively, the excavation of epistemic ruptures and messianic Marxism. Taken to their logical conclusion, they venture the impossible: to escape the prison of philology by locating those who were linguistically disfranchised in any given text. In his notes, Benjamin explained that his "method," historical materialism, "has as its foundation the book of life" and as its goal to "read what was never written."[50]

For Nietzsche, "life" itself—as opposed to the "power of history" represented by the state, science, and social engineering—flourishes only when it welcomes its "unhistorical" essence, that is, when, ignoring historical knowledge and "success," it inhabits its own ephemeral singularity instead: "A historical phenomenon, known clearly and completely and resolved into a phenomenon of knowledge, is, for him who has perceived it, dead[.] The study of history is something salutary and fruitful for the future only as the attendant of a mighty new current of life[.] Insofar as it stands in the service of life, history stands in the service of an unhistorical power."[51] Perhaps every literary text contains the trace of life in this sense, which not only exists in a perpetual state of emergency, always confronting the prospect of its own disappearance, but also contemplates this fate without blinking. In Benjamin's view, we will discern such traces only if we first recognize the essence of our own life to exist in precisely the same precarious state and to possess a similarly profound equanimity: "The true image of the past flits by[,] an irretrievable image of the past which threatens to disappear in any present that does not recognize itself as intended in that image."[52] This recognition will elude us, conversely, to the precise extent we identify with philological power rather than what it has suppressed. More broadly, every effort to understand the history of the present will need to be conscious of the fact—as Nietzsche, Benjamin, and Agamben all are—that what comes before or remains uncontaminated by this history cannot, by definition, be historically attested.[53]

In Benjamin's essay, "a conception of history that accords with this insight"—namely, that those who truly oppose the hegemonic tradition survive not in "history" conventionally defined but rather only in a perpetual state of emergency—is the precondition of revolutionary action. In this conception, history ceases to be a possible object of scholarly knowledge and becomes instead precisely that state of emergency, the ceaseless conflict of incommensurable discourses: on one side, sovereign speech; on the other, its repudiation. This conception of history is revolutionary because it shatters the aura that surrounds sovereign speech, in order to recognize a much deeper power within the traditions of the oppressed. In other words, it is aligned with the political praxis of those who suspend the law not to exercise their right to rule (as in Rancière's recuperation of "politics") but, on the contrary, to renounce the historical legacy of rule altogether. If the oppressed are, for Benjamin, those whom the historical record does not name, both their impotence and their power must lie precisely in this omission. Only those discursive practices that refuse to leave a mark on the historical record resist every form of philological co-optation. Only these practices keep faith with language's constituent power, because they have no desire to appropriate it to themselves alone. It is these unhistorical languages—these languages that, in other words, embrace unhistorical life—that reappear, in Benjamin's final essay, as emergency's antithesis. The discursive practice at stake here is—far from any literary or philological fetish—what the written tradition does not and in fact cannot attest.

☞

The imperial ideology of late eighteenth-century British India lay in the rule of law rather than the rule of men. This was the first empire that attempted to govern colonized populations according to their own law, and it produced the first legal codes anywhere in the modern world. But its rule of law merely cleared the way for the political paradigm of emergency. The legacy of this liberalism weighs on the living now more than ever. Perhaps it will become even more oppressive, as Chatterjee has suggested, in our immediate future. The argument here has been that philological approaches to languages, literatures, and religious traditions helped foster this history. To retreat from the historical trajectory of philology–colonial law–emergency, we would need to read texts differently. Whenever we see them in terms of privileged linguistic forms—as de Certeau, Cohn, Mignolo, and so many literary scholars inevitably do—we play into the hands of philology. We could attempt instead to read antiphilologically: to discern behind every type of textual authority the uncompromisingly unhistorical and therefore nameless power it needed to appropriate.

NOTES

Prologue

1. Jones, *Letters*, 2:721 (to C. W. Boughton Rouse, 24 October 1786).

2. Foucault, *Aesthetics*, 416.

3. Jones, *Works*, 10:359–60 ("Essay on the Poetry of Eastern Nations").

4. McGann, *New Oxford Book*, xxi. See also McGann, *Poetics of Sensibility*, 128–31.

5. Derrida, *Monolingualism*, 24.

6. Foucault, "Two Lectures," 20.

7. Althusser and Balibar, *Reading Capital*, 26.

8. Thompson, *Customs*, 106, 115, 133–36, 138, 161, 162, 164, 167.

9. Ibid., 167, 171.

10. Ibid., 15, 145, 151, 164.

11. Thompson, *Whigs*, 206, 207; Thompson, *Customs*, 12.

12. Thompson, *Whigs*, 207, 208, 209 (my emphases).

13. Ibid., 207.

14. Ibid., 207–8.

15. Ibid., 208.

16. Ibid., 204, 205, 206, 207, 209.

17. My thanks to Stanford University Press's anonymous reader for the quoted phrase.

18. Thompson, *Customs*, 10–11, citing Gramsci, *Selections from the Prison Notebooks*, 419–25.

19. Thompson, *Customs*, 6.

20. Thompson, *Whigs*, 208.

21. Thompson, *Customs*, 6–7, 100.

22. Ibid., 15, 182.

23. Ibid., 6, 98.

24. Ibid., 98.

25. Raman, "Law."

26. See Roy, *Capitalism*, 11–15, 52, 100. See also Human Rights Watch, *Getting Away with Murder*.

27. Volosinov, *Marxism and the Philosophy of Language*, 74; Schmitt, *Political Theology*, 6–7.

28. Dumézil, *Mitra-Varuna*, 23, 72, 78, 82; Deleuze and Guattari, *A Thousand Plateaus*, 388.

29. On this concept of performative language, see Austin, *How to Do Things with Words*; Searle, *Intentionality*, 166–67, and *Speech Acts*, 137–40; Derrida, "Signature Event Context"; Butler, *Excitable Speech*; and Esterhammer, *Romantic Performative*.

30. Schmitt, *Political Theology*, 6, 31–35.

31. Locke, *Essay Concerning Human Understanding*, 405. See Keach, *Arbitrary Power*, 2.

32. Locke, *Two Treatises*, 400. See Keach, *Arbitrary Power*, 4.

33. Keach, *Arbitrary Power*, 1, 2, 5–6.

34. Ibid., 16. Keach quotes, for example, Burke, *Philosophical Enquiry*, 60.

35. Keach, *Arbitrary Power*, 13, 15, 126; Wordsworth and Coleridge, *Lyrical Ballads*, 97. Keach quotes Wordsworth, *The Prelude* (1805), 10.107–11.

36. Keach, *Arbitrary Power*, 30, 35, 126, 129, 131–32, 148; Thompson, *Whigs*, 210.

37. Keach, *Arbitrary Power*, 17, 130.

38. Rancière, *Politics of Literature*, 13, 15, 17.

39. Benjamin, *Selected Writings*, 4:391–92, 406, 407.

40. Balakrishnan, *Enemy*, 13.

Introduction

1. De Man, "Return to Philology"; Barbara Johnson, "Philology: What Is at Stake?"; Patterson, "Return to Philology"; Holquist, "Why We Should Remember Philology"; Jonathan Culler, "Return to Philology"; Gumbrecht, *Powers of Philology*; Said, "Return to Philology"; Nichols, "Introduction: Philology"; Wenzel, "Reflections on (New) Philology"; Restall, "History of the New Philology"; Pollock, "Future Philology?"; McGann, "Philology in a New Key"; Mignolo, *Darker Side of the Renaissance*; Clines, "Philology and Power"; Harpham, "Roots, Races, and the Return to Philology; Bal, "Virginity: Toward a Feminist Philology"; Gurd, *Iphigenias at Aulis*; Mufti, "Orientalism"; Brennan, *Borrowed Light*. For other comparatists and classicists who have called for a return to philology, see also Hansen, *Changing Philologies*; Hamacher, "From '95 Theses on Philology'"; Copenhaver, "Valla Our Contemporary"; Gaisser, "Some Thoughts on Philology"; Turner, *Philology*.

2. Warner, "Professionalization"; Graff, *Professing Literature*; Guillory, "Literary Study."

3. De Certeau, *Writing of History*, 7.

4. Volosinov, *Marxism and the Philosophy of Language*, 74.

5. See Mufti, "Auerbach in Istanbul" and "Orientalism," 463; Cooppan, "World Literature," 16–17, and "Ghosts"; Arac, "Anglo-Globalism?," 40–44; Apter, *Translation Zone*, 41–81; Kadir, *Memos*, 19–40. Said, "Introduction," was reprinted as Said, "Erich Auerbach."

6. Said, *Orientalism*, xxiv–xv, 120, 261; "Introduction: Secular Criticism," in Said, *The World, the Text, and the Critic*, 1–30, 6–8; "Erich Auerbach," 13–17, 31.

7. Mufti, "Auerbach in Istanbul," 96–98.

8. Said, "Introduction: Secular Criticism," 21, and "Erich Auerbach," 18.

9. Auerbach, "Philology and *Weltliteratur*," 17, and *Gesammelte Aufsätze zur romanischen Philologie*, 310; Said, "Introduction: Secular Criticism," 7.

10. Derrida, *Demeure: Fiction and Testimony*, 20–21, and *Demeure: Maurice Blanchot*, 18. The comment prefaces a discussion of Auerbach's one-time colleague Ernst Robert Curtius. Derrida's elaboration on the Latinity of "literature" is relevant here: "Roman law and the Roman concept of the State [have] counted greatly in the institution and the constitution of literature" (*Demeure: Fiction and Testimony*, 21).

11. Derrida, *Demeure: Fiction and Testimony*, 19, and *Demeure: Maurice Blanchot*, 15. The implication is that "literature" is an originally Western mode of writing that finds its meaning in the letter and the voice and, by extension, in the *logos* and the law. See Derrida, *Grammatology*, 17.

12. Said, *Orientalism*, xxiv.

13. Auerbach, "Philology and *Weltliteratur*," 7.

14. Said, "Erich Auerbach," 20.

15. Auerbach, *Gesammelte Aufsätze*, 304.

16. Said, *Orientalism*, 120, and *Culture and Imperialism*, 44; Auerbach, "Philology and *Weltliteratur*," 4.

17. Said, *Orientalism*, 135–36, and "Islam, Philology, and French Culture: Renan and Massignon," in *The World, the Text, and the Critic*, 268–89, 269–74. See also Graff, *Professing Literature*, 69.

18. See Gadamer, *Truth and Method*, xxiii, 175–78, 198–200, 321, 333–34. See also Seebohm, *Hermeneutics*, 35–39. In the case of Renaissance humanism, though, the tradition may be normative, as in the work of Lorenzo Valla, or historically disjunct from the present, as in the work of Poliziano. Grafton, *Defenders of the Text*, 6–9, 33.

19. Auerbach, "Philology and *Weltliteratur*," 5, 4.

20. Auerbach, *Mimesis*, 573, and "Epilegomena zu *Mimesis*," 17.

21. The quotation describes indigenous languages from a European colonial perspective. Spivak, *Death of a Discipline*, 15.

22. Auerbach, "Philology and *Weltliteratur*," 6, and *Gesammelte Aufsätze*, 303.

23. For Said, the problem with Auerbach was his exclusive focus on history at the expense of geography. Said, "History, Literature, and Geography," in *Reflections on Exile*, 453–73, 47–51.

24. See also Erich Auerbach, *Scenes from the Drama*, 197.

25. Nietzsche was more caustic: "Philologists are eager slaves of the state" ("Notizen zu 'Wir Philologen,'" in Nietzsche, *Sämtliche Werke*, 8:11–130, 57 [my translation]). On Renaissance humanism and the early modern state, see Grafton and Jardine, *From Humanism to the Humanities*, xiii–xiv; and Grafton, *Bring Out Your Dead*, 102–5.

26. Gadamer, *Truth and Method*, 178.

27. Pollock, "Future Philology?," 938; Momma, *From Philology to English Studies*, 31–59, and "A Man on the Cusp." See also Hobsbawm, *The Age of Revolution*, 286.

28. Eco, *Search for the Perfect Language*, 341–44.

29. Hegel, *Lectures on the Philosophy of History*, 333, and *Philosophie der Weltgeschichte*, 728. See the discussion in Olender, *Languages of Paradise*, 9–10.

30. Eco, *Search for the Perfect Language*, 2.

31. Ibid., 17, and *La ricerca della lingua perfetta*, 23.

32. Errington, *Linguistics in a Colonial World*, 48, 57; Trautmann, *Aryans and British India*, 55.

33. Grafton, *New Worlds, Ancient Texts*, 33.

34. Said, *Orientalism*, 117; Trautmann, "Lives of Sir William Jones," 96. Foucault and Kristeva also locate the origins of comparatism here: Foucault, *Order of Things*, 291; Kristeva, *Language*, 193–95.

35. Müller, *Science of Language*, 2:513.

36. Ballantyne, *Orientalism and Race*, 32; Trautmann, "Lives of Sir William Jones," 99.

37. Schwab, *Oriental Renaissance*, 23.

38. Jones, "An Essay on the Poetry of Eastern Nations," in *Works*, 13:329–60, 347.

39. Errington, *Linguistics in a Colonial World*, 48.

40. Jones, "On the Literature of the Hindus," in *Works*, 4:93–113, 107.

41. Foucault, *Order of Things*, 240.

42. Ibid., 293.

43. Auerbach, "Philology and *Weltliteratur*," 2, 4; Said, "Erich Auerbach," 18, and *Orientalism*, xxiv; Cooppan, *Worlds Within*, 11, 13; Hoesel-Uhlig, "Changing Fields," 27, 28.

44. Damrosch, *What Is World Literature?*, 1–36; Hoesel-Uhlig, "Changing Fields," 31, 33, 36.

45. Hoesel-Uhlig, "Changing Fields," 39, 42–46.

46. Goethe, *Conversations with Eckermann*, 151.

47. Alan Jones, "Sir William Jones as an Arabist," 71; Trautmann, "Lives of Sir William Jones," 100; Arberry, *Asiatic Jones*, 33; Cannon, *Life and Mind of Oriental Jones*, 313; Aarsleff, *Study of Language*, 118.

48. Franco Moretti, "Conjectures on World Literature," 54.

49. Jones, "The Fourth Anniversary Discourse, on the Arabs, delivered 15th February, 1787," in *Works*, 3:47–70, 59.

50. Jones, "The Sixth Anniversary Discourse, on the Persians, delivered 19th February, 1789," in *Works*, 3:103–36, 107.

51. Jones, Preface to *Sacontalá*, in *Works*, 9:365–73, 367.

52. Olender, *Languages of Paradise*, 11–14.

53. Trautmann, *Aryans and British India*, 2; Eco, *Search for the Perfect Language*, 344; Foucault, *Order of Things*, 290; Bernal, *Black Athena*, vol. 1.

54. Humboldt, *On Language*, 24, and *Über die Verschiedenheit des menschlichen Sprachbaues*, 21.

55. Arendt, *Origins of Totalitarianism*, 271.

56. Ballantyne, *Orientalism and Race*, 6, 7, 32.

57. Vernant, "Foreword," x; Olender, *Languages of Paradise*, 8, 11; Eco, *Search for the Perfect Language*, 346.

58. Saussure, *Recueil des publications scientifiques*, 395 (Olender, *Languages of Paradise*, 8, contains the translation).

59. Errington, *Linguistics in a Colonial World*, 61; Ballantyne, *Orientalism and Race*, 30; Trautmann, *Aryans and British India*, 60.

60. Jones, "The Ninth Anniversary Discourse, on the Origin and Families of Nations, delivered 23d February, 1792," in *Works*, 9:185–204, 186. See also Jones, *Works* 3:53, 65.

61. Jones, *Works*, 9:199.

62. Jones, "The Fifth Anniversary Discourse, on the Tartars, delivered 21st February, 1788," in *Works*, 3:71–102, 101–2.

63. Dumézil, "Civilization Indo-européene," 222 (my translation).

64. Jones, *Works*, 9:194 (first italics, my emphasis); see also 196–97.

65. Steiner, *After Babel*, 73–86; Eco, *Search for the Perfect Language*, 9–10, 338; Genette, *Mimologics*, 115–41.

66. Eco, *Search for the Perfect Language*, 339, and *La ricerca della lingua perfetta*, 365.

67. Trautmann, *Aryans and British India*, 39.

68. Foucault, *Order of Things*, 240. The quotations that follow are from the same page.

69. Ibid., 304, and *Les mots et les choses*, 315–16. See Foucault's discussion of Babel, "Language to Infinity" (1963), in Foucault, *Language, Counter-Memory, Practice*, 53–67, 66 and passim.

70. Foucault, *Order of Things*, 299–300.

71. Ibid., xvii.

72. Ibid., 300, and *Les mots and les choses*, 313.

73. Vernant, "Foreword," viii, and "Préface," in Olender, *Les langues du Paradis*, 8.

74. Foucault, *Order of Things*, 300, and *Les mots et les choses*, 313.

75. De Man, "Return to Philology," 21, 24–25 (my emphasis).

76. Culler, "Anti-foundational Philology," 52.

77. Jones, *Works*, 3:68–69.

78. Ibid., 130–31.

79. Jones, "On the Mystical Poetry of the Persians and Hindus," in *Works*, 4:211–35, 230.

80. Schwab, *Oriental Renaissance*, 35–36, 38, 51, 56–61.

81. Derrida, *Psyche*, 199.

82. Ibid., 191, and *Psyché*, 203.

83. Heller-Roazen, *Echolalias*, 227, 230–31.

84. Ibid., 12.

85. Benjamin, "The Translator's Task," 163, and "Die Aufgabe des Übersetzers," in Benjamin, *Gesammelte Schriften*, 4:9–21, 19. Foucault also uses the term "pure language" (*un pur langage*)—and "the brute being of language"—to define "literature": Foucault, *Order of Things*, 89, 119, and *Les mots et les choses*, 103.

86. Benjamin, "Die Aufgabe des Übersetzers," 16, and "Translator's Task," 159.

87. Cohn, *Colonialism and Its Forms of Knowledge*, 18. The same point is made by Anderson, *Imagined Communities*, 14.

88. Cohn, *Colonialism and Its Forms of Knowledge*, 56; Zvelebil, *Tamil Literature*, 2–4.

89. Foucault, *Order of Things*, 238, 306–7.

90. Holwell, *Interesting Historical Events*, 2:9.

91. Jones, *Grammar of the Persian Language*; Hadley, *Grammatical Remarks*; Halhed, *Grammar of the Bengal Language*; Richardson, *Dictionary, English, Persian and Arabic*; Balfour, *Inshā-yi Harkaran*; Kirkpatrick, *Vocabulary, Persian, Arabic and English*; Gilchrist, *Dictionary, English and Hindustanee*.

92. See, in particular, Halhed, *Code of Gentoo Laws*; Wilkins, *Bhagvat-Geeta*; Gladwin, *Ayeen Akbery*; Hamilton, *Hèdaya*; and Jones's works listed below. See also Singha, *Despotism of Law*, viii–x, 81–82.

93. Baxi, "'The State's Emissary,'" 249–50, 252; Hussain, *Jurisprudence of Emergency*, 41.

94. Cohn, *Colonialism and Its Forms of Knowledge*, 22.

95. Comaroff, "Colonialism, Culture, and the Law," 306, 309.

96. Jones, *Al Sirájiyyah*; Colebrooke, *Digest of Hindu Law* (1798); Cohn, *Colonialism and Its Forms of Knowledge*, 71; Trautmann, "Lives of Sir William Jones," 102; Ibbetson, "Sir William Jones as Comparative Lawyer," 21.

97. Jones, *Letters*, 2:795; Strawson, "Islamic Law and English Texts," 122; Jon Wilson, *Domination of Strangers*, 80.

98. Jones, *Letters*, 2:721.

99. Comaroff, "Colonialism, Culture, and the Law," 309.

100. Cohn, *Colonialism and Its Forms of Knowledge*, 3, and *Anthropologist among the Historians*, 124, 228–29, 618.

101. Herzfeld, *Anthropology through the Looking-Glass*, 31.

102. Guha, "Chandra's Death," 141.

103. Auerbach, *Introduction aux études*, 9 (my translation).

104. White, *Figural Realism*, 99.

105. Said, "Introduction: Secular Criticism," 6. See "Reflections on Exile," in Said, *Reflections on Exile*, 173–86, 185.

106. For example, he pointedly criticized nineteenth-century philology's politics, not its epistemology. "Raymond Schwab and the Romance of Ideas," in Said, *The World, the Text, and the Critic*, 248–67, 264.

107. See Said, *Orientalism*, 136; *The World, the Text, and the Critic*, 260, 278; and "Erich Auerbach," 13–15.

108. Said, *Beginnings*, 315–16, 364, 366; *Orientalism*, 120–21, 138–39; "Introduction: Secular Criticism," 24; *The World, the Text, and the Critic*, 260, 273–74, 278, 288; *Culture and Imperialism*, 161; "Erich Auerbach," 29–30.

109. Asad, *Formations of the Secular*, 23–27, 37–43, 211–15, 235–36, 253; Bremer, *Greek Religion*, 5–6; Chadwick, *Secularization*, 88–93; Waterhouse, "Secularism," 347–50.

110. Said, *Beginnings*, 6; "Introduction: Secular Criticism," 3; *Culture and Imperialism*, 61; *The World, the Text, and the Critic*, 288; "The Future of Criticism," in *Reflections on Exile*, 165–72, 170; Brennan, *Wars of Position*, 109, 114. Recall Lévi-Strauss's argument that Sartre's *Critique of Dialectical Reason* remained Eurocentric despite its best intentions: historical method, though identified with reason as such, reflects Europe's development alone and excludes people without history from the category of the human. Lévi-Strauss, *Savage Mind*, 262.

111. Agamben, *Infancy and History*, 161–62. Nietzsche's vision was similar: "The philologist of the future [must be] the destroyer [*Vernichter*] of the discipline of philology"; "I dream of a human collective [that] wants to be called 'destroyer'" (Nietzsche, *Sämtliche Werke*, 8:56, 48 [my translation]).

112. Wellek, *Rise of English Literary History*, 71, 130.

113. Schwab, *Oriental Renaissance*, 57–64.

114. In regard to the relationship of psychoanalysis to philology, see Forrester, *Language*.

115. See Spivak, *Critique*, 141–42, on "ab-using" the Enlightenment.

116. Porter, "Introduction," xiii; see also xii–xiv, xvii, xix, xxvii, xxxviii–xxxix.

117. Auerbach, *Literary Language*, 337.

118. Said, "Return to Philology," 68.

119. Ibid., 59–60.

120. Ibid., 61.

121. Pollock, "Future Philology?," 948.

122. Mufti, "Orientalism," 488–89.

123. Young, *Postcolonialism*; Denning, *Culture*.

First Stratum

1. Anderson, *Imagined Communities*, 70; Said, *Orientalism*, 135.

2. Hodgson, *Venture of Islam*, 2:293.

3. Cannon, *Oriental Jones*, 25. The claim that follows draws on the same volume, 25, as well as Cohn, *Colonialism and Its Forms of Knowledge*, 23; Cannon, "Sir William Jones, Persian, Sanskrit," 86.

4. Aarsleff, *Study of Language*, 127; Gramsci, *Gramsci Reader*, 358.

5. Foucault, *Order of Things*, 299–300.

6. Ibid., 300.

7. Rancière, *Politics of Literature*, 14.

8. Foucault, *Order of Things*, 300, and *Les mots et les choses*, 313.

9. On this opposition in I. A. Richards and Roman Jakobsen, see Guillory, "Literary Study," 37.

10. Hamacher, *Minima Philologica*, 11, 18, 45, 47–48, 51, 54.

11. See Bauer and Neuwirth, *Ghazal as World Literature I*, and Neuwirth et al., *Ghazal as World Literature II*.

12. Asani, "South Asian Literatures," 97. Unless otherwise indicated, the claims that follow draw on the same source, as well as Lewisohn, "Prolegomenon to the Study of Ḥāfiẓ 1," 16, 18; Khorramshahi, "Hafez's Life and Times," 465–66; Alam and Subrahmanyam, *Indo-Persian Travels*, 309–10.

13. Nwyia, *Ibn 'Aṭā' Allāh* (cited by Asani, "South Asian Literatures," 97).

14. Cannon, "Sir William Jones's Persian Linguistics," 265–71; see also Cannon, "Sir William Jones, Persian, Sanskrit," 84.

15. Jeremiás, *"Persian Grammar of Sir William Jones,"* 277–88.

16. Campbell, "History of Linguistics," 89, 94.

17. Foucault, *Order of Things*, 240; Aarsleff, *Study of Language*, 112, 127, 134; Guillory, "Literary Study," 29; Pollock, "Future Philology," 938; Momma, *From Philology to English Studies*, 31–59.

18. Windfuhr, *Persian Grammar*, 14, 24.

19. Campbell, "History of Linguistics," 88–89.

20. Ibid., 84–85; Aarsleff, *Study of Language*, 14, 15.

21. Campbell, "History of Linguistics," 85–87.

22. Jones, *Grammar of the Persian Language*, xiv.

23. Jones, "The History of the Persian Language," in *Works*, 5:407–46, 441.

24. Ibid., 446.

25. Ibid., 409–10 (emphasis in the original).

26. Jones, *Grammar*, xxiii–xiv.

27. Jones, *Poems Consisting Chiefly of Translations*, 194 ("On the Poetry of Eastern Nations").

28. Volosinov, *Marxism and the Philosophy of Language*, 72, 75, 76; see also 66, 71, 77.

29. Ibid., 75.

30. Ibid.

31. Arendt, *On Revolution*, 163; Negri, *Insurgencies*, 146.

32. Campbell, "History of Linguistics," 81–84.

33. Jones, *Poems Consisting Chiefly of Translations*, 198–99.

34. Ibid., 195. Jones reiterated this argument in the preface to *Poems Consisting Chiefly of Translations*, while alluding to Hafiz's specific place in his aesthetic project; see Jones, *Works*, 10:204–5.

35. Jones, *Grammar*, xi. The claim that follows draws on the same volume, xii; Cohn, *Colonialism and Its Forms of Knowledge*, 18.

36. Jones, *Grammar*, xiii; Cannon, "Sir William Jones, Persian," 85.

37. Jones, *Grammar*, xviii. The claim that follows draws on Cannon, "Sir William Jones, Persian, Sanskrit," 85.

38. Cannon, "Sir William Jones, Persian, Sanskrit," 86 (citing a letter of 30 December 1770 to the East India Company Court of Directors).

39. Rahman, *Language, Ideology, and Power*, 134; see also Alam, "The Pursuit of Persian." The claims that follow draw on Alam and Subrahmanyam, *Indo-Persian Travels*, 101, 103; Cohn, *Colonialism and Its Forms of Knowledge*, 29; Rahman, "Decline of Persian," 50, 55, which cites David Lelyveld, *Aligarh's First Generation*, 33. See also Rahman, "British Language Policies."

40. Rahman "Decline of Persian," 53.

41. Cohn, *Colonialism and Its Forms of Knowledge*, 21; Jones, *Grammar*, xii.

42. Jones, *Works*, 5:433.

43. Ibid., 3:312, and *Grammar*, xiii, 132–33. See also Jones, *Works*, 5:433, 436.

44. Jones, *Grammar*, xiii. The claims that follow draw on Davis, "Persian: Literary Translations," 1057–58; Cohn, *Colonialism and Its Forms of Knowledge*, 24; Loloi, "Ḥāfiẓ and the Religion of Love," 279; Rahman, "Decline of Persian," 49; Jones, *Grammar*, iii, 133, and *Works*, 5:433.

45. Davis, "Persian: Literary Translations," 1057, citing Arberry, *British Contributions*; Firoze, "Contribution of Jones"; Nair, "Calcutta's Contribution."

46. Dharwadker, "Orientalism," 172–73; Jaroslav Stetkevych, *Arabic Poetry*, 36.

47. Arberry, *Asiatic Jones*, 10.

48. Rahman, "Decline of Persian," 49.

49. Qur'ān 55:26–27 (*Surat al-Rahman*).

50. Rahman, "Decline of Persian," 52.

51. Shahab Ahmed, *What Is Islam?*, 32. The claim that follows draws on Lewisohn, "Prolegomenon to the Study of Ḥāfiẓ 1," 14; Rahman "Decline of Persian," 61–62.

52. Jones, *Grammar*, 133.

53. Ibid., 137. The claims that follow draw on Arberry, "Orient Pearls," 699, 700; Loloi, "Ḥāfiẓ and the Religion of Love," 281; de Sola Pinto, "Sir William Jones and

English Literature," 687–88; Paden, "Tennyson and Persian Poetry," 652–56; Lewisohn, "Editor's Introduction," xxvii.

54. Marx and Engels, *Collected Works*, 39:341 (6 June 1853).

55. Arberry, "Orient Pearls," 699.

56. De Sola Pinto, "Sir William Jones and English Literature," 687.

57. Franklin, *Orientalist Jones*, 72.

58. Jones, *Poems Consisting Chiefly of Translations*, 201, 202.

59. Ibid., 189.

60. Wordsworth and Coleridge, *Lyrical Ballads*, iii.

61. Jones, *Poems Consisting Chiefly of Translations*, 206–7.

62. Ibid., 211.

63. Ibid., 202.

64. Abrams, *Mirror and the Lamp*, 70–99. On this transformation in Romanticism in general, see Agamben, *Man without Content*, 21.

65. Abrams, *Mirror and the Lamp*, 87–88; see, for example, Mufti, "Orientalism," 466, and Franklin, *Sir William Jones*, 337.

66. Black et al., *Broadview Anthology*, 4:39, 40.

67. Taylor, *Sources of the Self*, 368–69; see also 377. See also Wellek, *Rise of English Literary History*, 51–52, 71–72, 130.

68. Abrams, *Mirror and the Lamp*, 87.

69. Meisami, *Structure and Meaning*, 4.

70. Rancière, *Politics of Literature*, 4, 11–14.

71. Jones, *Poems Consisting Chiefly of Translations*, 216; see also 207.

72. Ibid., 213.

73. Dharwadker, "Orientalism," 160–61, 164; Williams, *Keywords*, 185; Wellek, "Literature and Its Cognates," 82.

74. Williams, *Keywords*, 185–86.

75. Dharwadkar, "Orientalism," 163.

76. Rancière, *Politics of Literature*, 13; the claims that follow draw on the same volume, 15, 16, 19–20.

77. Ibid., 13, 14.

78. McGann, *New Oxford Book*, xix.

79. Nietzsche, *Anti-Christ*, 169.

80. Ibid., 170.

81. Jones, *Works*, 11:302.

82. Nietzsche, *Briefwechsel*, pt. 3, vol. 1 (*Briefe von Friedrich Nietzsche Januar 1880–Dezember 1884*), 68 (letter to Köselitz, 13 March 1881; my translation and emphasis). See the discussion in Almond, *New Orientalists*, 8.

83. Nietzsche, *Philosophical Writings*, 243 (notebook entry 1051, August/September 1885).

84. "An Hafis. Frage eines Wassertrinkers": Nietzsche, *Briefwechsel*, pt. 3, vol. 7.3 (*Briefe von und an Friedrich Nietzsche Januar 1887–Januar 1889*), 481; Nietzsche, *Fragmente*, 278.

85. Nietzsche, *Philosophical Writings*, 241.

86. Nietzsche, *Gay Science*, 330–31 (sec. 370).

87. Ibid., 329.

88. Ibid.

89. Nietzsche, *Genealogy of Morality*, 69. See Almond, *New Orientalists*, 20, 21.

90. Nietzsche, *Gay Science*, 329. The claims that immediately follow draw on the same volume, 331 (see Walter Kaufmann's footnote on this page).

91. Ibid., 328.

92. Nietzsche, *Philosophical Writings*, 243.

93. Nietzsche, *Gay Science*, 330.

94. Ibid.

95. Ibid., 331.

96. Nietzsche, *Philosphical Writings*, 243 (first italics mine).

97. Nietzsche, *Briefwechsel*, pt. 3, vol. 5 (*Briefe von Friedrich Nietzsche Januar 1887–Januar 1889*), 574; Kaufmann, *Nietzsche*, 67.

98. Williamson, *Longing for Myth*, 133, 169, 172–73, 227, 250–51, 258.

99. Jones, *Grammar*, 45, 132, 437.

100. Jaroslav Stetkevych, *Arabic Poetry*, 32.

101. Goethe, *Selected Poetry*, 146–47.

102. Lewisohn, "Prolegomenon to the Study of Ḥāfiẓ 1," 16.

103. "Notizen zu 'Wir Philologen,'" in Nietzsche, *Sämtliche Werke*, 8:76. See also Almond, *History of Islam*, 154.

104. Gramsci, *Gramsci Reader*, 358.

105. Ibid., 354.

106. Ibid., 357.

107. Spivak, *Aesthetic Education*, 463.

108. Ibid., 464.

109. Jones, *Poems Consisting Chiefly of Translations*, 212, and *Grammar*, 137.

110. Hammer-Purgstall, *Der Diwan*; Bell, *Poems*; Arberry, "Orient Pearls"; Payne, *Poems*; Le Gallienne, *Odes*; Hillmann, "Ḥāfez's 'Turk of Shiraz,'" *Unity in the Ghazals*, 26, 141–42, and "Pseudo-Scholarship"; Meisami, *Medieval Persian Court Poetry* and "Persona and Generic Conventions," 136–37; Dabashi, *Being a Muslim*, 21–25, 126. See the discussion in Loloi, *Hâfiz, Master of Persian Poetry*, 17.

111. Limbert, *Shiraz*, 105, 121. The claims that follow draw on the same volume, 72, 76, 93, 115, 122; Lewisohn, "Prolegomenon to the Study of Ḥāfiẓ," 35; Green, *Sufism*, 188, 191, 192, 194–95. See also Yarshater, "Hafez (i): An Overview," 461–65.

112. Lewisohn, "Religious Sources of Love," 159, 160; Lewis, "Hafez and *Rendi*,"

485–86; Limbert, *Shiraz*, 86. I take the claims that follow from the same volume, 70, 81, 83, 96, unless otherwise noted.

113. Yarshater, "Hafez (i): An Overview," 462.

114. Bashiri, "'Hafiz' Shirazi Turk,'" 266. See also Bashiri, "Hafiz and the Sufic Ghazal."

115. Often, the number of recitations and readers is said instead to be seven. See Leemhuis, "Readings of the Qur'ān"; Gade, "Recitation of the Qur'ān"; and Melchert and Afsaruddin, "Reciters of the Qur'ān."

116. Lewisohn, "Prolegomenon to the Study of Ḥāfiẓ 1," 17. This verse is found in five of the manuscripts used by Khānlarī, *Dīwān-i Ḥāfiẓ*, *ghazal* 312.

117. This is Shahab Ahmed's graceful translation (which I have slightly modified), of *ghazal* 312, in Khānlarī, *Dīwān-i Ḥāfiẓ*: see Shahab Ahmed, *What Is Islam?*, 34. For other versions see Avery, *Collected Lyrics*, 388, and Bly and Lewisohn, *Angels*, 62. See also "*Eros* come to your rescue, even if you,/Like Ḥāfiẓ, can chant the Qur'ān by heart/In all its fourteen different lections": Lewisohn, "Prolegomenon to the Study of Ḥāfiẓ 1," 17; Khānlarī *ghazal* 93.

118. Berg, "Polysemy in the *Qur'ān*," 155.

119. Ibid., 156.

120. Lewisohn, "Prolegomenon to the Study of Ḥāfiẓ 1," 28 (Khānlarī *ghazal* 110). The claims that follow draw on the same source, 11–12; Morris, "Transfiguring Love," 228.

121. Ali, "Introduction," 5, 8.

122. Arberry, "Orient Pearls," 705.

123. On amphiboly/punning, see Boyce, "A Novel Interpretation," 279–88.

124. Ali, "Introduction," 12.

125. Bashiri, "'Hafiz' Shirazi Turk,'" 191–92.

126. Ibid., 192, 196.

127. Avery and Heath-Stubbs, *Hafiz of Shiraz*, 22–23.

128. Bashiri, "'Hafiz' Shirazi Turk,'" 249. The claims that follow in this paragraph draw on the same essay, 250, 256, 257. For other readings of "The Shirazi Turk," see Arberry, "Orient Pearls"; Wickens, "Analysis"; Boyce, "A Novel Interpretation"; Rehder, "Unity"; Schimmel, "Ḥāfiẓ," 30–31; Pritchett, "Orient Pearls"; Loloi, *Hāfiz, Master of Persian Poetry*, 22–48; Anushiravani and Atashi, "Cultural Translation."

129. Berkey, *Formation of Islam*, 245; Karamustafa, *God's Unruly Friends*, 2–3, 14, 15, 18–20, 33, and *Sufism*, 164, 165.

130. Karamustafa, *Sufism*, 48, 156–59, 162, 169, and *God's Unruly Friends*, 32.

131. Qur'ān 5:54 (*Sūrat al-Mā'idah*); Morris, "Transfiguring Love," 237.

132. Meisami, "Persona and Generic Conventions," 136. For different translations, see Avery and Heath-Stubbs, *Hafiz of Shiraz*, 23: "Though you give me harsh words, bad names, God's blessings upon you:/A bitter answer comes sweet on a sweet lip"; Avery,

Collected Lyrics, 21: "You spoke ill of me and I do not mind. God forgive you! You spoke well:/The bitter answer is becoming from sugar-crunching ruby lips."

133. John 3:17, quoted in Agamben, *Pilate and Jesus*, 37.

134. Agamben, *Pilate and Jesus*, 19.

135. Ibid., 44–45, 31.

136. Ibid., 42 (see also 41, 17); John 18:36.

137. Agamben, *Pilate and Jesus*, 57, 20.

138. Ibid., 42.

139. Kierkegaard, *The Moment*, 6 (translation slightly modified).

140. Karamustafa, *God's Unruly Friends*, 16, 21.

141. Agamben, *Pilate and Jesus*, 54.

142. Lewis, "Hafez and *Rendi*," 485; Khānlarī *ghazal* 385. See Avery, *Collected Lyrics*, 470, for another translation.

143. Agamben, *Homo Sacer*, 8 (my emphasis).

144. Ibid., 187.

145. Ibid.

146. Ibid., 188.

147. Agamben, *Use of Bodies*, 263–66.

148. Karamustafa, *God's Unruly Friends*, 13, 14, 17, 18, 22, 27, 32, 99. The claims that follow draw on the same source, as well as Karamustafa, *Sufism*, 165–66, 174–77.

149. Karamustafa, *God's Unruly Friends*, 13.

150. Ibid., 29, 101. For an even more direct connection between Christian monks (in Syria and Egypt) and Sufis, see also Hodgson, *Venture of Islam*, 1:394.

151. Agamben, *Highest Poverty*, 110, 93; see also 94.

152. Ibid., 73–75.

153. Ibid., 110.

154. Karamustafa, *Sufism*, 48, 62, 63, 159, 160, 161, 165, and *God's Unruly Friends*, 9, 51, 97.

155. Lewisohn, "Prolegomenon to the Study of Ḥāfiẓ 2," 37 (Khānlarī *ghazal* 479). Compare with Avery, *Collected Lyrics*, 580: "Footloose rascal dervishes [*qalandars*] are at the tavern door,/Who the imperial diadem take and give."

156. Morris, "Transfiguring Love," 247.

157. Ibid., 229. The claims that follow draw on the same essay, 230, 234, 239.

158. Avery, *Collected Lyrics*, 21 (translation slightly modified). For other translations, see Ordoubadian, *Poems of Hafez*, 82: "Hafez, you sang ghazal, made pearls of words; come and sing:/the Universe graces your verse with a marriage to the Pleiades"; Avery and Heath-Stubbs, *Hafiz of Shiraz*, 23: "You have made a poem, Hafiz, and threaded pearls; recite it deftly:/And on your verse Heaven scatter the knot of Pleiades."

159. Bashiri, "'Hafiz' Shirazi Turk,'" 260. The claims that follow draw on the same essay, 259–61.

160. Karamustafa, *Sufism*, 163.

161. Avery, *Collected Lyrics*, 470 (*ghazal* 385, translation slightly modified). For another translation, see Bly and Lewisohn, *Angels*, 21.

162. Karamustafa, *God's Unruly Friends*, 5.

163. Agamben, *Sacrament of Language*, 51. The claims that follow draw on the same source.

164. Benjamin, *Selected Writings*, 1:72. See also "On Language as Such and on the Language of Man," in Benjamin, *Reflections*, 314–32, 328, and "Über Sprache überhaupt und die Sprache des Menschen," in Benjamin, *Gesammelte Schriften*, 2:140–57.

165. Benjamin, *Selected Writings*, 1:72.

166. Bly and Lewisohn, *Angels*, 6 (Khānlarī *ghazal* 385, translation slightly modified); Lewisohn, "English Romantics," 15–52, 45; Lewisohn, "Religious Sources of Love," 164, 165.

167. Avery, *Collected Lyrics*, 68 (Khānlarī *ghazal* 37).

168. Foucault, *Language, Counter-Memory, Practice*, 66.

Second Stratum

1. Hegel, *Aesthetics*, 2:1044, 1045 (translation slightly modified). See the discussion in Pollock, *Language of the Gods*, 542–48.

2. Lukács, *Theory of the Novel*, 56.

3. Anderson, *Imagined Communities*, 24–35.

4. Gellner, *Nations and Nationalism*, 8, 27–29, 34–35, 46, 54–55, 66.

5. See Hallaq, *Sharī'a*, 372.

6. Franklin, *Orientalist Jones*, 185. The claims that follow draw on Cohn, *Colonialism and Its Forms of Knowledge*, 29, 69. "The Best Practicable System of Judicature" is reprinted in Jones, *Collected Works*, 1:cxxxiii–cxxxv.

7. Cohn, *Colonialism and Its Forms of Knowledge*, 57.

8. Ibid.

9. Fisch, "Law as a Means," 23 (emphasis added); see also 29–30.

10. Anderson, *Imagined Communities*, 71, 84. The terms "vertical" and "horizontal" are adapted from the seminal distinction in regard to the medieval and modern apprehension of time in Auerbach, *Mimesis*, 17, 74.

11. Said, *Orientalism*, 136.

12. Ibid.

13. Anderson, *Imagined Communities*, 42–44.

14. Ibid., 72, 83, 84.

15. Wellek, "Literature and Its Cognates," 83.

16. Anderson, *Imagined Communities*, 81.

17. Ibid., 25.

18. Gramsci, *Selections*, 256–57.

19. Jones, *Mohamedan Law of Succession* and *Moallakát*.

20. Rancière, *Politics of Literature*, 16.

21. Dharwadker, "Orientalism," 167.

22. Rancière, *Politics of Literature*, 13.

23. Anderson, *Imagined Communities*, 23.

24. Cohn, *Colonialism and Its Forms of Knowledge*, 62–65.

25. Gleig, *Memoirs*, 1:400 (to Lord Mansfield, 21 March 1774); Cohn, *Colonialism and Its Forms of Knowledge*, 65–66.

26. Gleig, *Memoirs*, 1:400.

27. Hallaq, *Shari'a*, 372.

28. Halhed, *Code* (1781), lxxiv.

29. Jones, *Letters*, 2:795 (to the first Marquis of Cornwallis, 19 March 1788).

30. Cannon, "Sir William Jones, Persian, Sanskrit," 93.

31. Jones, *Works*, 8:162, 165.

32. Ibid., 162–63.

33. Jones, *Letters*, 2:795–96 (to the first Marquis of Cornwallis, 19 March 1788).

34. Ibid., 2:643 (to William Pitt the Younger, 5 February 1785).

35. Jones, *Collected Works*, 1:cxxxiii–cxxxiv (the tenth point of the "Best Practicable System of Judicature for India" (1784): "The *laws* of the natives must be preserved inviolate; but the learning and vigilance of the *English* judge must be a check upon the native interpreters."

36. Ibid.

37. Jones, *Letters*, 2:797 (to the first Marquis of Cornwallis, 19 March 1788); see also 2:664.

38. Jones, *Works*, 2:128 (to Thomas Caldicott, 27 September 1787).

39. Jones, *Letters*, 2:720 (to C. W. Boughton Rouse, MP for Evesham and Secretary to the Board of Control for India, 24 October 1786).

40. Jones, *Letters*, 2:699; Hallaq, *Shari'a*, 372; Cohn, *Colonialism and Its Forms of Knowledge*, 70. The claim that follows draws on the former volume, 374.

41. Hussain, *Jurisprudence of Emergency*, 3–4; Fisch, "Law as a Means," 24; Kugle, "Framed," 277.

42. Jones, *Works*, 7:4, 5, 3 ("Charge to the Grand Jury, at Calcutta," 4 December 1783).

43. Jones, "Notes on Cases," 2 overleaf (dated 11 March 1785).

44. Brewer and Styles, *An Ungovernable People*, 14. See Hussain, *Jurisprudence of Emergency*, 3.

45. Zaman, *Ulama*, 22, which cites Singha, *Despotism of Law*; Hallaq, *Shari'a*, 372.

46. Zaman, *Ulama*, 23; Bhattacharyya-Panda, *Invention and Appropriation*, 7.

47. Franklin, *Orientalist Jones*, 306; Jones, *Letters*, 2:684.

48. Hefner, "Human Rights and Democracy," 45. The claims that follow draw on Michael Anderson, "Islamic Law," 171; Kugle, "Framed," 263, 270, 276, 287–89, 291, 296,

305; Bhattacharyya-Panda, *Invention and Appropriation*, 17–19, 24, 27; Hallaq, *Sharī'a*, 372–73; de Certeau, *Writing of History*, xiii, unless otherwise noted.

49. Kugle, "Framed," 305.

50. Dow, *History of Hindostan*, 3:civ.

51. This is proposal XX of Hastings' "A Plan for the Administration of Justice": see *Proceedings of the Governor*, 23.

52. Kugle, "Framed," 267–68. The claims that follow draw on the same essay, 293; Washbrook, "Sovereignty, Property, Land and Labour," 73–74, 83, 86, 88, 90, and "Law, State and Agrarian Society," 652.

53. Schmitt, *Nomos*, 127, 140.

54. Ibid., 148.

55. Bhattacharyya-Panda, *Invention and Appropriation*, 8–9; Price, "'Popularity' of the Imperial Courts," 185.

56. Jones, *Al Sirájiyyah*, ix, xi; *Works*, 8:206, 207.

57. Bhattacharyya-Panda, "Invention and Appropriation," 81, 209. See also Hallaq, *Sharī'a*, 374. The claims that follow draw on the former volume, 81, 209–12, 215, 216. On the translations of *al-Hidāyah* and *al-Sirājiyyah*, see Michael Anderson, "Legal Scholarship," 74, and Kolff, "Indian and British Law Machines," 213–14.

58. See Siraj Ahmed, "Orientalism," 167–205, and *Stillbirth of Capital*, 161–88. The claims that follow draw on Hallaq, *Sharī'a*, 372; Mufti, "Invention," 478.

59. Jones, *Letters*, 2:664 (to William Pitt the Younger, 5 February 1785).

60. Jones, *Institutes of Hindu Law* (1794), xix–xx.

61. Hallaq, *Sharī'a*, 373, which cites Weber, *Economy and Society*, 2:818–22. The claim that follows draws on the former volume, 372.

62. Baxi, "'The State's Emissary,'" 252; Singha, *Despotism of Law*, 81–82; Benton, *Law and Colonial Cultures*, 127–31. See also Kugle, "Framed," 275. The claims that follow draw on Bhattacharyya-Panda, *Appropriation and Invention*, 250; Jones, *Letters*, 2:796 (to the first Marquis of Cornwallis, 19 March 1788). See also Ibbetson, "Sir William Jones and the Nature of Law."

63. Bayly, *Indian Society*, 76; Kugle, "Framed," 281, 276. The claims that follow draw on the same essay, 257, 267, 276–78.

64. Stokes, *English Utilitarians*.

65. Mamdani, *Define and Rule*, 2.

66. Ibid.

67. Ibid., 44.

68. Ibid.

69. Ibid., 1.

70. Ibid., 2. The claims that immediately follow draw on the same volume, 3, 28, 49, 50; Cohn, *Colonialism and Its Forms of Knowledge*, 70.

71. Jones, *Letters*, 2:720.

72. Ibid., 2:720–21.

73. Kugle, "Framed," 280. The claims that follow draw on the same essay, 280, 283; Jones, *Letters*, 2:720; Cohn, *Colonialism and Its Forms of Knowledge*, 71.

74. Michael Anderson, "Islamic Law," 170.

75. Ibid., 176.

76. Dirks, *Castes of Mind*, 43; Mamdani, *Define and Rule*, 30–31. The claims that follow draw on the latter volume, 10, 31; Michael Anderson, "Islamic Law," 176–80.

77. Maine, *Village-Communities*, 220.

78. Ibid., 224.

79. Reyntjens, "Development of the Dual Legal System," 111; Price, "'Popularity' of the Imperial Courts," 181, 185. The claims that follow draw on the former essay, 112; Miège, "Legal Developments," 103, 104, 107.

80. Comaroff, "Colonial, Culture, and the Law," 306. The claims that follow draw on the same essay, 306–7; Price, "'Popularity' of the Imperial Courts," 184.

81. Kugle, "Framed," 258, 304; Michael Anderson, "Islamic Law," 171–72, 180. The claims that follow draw on the latter essay, 175; Mamdani, *Define and Rule*, 34–42.

82. Hallaq, *Sharī'a*, 376.

83. Zaman, *Ulama*, 24. The claims that follow draw on the same volume, 23–24.

84. Ibid., 21. The claims that follow draw on the same volume, 24, 26–27, 31.

85. Michael Anderson, "Islamic Law," 180–81. The claims that follow draw on Zaman, *Ulama*, 31–32, 37; Kugle, "Framed," 288, 308–9. See also Geertz, *Islam Observed*; Ahmad, *Islamic Modernism*; Rafiuddin Ahmed, *Bengal Muslims*; Brown, "Shari'a and State."

86. Nehru, *Discovery of India*, 330.

87. Kugle, "Framed," 302–3.

88. Metcalf, *"Traditionalist" Islamic Activism*, 1, and *Islamic Contestations*, 265. See also Metcalf, *Islamic Revival*.

89. Mamdani, *Define and Rule*, 50.

90. Kugle, "Framed," 259, 307; Bhattacharyya-Panda, *Invention and Appropriation*, 3. But see Said, *Orientalism*, 77–79.

91. Said, *Orientalism*, 78; see also 2, 5.

92. Abou El Fadl, "Shari'ah," 10; Kugle, *Homsexuality in Islam*, 132–33. The claims that follow draw on the former source, 12; Hefner, "Human Rights and Democracy in Islam," 41; Hallaq, *History of Islamic Legal Theories*, 10.

93. Messick, *Calligraphic State*, 6–7, 30–36; Zaman, *Ulama*, 39; Vikor, "Shari'a and the Nation-State," 221–22. The claims that follow draw on Abou El Fadl, "Shari'ah," 13, 14; Kugle, "Framed," 274, 285–87, 295–97; Hallaq, *Sharī'a*, 375, and *Authority, Continuity and Change*, 240; Michael Anderson, "Islamic Law," 173.

94. Zaman, *Ulama*, 37–38. The claims that follow draw on Messick, *Calligraphic State*, 17–18, 30, 31; Hallaq, *Authority, Continuity and Change*, xii, 239, 240.

95. Abou El Fadl, "Shari'ah," 14.

96. Messick, *Calligraphic State*, 30, 33.

97. Ibid., 22. The claims that follow draw on the same volume, 21–22.

98. Ibid., 241. The claims that follow draw on the same volume, 15, 23, 24, 249.

99. Hallaq, *Shari'a*, 375. The claims that follows draw on Reid, *Law and Piety*, 1.

100. Reid, *Law and Piety*, 10, 131; Chamberlain, *Knowledge and Social Practice*, 106–7, 122–25. See also Berkey, *Transmission of Knowledge*.

101. Reid, *Law and Piety*, 19, 131.

102. Chamberlain, *Knowledge and Social Practice*, 123.

103. Messick, *Calligraphic State*, 241, 249.

104. On the scholarly warning about "the disease of corruption of the text," see Messick, *Calligraphic State*, 23. He takes the quotation from the entry on "Hadith" by Ignaz Goldziher in Gibb and Kramers, *Shorter Encyclopedia of Islam*, 120.

105. Reid, *Law and Piety*, 2–3, 6. The period in question here is 1170–1500 A.D. The claims that follow draw on the same volume, 1, 6–9, 13, 20, 96, 197, 203, 205–7, 209–10; Chamberlain, *Knowledge and Social Practice*, 130–32; Abou El Fadl, "Shari'ah," 17. See also Geoffrey, *Le soufisme*; Pouzet, *Damas aux VII/XIII siècle*; Meri, *Cult of Saints*; and Talmon-Heller, *Islamic Piety*.

106. Abou El Fadl, "Shari'ah," 9. The claim that ends this paragraph draws on Hallaq, *Authority*, 240.

107. See Hallaq, *Authority*, 240.

108. Ibid., 16, 19. The claims that follow draw on Abou El Fadl, "Shari'ah," 8–9.

109. Hallaq, *Shari'a*, 376; Messick, *Calligraphic State*, 3. The claims that follow draw on the former source, 375; the latter, 31; Kugle, "Framed," 274, 296, 297; Cannon, *Oriental Jones*, 173.

110. Jones, *Works*, 8:200 (preface to *Al Sirájiyyah; or, the Mohammedan Law of Inheritance*). On the *Kitab al-Farā'id al-Sirajiyya*, see Zaman, *Ulama*, 22; Pirbhai, *Reconsidering Islam*, 126, who dates it incorrectly; Jones, *Letters*, 2:721.

111. Jones, *Works*, 8:201–2.

112. Kugle, "Framed," 284–85. The claim that follows draws on the same essay, 286, 300.

113. Asad, *Formations of the Secular*, 255. The claims that follow draw on Kugle, "Framed," 297, 299, 308; Zaman, *Ulama*, 18; Abou El Fadl, "Shari'ah," 21; Messick, *Calligraphic State*, 3. See also Hallaq, *Authority*, 238–39, and "Was the Gate of Ijtihad Closed?," reprinted in Hallaq, *Law and Legal Theory*.

114. Zaman, *Ulama*, 22; Cannon, *Oriental Jones*, 173, which cites Vesey-FitzGerald, "Sir William Jones, the Jurist," 814. See also Strawson, "Islamic Law and English Texts."

115. Baillie, *Digest of Moohummudan Law* (1865). See Michael Anderson, "Islamic Law," 175, and Hallaq, *Shari'a*, 377.

116. Hallaq, *Shari'a*, 375–76. The claims that follow draw on Abou El Fadl, "Shari'ah," 19–20. See also Devji, *Landscapes of Jihad* and *Terrorist in Search of Humanity*.

117. Foucault, *Security, Territory, Population*, 364–66, and "The Subject and Power," 782–84.

118. Abou El Fadl, "Shari'ah," 23.

119. Fynes, "Sir William Jones," 50.

120. Jones, *Moallakât*, 73; Arberry, *Seven Odes*, 8.

121. Jones, *Poems Consisting Chiefly of Translations*, 174, 179 ("On the Poetry of Eastern Nations").

122. Ibid., 179.

123. Ibid.

124. Rancière, *Politics of Literature*, 16.

125. Wellek, "Literature and Its Cognates," 83. See also Dharwadker, "Orientalism," 167.

126. Fynes, "Sir William Jones," 53–54; de Sola Pinto, "Sir William Jones and English Literature," 690–91.

127. Jones, *Works*, 10:389–90.

128. Dumézil, *Mitra-Varuna* and *Destiny of the Warrior*; Clastres, *Society against the State* and *Archeology of Violence*; Deleuze and Guattari, *A Thousand Plateaus*, 390–97.

129. Jones, *Works*, 8:207.

130. Rancière, *Politics of Literature*, 16.

131. Ibid., 18.

132. Ahlwardt, *Über Poesie und Poetik*, 1–2 (quoted in Jaroslav Stetkevych, *Arabic Poetry*, 38).

133. Jaroslav Stetkevych, *Arabic Poetry*, 38.

134. Nöldeke, *Beiträge*, xxiv.

135. Jaroslav Stetkevych, *Arabic Poetry*, 37, 40–41. The claims that follow draw on the same volume, 38–39.

136. Wellhausen, *Skizzen und Vorarbeiten*, 105 (quoted in Jaroslav Stetkevych, *Arabic Poetry*, 45).

137. Melas, *All the Difference*, 7, 14; Guillory, "Literary Study," 29–37; Graff, *Professing Literature*, 55–144.

138. Suzanne Stetkevych, *Mantle Odes*, 6.

139. Mufti, "Orientalism," 486.

140. De Certeau, *Writing of History*, 36–37. That claim that follows draws on the same volume, 38, 40, 48.

141. Tuetey, *Classical Arabic Poetry*, 6, 20.

142. Arberry, *Seven Odes*, 209.

143. Suzanne Stetkevych, *Mantle Odes*, 14. The claim that ends this paragraph draws on Suzanne Stetkevych, *Mute Immortals Speak*, 18, 19, 24.

144. Arberry, *Seven Odes*, 142.

145. Suzanne Stetkevych, *Mute Immortals*, 20, 22, 23. The claims that follow draw on the same volume, 18.

146. Arberry, *Seven Odes*, 61 (the *mu'allaqa* of Imr Al-Qais, "The Wandering King").

147. Suzanne Stetkevych, *Mute Immortals*, 26, and *Mantle Odes*, 23–24. The claims that follow draw on the former volume, 22–23, 26; Irwin, *Night and Horses*, 6.

148. Arberry, *Seven Odes*, 83 (the *mu'allaqa* of Tarafa, "Whom the Gods Loved?").

149. Suzanne Stetkevych, *Mute Immortals*, 23.

150. Arberry, *Seven Odes*, 145; O'Grady, *Golden Odes*, 32.

151. Arberry, *Seven Odes*, 86.

152. Ibid., 143.

153. Badawi, "Abbasid Poetry," 147, 149.

154. Bamyeh, *Social Origins*, 4, 8, 65.

155. Ibid., 28.

156. Ibid., xii.

157. Suzanne Stetkyvech, *Mute Immortals*, xii. The claims that follow draw on Arberry, *Seven Odes*, 231; Suzanne Stetkevych, *Mantle Odes*, 30.

158. Hallaq, *Origins*, 17; see also 4.

159. Ibid., 12, 14; Irwin, *Night and Horses*, 6; Tuetey, *Classical Arabic Poetry*, 7; Suzanne Stetkevych, *Mantle Odes*, 3.

160. Suzanne Stetkevych, *Mantle Odes*, 33. See also Abu-Lughod, *Veiled Sentiments*, 28–29.

161. Suzanne Stekevych, *Mantle Odes*, 18–19; Mauss, *Gift*, 1.

162. Abu-Lughod, *Veiled Sentiments*, xvii, 26, 32, 35, 235. The claims that follow draw on the same volume, xxi, xxvi, 30–31.

163. Ibid., 27, 173, 180. The claims that follow draw on the same volume, 27, 28, 31, 171, 173, 174, 175, 177, 180, 236. The vitality of poetry within everyday Arab life has repeatedly been invoked by ethnography, both old and new. Abu-Lughod cites Granqvist, *Marriage Conditions*; Musil, *Manners and Customs*; Evans-Pritchard, *Sanusi of Cyrenaica*; Meeker, *Literature and Violence*; Caton, "Tribal Poetry." See also Sowayan, *Nabati Poetry*; Finnegan, *Oral Poetry*; Zwettler, *Oral Tradition*; Caton, *"Peaks of Yemen"*; Gilsenan, *Lords*; Reynolds, *Heroic Poets*; Shryock, *Nationalism*; Slyomovics, *Merchant of Art*.

164. Abu-Lughod, *Veiled Sentiments*, 33, 46, 238. The claims that follow draw on the same volume, 103, 236.

165. Ibid., 270. The claims that follow draw on the same volume, 34, 269, 270.

166. Ibid., 69, 179, 180, 235, 239.

167. Badiou, *Handbook*, 51, 54.

168. Ibid., 52, 53, 54.

169. Badiou, *Ethics*, 102, 103. The claims that follows draw on the same volume, 143.

170. Badiou, *Handbook*, 55, 50.

171. Ibid., 54.

172. Ibid., 51, 54.

173. Ibid., 54. See also Badiou, *Conditions*, 33–90.

174. Badiou, *Handbook*, 56.

175. Badiou, *Metapolitics*, 76.

176. Hobsbawm and Ranger, *The Invention of Tradition*.

177. Bayly, *Indian Society*, 150; see also 156, 158.

178. O'Hanlon and Washbrook, "Histories in Transition," 115.

179. Ibid., 116.

180. Ibid., 116, 125.

181. Inden, *Imagining India*, 4, 5.

182. Bhattacharyya-Panda, *Appropriation and Invention*, 5, 6 (my emphasis).

Third Stratum

1. Kaiwar, "Aryan Model," 13.

2. See Said, *Orientalism*, 136–37.

3. Schwab, *Oriental Renaissance*, 4.

4. Aarsleff, *Study of Language*, 148.

5. Agamben, *Infancy and History*, 149.

6. Kaiwar, "Aryan Model," 15.

7. Benveniste, *Indo-European Language*, 379, 399, 407, 416.

8. Anderson, *Imagined Communities*, 70.

9. Gramsci, *Selections*, 226.

10. Geertz, *Interpretation of Cultures*, 260, 262, 268, 271, 272, 276. See the discussions of Gramsci and Geertz in Pollock, *Language of the Gods*, 505–8.

11. Ranajit Guha, *Dominance without Hegemony*, 190.

12. Dirks, *Castes of Mind*, 14.

13. Foucault, "Nietzsche, Genealogy, History," 78.

14. Olivelle, "Introduction," xxii–xxiii, xxiii.

15. Colebrooke, *Digest of Hindu Law* (1874), 1:xx, xxi.

16. Jones, *Letters*, 2:664, 680, 687, 706, 712–13, 718, 727, 748, 784, 792; Cannon and Pandey, "Sir William Jones Revisited," 528; Rocher, "Weaving Knowledge," 54–60.

17. Jones, *Letters*, 2:795 (to the first Marquis of Cornwallis, 19 March 1788). See also Jones, *Works*, 7:3–6 ("Charge to the Grand Jury, at Calcutta," 4 December 1783), 20 ("Charge to the Grand Jury, at Calcutta," 10 June 1785).

18. Doniger, *Hindus*, 596; Majeed, *Ungoverned Imaginings*, 16.

19. Jones, *Sacontalá* and "Gítagóvinda." See also *Hitópadésa of Vishnusarman*, in Jones, *Works*, 13:1–210. He originally translated this work, a collection of medieval Sanskrit beast fables on statecraft, in 1786: see Cannon and Pandey, "Sir William Jones Revisited," 529.

20. Wilkins, *Bhagvat-Geeta* and *Heetopades*.

21. Aarsleff, *Study of Language*, 4–5, 33–35, 43, 143.

22. Jones, *Works*, 3:207, 236.

23. Ibid., 3:230.

24. Ibid., 1:338; see also 3:32. For a discussion of Jones's view in this regard, see Aarsleff, *Study of Language*, 87, 124–27.

25. Aarsleff, *Study of Language*, 96; Del Valle, "Language, Politics and History," 3.

26. Müller, *History of Ancient Sanskrit Literature*, 8. See the discussions in Dharwadker, "Orientalism," 176, and Kaiwar and Mazumdar, "Race, Orient, Nation," 269.

27. For the quoted words, see Jones, *Works*, 3:34 (from the "Third Anniversary Discourse" [1786], where he first articulated the Indo-European hypothesis). For the study of cognates, see this discourse, as well as the "Fourth" (1787) and the "Sixth" (1789): Jones, *Works* 3:24–70 and 3:103–36. For discussions, see Cannon, "Introduction," xxxvii–xxxviii, and Aarsleff, *Study of Language*, 157.

28. Aarsleff, *Study of Language*, 152; Del Valle, "Language, Politics, History," 4.

29. Del Valle, "Language," 4.

30. Dharwadker, "Orientalism," 175.

31. Jones, *Works*, 3:203, 28.

32. Schwab, *Oriental Renaissance*, 216. See also Herling, *German Gita*, 123–24.

33. Bopp, *Comparative Grammar* and *Grammaire comparée*; Burnouf, *Le lotus de la bonne loi* (cited by Schwab, *Oriental Renaissance*, 121); Kaiwar, "Aryan Model," 25, 55.

34. Dharwadker, "Orientalism," 175–76.

35. Ibid., 175.

36. Foucault, "Nietzsche, Genealogy, History," 79.

37. Jones, *Institutes of Hindu Law* (1796), iv.

38. Ibid., v, ix.

39. Ibid., viii, x.

40. Rocher, "British Orientalism," 229.

41. Olivelle, "Introduction," xvii. The claims that follow draw on the same source; Dharwadker, "Orientalism," 176–77 (who also cites Müller and Winternitz); Doniger, *Hindus*, 87. See Schwab, *Oriental Renaissance*, 52, for a brief publication and retranslation history of Jones's version.

42. Müller, *History of Ancient Sanskrit Literature*, 3.

43. Winternitz, *History of Indian Literature*, 5–6.

44. Dharwadker, "Orientalism," 175–76 (he takes the idea of philology as "master-science" from the *Athenäum*, 25 June 1892); Said, *Orientalism*, 139 (he takes the second quotation from Renan, *Questions contemporaines*, 170).

45. See Arvidsson, *Aryan Idols*; Leon Poliakov, *Aryan Myth*; Trautmann, *Aryan Debate*; Hutton, *Linguistics and the Third Reich* and *Race and the Third Reich*; Lincoln, *Theorizing Myth*.

46. Aarsleff, *Study of Language*, 152. The claims that follow draw on Kaiwar, "Aryan Model," 15–16, 23, 49.

47. Dirks, *Castes of Mind*, 14, 42; the claims that follow draw on 37–38, 118.

48. Ibid., 118, 122.

49. See Mill, *History of British India* (1820) and *History of British India*, continuation by Wilson (1858).

50. "I believe in the Vedas, the Upanishads, the Puranas, and all that goes by the name of Hindu scripture"; "I believe in the *Varnashrama Dharma*." Gandhi, *Gandhi Reader*, 168 (from an article published in *Young India*, 6 October 1921). See also Joseph Lelyveld, *Great Soul*, 185, and Dirks, *Castes of Mind*, 299.

51. The first two quotation are from Dirks, *Castes of Mind*, 54; the final two from Inden and Marriott, "Interpreting Indian Society," 191 (quoted by Dirks, *Castes of Mind*, 55). See also Marriott and Inden, "Caste Systems."

52. See Savarkar, *Hindutva*, 84–85; Saraswati, *Light of Truth*, 248; Ghose, *Speeches*, 76–80; Tilak, *Orion*, 1 (all cited by Kaiwar, "Aryan Model," 41, 44, 45, 48).

53. Kaiwar, "Aryan Model," 49.

54. Geertz, *Interpretation of Cultures*, 262. The claims that follow draw on the same volume, 290, and Pollock, *Language of the Gods*, 506–8.

55. Pollock, *Language of the Gods*, 507, drawing from Appadurai, *Modernity at Large*, 146.

56. Pollock, "Language of the Gods," 507.

57. On this point, see also Beecroft, "Sanskrit Ecumene," 157, and Pollock, *Language of the Gods*, 541–42, 545, 547–48.

58. Mufti, "Invention," 472, 474–75.

59. Cannon and Pandey, "Sir William Jones Revisited, 535; Thapar, *Śakuntalā*, 199. See also Cannon, "Sir William Jones and the Sakuntala" and "Sir William Jones's Summary of Sakuntala."

60. Jones, *Works*, 9:367, 368, 369, 370.

61. Ibid., 367, 369, 370.

62. Ibid., 366, 367.

63. Bose, "Staging *Abhijñānaśākuntalam*," 40; Miller, "Preface," ix–x; Krishnamoorthy, *Kalidasa*, 11.

64. See Thapar, *Śakuntalā*, 199, and Mahadevan, "Gadamerian Hermeneutics," 103.

65. Jones, *Works*, 3:369; Dharwadker, "Orientalism," 178. See also Mufti, "Invention," 468.

66. Jones, *Works*, 3:367.

67. Trautmann, *Aryans and British India*, 29.

68. Schwab, *Oriental Renaissance*, 51; Cannon and Pandey, "Sir William Jones Revisited," 528; Trautmann, *Aryans and British India*, 29; McGetchin, *Indology*, 57.

69. Mill, *History of British India* (1820), 2:48–53. See the discussion in Viswanathan, *Masks of Conquest*, 121–24.

70. Thapar, "Creating Traditions," 169–70; Mahadevan, "Gadamerian Hermeneutics," 104.

71. Monier-Williams, "Introduction," 221, 223–24.

72. Monier-Williams, *Sakoontala*, vi–vii: "India's most cherished drama [elucidates] and explains the conditions of the millions of Hindus who [are] governed by English laws" (cited by Thapar, *Śakuntalā*, 233).

73. Dharwadker, "Orientalism," 178, referring to Keith, *History of Sanskrit Literature*.

74. Gerow, "Plot Structure," 564 (quoted in Franklin, *Orientalist Jones*, 272).

75. Trautmann, *Aryans and British India*, 29; McGetchin, *Indology*, 57; Cannon, *Oriental Jones*, 165; Mahadevan, "Gadamerian Hermeneutics," 103; Miller, "Preface," x. For early German, French, and Italian retranslations, see Jones, *Sakontala*, trans. Forster (Mainz, 1791); *Sacontala*, trans. Bruguière (Paris, 1803); *Sacontala*, trans. Doria (Darmstadt, 1815), respectively.

76. Schwab, *Oriental Renaissance*, 59; McGetchin, *Indology*, 57, 58, 65, 115, 223.

77. Herder, *Sämmtliche Werke* (1807), 9:226 (quoted by Müller, *History of Ancient Sanskrit Literature*, 5). See also Dharwadker, "Orientalism," 179; Thapar, *Śakuntalā*, 210; Sedlar, *India in the Mind of Germany*, 26.

78. Schwab, *Oriental Renaissance*, 53, 59, 204, 205, 216, 217.

79. The first quotation is cited in McGetchin, *Indology*, 65, as a letter from 15 September 1803; the second ("alles, ja alles ohne Ausnahme seinen Ursprung in Indien hat") from Friedrich Schlegel, *Kritische Ausgabe*, 14:xxxi (also a letter of September 1803) is quoted in Aarsleff, *Study of Language*, 155. See also Said, *Orientalism*, 137, who refers to the claim in Benjamin Constant's *Journal intime* (1804) that "the English who owned the place and the Germans who studied it indefatigably had made India the *fons et origo* of everything"; and Franklin, *European Discovery*, 1:ix–x.

80. Schwab, *Oriental Renaissance*, 57–64.

81. Thapar, *Śakuntalā*, 210.

82. Herder, *Sämtliche Werke* (1967), 24:577; see also 578 (quoted by McGetchin, *Indology*, 61).

83. Goethe, *Werke*, 1:206 (my translation [originally published in the *Deutche Monatschrift* (1791)]). See Franklin, *Orientalist Jones*, 251.

84. Goethe to Antoine-Léonard de Chézy, 9 October 1830 (quoted in A. Leslie Wilson, *Mythical Image*, 69). See Thapar, *Śakuntalā*, 207; Franklin, *Orientalist Jones*, 259.

85. See Tagore, "Sakuntala: Its Inner Meaning," xiv.

86. Thapar, *Śakuntalā*, 211, and Franklin, *Orientalist Jones*, 261, for example, use the former opposition to describe the Romantic project; Miller, "Preface," ix, the latter.

87. Franklin, *European Discovery*, 1:ix–x; Said, *Orientalism*, 137. For the quotation, see Schlegel and Schlegel, *Athenäum*, 3:103; Franklin, *Orientalist Jones*, 261. See also the opening of Friedrich Schlegel, *Über die Sprache und Weisheit*.

88. Jones, *Institutes of Hindu Law* (1796), xv–xvi.

89. Franklin, *Representing India*, 9:x. See also Schwab, *Oriental Renaissance*, 195. The claims that follow draw on the same volume, 121, 206, 207; Thapar, *Śakuntalā*, 210; Kaiwar, "Aryan Model," 25–28; Olender, *Languages of Paradise*, 139.

90. See, for example, Pictet, *Les origines indo-européennes*.

91. Thapar, *Śakuntalā*, 235, 257–58.

92. Doniger, *Hindus*, 598; Mufti, "Invention," 474. The claims that follow draw on the latter source, 472; Kaiwar, "Aryan Model," 14; Thapar, *Śakuntalā*, 234–36, 255–57; Mahadevan, "Gadamerian Hermeneutics," 100; Sengupta and Tandon, "Introduction," 13. See also Dalmia, *Nationalisation of Hindu Traditions*, and Sawhney, *Modernity of Sanskrit*, 21–70, 51.

93. Kālidāsa, *Abhijñānaśākuntalam*, ed. M. R. Kale, 49.

94. Tagore, "Sakuntala: Its Inner Meaning," xvi.

95. Thapar, *Śakuntalā*, 259.

96. Sawhney, "Who Is Kalidasa?," 297.

97. Elst, "Manu as a Weapon," 561; Doniger, "Introduction," xix.

98. Nietzsche, *Twilight of the Idols*, 68.

99. Nietzsche, *Anti-Christ*, 56.

100. Ibid.

101. Ibid., 58. On *Manu*, see also Nietzsche, *Will to Power*, 91–92, 382.

102. Olivelle, "Introduction," xxix, xxviii, xxxix. The claims that follow draw on the same volume, xvi, xlii, and Doniger, "Introduction," xviii.

103. Olivelle, "Introduction," x–xl, xli. The claims that follow draw on Parry, "Brahmanical Tradition," 208; Doniger, "Introduction," xvii, xviii, xlvii, lvii, and *Hindus*, 105–6.

104. Doniger, "Introduction," lx, lxi. The claims that follow draw on the same essay, lvii–lviii; Bhattacharyya-Panda, *Appropriation and Invention*, 19, 24, 97, 206–7; Derrett, *Essays*, 174; Parry, "Brahmanical Tradition," 212; Olivelle, "Introduction," xviii, xxxvii, lvii. See also Lingat, *Classical Law*.

105. Mufti, "Invention," 470.

106. Parry, "Brahmanical Tradition," 213.

107. Doniger, *Hindus*, 596.

108. Hiltebeitel, *Dharma*, 54–55. The claims that follow draw on the same volume, 54–57.

109. Doniger, "Introduction," xxx. The claims that follow draw on the same volume, xxiii, xxvii, xxviii; Doniger, *Hindus*, 108; Parry, "Brahmanical Tradition," 209. See also Heesterman, *Inner Conflict*, and Brian Smith, "Eaters, Food and Social Hierarchy."

110. Parry, "Brahmanical Tradition," 210.

111. Gadgil and Guha, *Fissured Land*, 78. The claims that follow draw on the same volume, 79; Sengupta and Purkayastha, "When the King," 151, 156–57; Doniger, *Hindus*, 266; Thapar, *Śakuntalā*, 49; Olivelle, "Semantic History"; Hiltebeitel, *Dharma*, 36.

112. John Smith, *Mahābhārata*, 82–83.

113. Kosambi, "Basis of Ancient Indian History," 40.

114. Doniger, "Introduction," xxxii and xxxiii, cites Zimmerman, *Jungle*, 1–2. The claims that follow draw on Doniger, *Hindus*, 186, and Gadgil and Guha, *Fissured Land*, 81, 88.

115. Gadgil and Guha, *Fissured Land*, 88. The claims that follow draw on Doniger, "Introduction," xxxv; Olivelle, "Introduction," xxv, xlii, xliv, xlv; Hiltebeitel, *Dharma*, 51.

116. Olivelle, "Introduction," xliii; Hiltebeitel, *Dharma*, 191. The claims that follow draw on the latter volume, 9, 29, 34, 36, 40, 42–47, 49; Gadgil and Guha, *Fissured Land*, 85; Padel and Das, *Out of This Earth*, 55, which cites Thapar, *Aśoka*, 255–57.

117. Hiltebeitel, *Dharma*, 6. The claims that follow draw on the same volume, 6, 30; Doniger, *Hindus*, 186, and "Introduction," xxxv, xxxvi, xlii–xliii, li; Dumont, *Homo Hierarchicus*, 70; Thapar, "Forests and Settlements," 38.

118. Sengupta and Tandon, "Introduction," 2; Chakravarti, "A Royal Hunt," 238, 239; Hiltebeitel, *Dharma*, 11, 379. The claims that follow draw on the latter volume, 18–19; Doniger, *Hindus*, 136–38, 220; Thapar, *Śakuntalā*, 7, 8; Sengupta and Purkayastha, "When the King," 156; Sengupta and Tandon, "Introduction," 4. See also Kumkum Roy, *Emergence of Monarchy*.

119. Sengupta and Purkayastha, "When the King," 149; Doniger, *Hindus*, 376. The claims that follow draw on the latter source, 138, 371, 372, 374, 383.

120. Thapar, *Śakuntalā*, 45, 48–49.

121. Jones, *Sacontalá* (1995), 240, 255, 257, 258, 259; Kālidāsa, *Abhijnāna Śākuntalam*, 260, and *Recognition of Śakuntalā*, 85; Sengupta and Tandon, "Introduction," 11.

122. Kālidāsa, *Abhijnānaśākuntalam*, 237, and *Recognition of Śakuntalā*, 64.

123. Doniger, *Hindus*, 376.

124. Sengupta and Tandon, "Introduction," 11; Sengupta and Purkayastha, "When the King," 161, 165–66; Thapar, *Śakuntalā*, 48.

125. Kālidāsa, *Recognition of Śakuntalā*, 27, and *Abhijnānaśākuntalam*, 194.

126. Kālidāsa, *Recognition of Śakuntalā*, 9, and *Abhijnānaśākuntalam*, 174; Sengupta and Purkayastha, "When the King," 150.

127. Kālidāsa, *Abhijnāna Śākuntalam*, 272, and *Recognition of Śakuntalā*, 96; Sengupta and Tandon, "Introduction," 7.

128. Kālidāsa, *Abhijnāna Śākuntalam*, 281, and *Recognition of Śakuntalā*, 105.

129. Doniger, *Hindus*, 4, 100–101, 375, 382; Parry, "Brahmanical Tradition," 203. The claim that follows draws on Bose, "Staging *Abhijñānaśākuntalam*," 43, 44, 46.

130. Sengupta and Tandon, "Introduction," 3. The claim about actresses draws on Doniger, *Hindus*, 376, and Kuritz, *Making of Theatre History*, 73, 74.

131. Kālidāsa, *Recognition of Śakuntalā*, 61, and *Abhijnāna Śākuntalam*, 235; Jones, *Sacontalá* (1995), 266.

132. Chakravarti, "Royal Hunt," 248, 249, 251.

133. Ibid., 252, drawing on Insler, "Shattered Head Split."

134. Jones, *Sacontalá* (1995), 269; Kālidāsa, *Abhijnāna Śākuntalam*, 240, and *Recognition of Śakuntalā*, 66.

135. Doniger, *Hindus*, 2, 5.

136. Dumézil, *Mitra-Varuna*, 17, 22, 24, 27, 34, 35.

137. Deleuze and Guattari, *Anti-Oedipus*, 199.

138. Doniger, *Hindus*, 107; Dumézil, *Mitra-Varuna*, 30, 44

139. Dumézil, *Mitra-Varuna*, 27, 45.

140. Ibid., 45, 38.

141. Lincoln, *Theorizing Myth*, 260.

142. Deleuze and Guattari, *A Thousand Plateaus*, 388.

143. Ibid., 387; Dumézil, *Mitra-Varuna*, 73.

144. Deleuze and Guattari, *A Thousand Plateaus*, 388, 389.

145. Ibid., 415; see also 391.

146. Kālidāsa, *Abhijñāna Śākuntalam*, 175, and *Recognition of Śakuntalā*, 10; Sengupta and Purkayastha, "When the King," 156.

147. See Thapar, *Śakuntalā*, 36; Chakaravarti, "Royal Hunt," 240, 242. The claim that follows draws on Hopkins, *Epic Mythology*, 46. See also Kosambi, "Autochthonous Element"; Thapar, *Early India*; Pollock, "Ramayana."

148. Kālidāsa, *Abhijñāna Śākuntalam*, 266–67 ("titans"), and *Recognition of Śakuntalā*, 90–91 ("demons"); Wilmot, *Mahābhārata Book Two*, 101, 213, 269, 301; Johnson, *Mahābhārata Book Three*, 39, 79; Sengupta and Purkayastha, "When the King," 152, 154, 155. See also Thapar, "Sacrifice, Surplus and the Soul."

149. Freeman, "Gods, Groves," 295–96; Kent, *Sacred Groves*, 7. The quoted words in the following sentence are from Baviskar, "Indian Indigeneities," 275. The claims that follow draw on the same essay, 275, 278, 282, 291; Padel and Das, *Out of This Earth*, 591; Freeman, "Gods, Groves," 278, 285. See also Povinelli, *Cunning of Recognition*; Redford, "Ecologically Noble Savage"; Sumit Guha, *Environment and Ethnicity*; Prasad, *Against Ecological Romanticism*; Sundar, *Subalterns and Sovereigns*; Ghurye, *Scheduled Tribes*; Skaria, *Hybrid Histories*; Béteille, "Concept of Tribe" and "Idea of Indigenous People."

150. Quoted in Baviskar, "Indian Indigeneities," 287.

151. Gadgil and Vartak, "Sacred Groves," 318; Chandran and Hughes, "Sacred Groves and Conservation," 180–82; Kent, *Sacred Groves*, 2, 3; Gajula, "Sacred Grove Lore," 21–22. The claims that follow draw on these sources as well as Chandran and Hughes, "Sacred Groves of South India," 414.

152. Chandran and Hughes, "Sacred Groves and Conservation," 172, 173, 176, 178, 180; Chandran and Hughes, "Sacred Groves of South India," 416, 421; Kent, *Sacred Groves*, 7; Gadgil and Vartak, "Sacred Groves," 315, 317. The claims that follow draw on these sources; Padel and Das, *Out of This Earth*, 594; Gadgil and Guha, *Fissured Land*, 78–79, 81, 82.

153. Doniger, *Hindus*, 87. The claims in the following paragraph draw on the same volume, 88, 89.

154. Ibid., 88.

155. Olivelle, *Manu's Code of Law*, 7, 19; Hiltebeitel, *Dharma*, 13–14.

Conclusion

1. Nkrumah, *Neo-colonialism*, is the earliest example of such an effort. See the discussion in Chatterjee, *Black Hole of Empire*, 336, 339–40.

2. We could place Baran and Sweezy, *Monopoly Capital*; Kemp, *Theories of Imperialism*; and Magdoff, *Age of Imperialism* and *Imperialism* in the former camp. They extend the earlier arguments of Hilferding, *Finance Capital*, and Lenin, *Imperialism*. Frank, *Capitalism and Underdevelopment*, and Amin, *Imperialism and Unequal Development*, are in the latter camp. Most of these works are cited and discussed by Chatterjee, *Black Hole*, 339.

3. Chatterjee, *Black Hole*, 194; see also 337; Schmitt, *Politische Theologie*, 13. Schmitt had also already made Chatterjee's argument for him: see Schmitt, *Roman Catholicism*, 30. See also Schmitt, *Nomos of the Earth*, 227.

4. Chatterjee, *Black Hole*, 194; see also xi, 195, 212, 214, 216, 345.

5. Ibid., 336, 338, 341, 344; the quotation is from Hussain, *Jurisprudence of Emergency*, 143.

6. Chatterjee, *Black Hole*, 343.

7. Mbembe, *On the Postcolony*, 28.

8. Ibid, 35.

9. Ibid., 28.

10. Ibid., 26.

11. The first quotation is from Raman, "Law," the second from Hussain, *Jurisprudence of Emergency*, 134.

12. Raman, "Law." Raman here tacitly alludes to Agamben's claim that "the immediately biopolitical significance of the state of exception as the original structure in which law encompasses living beings by means of its own suspension emerges clearly in the 'military order'" (Agamben, *State of Exception*, 3).

13. Agamben, *State of Exception*, 7. See also Morton, *States of Emergency*.

14. Agamben, *State of Exception*, 5.

15. Schmitt, *Politische Theologie*, 13 (Souverän ist, wer über den Ausnahmezustand entscheidet).

16. Schmitt, *Nomos of the Earth*, 44–48, 67, 70, 73, 325, 326, 342.

17. Cohn, *Colonialism and Its Forms of Knowledge*, 19.

18. Ibid.

19. Mignolo, *Darker Side*, 82, 86, 96.

20. Asad, *Formations of the Secular*, 251.

21. Ibid., 249, 250.

22. De Certeau, *Writing of History*, 6–7.

23. Asad, *Formations of the Secular*, 251; de Certeau, *Writing of History*, 3–4, 6, 14, 47.

24. Asad, *Formations of the Secular*, 222.

25. De Certeau, *Writing of History*, 4.

26. Ibid.

27. Ibid.

28. Asad, *Formations of the Secular*, 222.

29. Chakrabarty, "Time of History," 47. This essay became the third chapter of Chakrabarty, *Provincializing Europe*, 72–96.

30. Chakrabarty, "Time of History," 46, 47.

31. Ibid., 43, 47, 48.

32. Mignolo, *Darker Side*, 8, 11; see also 9 and 331.

33. Volosinov, *Marxism and the Philosophy of Language*, 74.

34. Arrighi, *Long Twentieth Century*.

35. Rancière, *Dissensus*, 27–28.

36. Ibid., 15, 27, 40, 41, 68, 78, 150; Žižek, *Ticklish Subject*, 187–88, which cites Rancière, *La mésentente*.

37. Rancière, *Dissensus*, 16.

38. Ibid., 31.

39. Ibid., 31, 34

40. Vernant and Vidal-Naquet, *Myth and Tragedy*, 30–31 (my emphasis).

41. Deleuze's argument draws on the classical philologist Laroche, who interpreted the etymology of *nomos* differently from Schmitt: Deleuze, *Difference and Repetition*, 37, 309; Laroche, *Histoire de la racine* NEM-, 264. Deleuze and Guattari, *A Thousand Plateaus*, 530–46, 621, returns to and elaborates this argument. On the relevance of Indo-European philology to this argument, see the same volume, 21–22. For other disagreements with Schmitt in this regard, see Ostwald, *Nomos*, 155–60, and Wood, *Citizens to Lords*, 36.

42. Benjamin, *Selected Writings*, 4:392. Benjamin might have carried this essay in his valise as he crossed the Pyrénées from Vichy France, the "new manuscript" he considered "more important" than his own life. See Buck-Morss, *Dialectics of Seeing*, 332, 334; Benjamin, *Gesammelte Schriften*, 5:1191–92; Tiedemann, "Historical Materialism."

43. See, for example, Agamben, *State of Exception*, 3, 4, 11.

44. Schmitt, Benjamin, and Rancière all overturn, in this way, the Enlightenment concept of the political: see Bates, *States of War*, 12, 18, 19, which argues that Enlightenment political thought was concerned not just with the elaboration of the constitutional state but, more importantly, with the relationship between an otherwise autonomous political realm and the rule of law.

45. Agamben, *State of Exception*, 48.

46. Benjamin, *Selected Writings*, 1:246, 249–52. See Agamben, *State of Exception*, 53, 59.

47. Benjamin, *Selected Writings*, 4:406, 407.

48. Ibid., 4:391–92, and Benjamin, *Gesammelte Schriften*, 1:696.

49. Nietzsche, *Untimely Meditations*, 104, 114. On Nietzsche and Benjamin's common ground in these regards, see McFarland, *Constellation*, 66–74, 126–28, 145–55.

50. Benjamin, *Selected Writings*, 4:405. For a discussion, see Heller-Roazen, "Editor's Introduction," 1.

51. Nietzsche, *Untimely Meditations*, 105, 67.

52. Benjamin, *Selected Writings*, 4:390–91.

53. See Agamben, *State of Exception*, 60, and *Sacrament of Language*, 9, 11.

BIBLIOGRAPHY

Aarsleff, Hans. *The Study of Language in England, 1780–1860*. Princeton, NJ: Princeton University Press, 1967.

Abou El Fadl, Khalid. "The Shari'ah." In *The Oxford Handbook of Islam and Politics*, edited by John Esposito and Emad El-Din Shahin, 7–26. Oxford: Oxford University Press, 2013.

Abrams, M. H. *The Mirror and the Lamp: Romantic Theory and the Critical Tradition*. Oxford: Oxford University Press, 1953.

Abu-Lughod, Lila. *Veiled Sentiments: Honor and Poetry in a Bedouin Society*. Berkeley: University of California Press, 1999.

Agamben, Giorgio. *The Highest Poverty: Monastic Rules and the Form-of-Life*. Stanford, CA: Stanford University Press, 2013.

———. *Homo Sacer: Sovereign Power and Bare Life*. Stanford, CA: Stanford University Press, 1998.

———. *Infancy and History: On the Destruction of Experience*. London: Verso, 1993.

———. *Infanzia e storia: Distruzione dell'esperienza e origine della storia*. Turin: Einaudi, 2001.

———. *The Man without Content*. Stanford, CA: Stanford University Press, 1999.

———. *Pilate and Jesus*. Stanford, CA: Stanford University Press, 2015.

———. *The Sacrament of Language: An Archaeology of the Oath*. Stanford, CA: Stanford University Press, 2010.

———. *State of Exception*. Chicago: University of Chicago Press, 2005.

———. *The Use of Bodies*. Stanford, CA: Stanford University Press, 2016.

Ahlwardt, Wilhelm. *Über Poesie und Poetik der Araber*. Gotha: F. A. Perthes, 1856.

Ahmad, Aziz. *Islamic Modernism in India and Pakistan, 1857–1964.* London: Oxford University Press, 1967.

Ahmed, Rafiuddin. *The Bengal Muslims 1871–1906: A Quest for Identity.* Delhi: Oxford University Press, 1982.

Ahmed, Shahab. *What Is Islam? The Importance of Being Islamic.* Princeton, NJ: Princeton University Press, 2016.

Ahmed, Siraj. "Orientalism and the Permanent Fix of War." In *The Postcolonial Enlightenment: Eighteenth-Century Colonialism and Postcolonial Theory*, edited by Daniel Carey and Lynn Festa, 167–205. Oxford: Oxford University Press, 2009.

———. *The Stillbirth of Capital: Enlightenment Writing and Colonial India.* Stanford, CA: Stanford University Press, 2012.

Alam, Muzaffer. "The Pursuit of Persian: Language in Mughal Politics." *Modern Asian Studies* 32.2 (May 1998): 317–49.

Alam, Muzaffar, and Sanjay Subrahmanyam. *Indo-Persian Travels in the Age of Discoveries, 1400–1800.* Cambridge: Cambridge University Press, 2007.

Ali, Aga Shahid. Introduction to *Ravishing Disunities: Real Ghazals in English*, edited by Aga Shahid Ali, 1–14. Middletown, CT: Wesleyan University Press.

Almond, Ian. *History of Islam in German Thought: From Leibniz to Nietzsche.* London: Routledge, 2010.

———. *The New Orientalists: Postmodern Representations of Islam from Foucault to Baudrillard.* London: I. B. Tauris, 2007.

Althusser, Louis, and Étienne Balibar. *Reading Capital.* London: New Left Books, 1970.

Amin, Samir. *Imperialism and Unequal Development.* New York: Monthly Review Press, 1977.

Anderson, Benedict. *Imagined Communities: Reflections on the Origin and Spread of Nationalism.* London: Verso, 1991.

Anderson, Michael. "Islamic Law and the Colonial Encounter in British India." In *Institutions and Ideologies: A SOAS South Asia Reader*, edited by David Arnold and Peter Robb, 165–85. Richmond, UK: Curzon Press, 1993.

———. "Legal Scholarship and the Politics of Islam in British India." In *Perspectives on Islamic Law, Justice, and Society*, edited by Ravindra Khare, 65–91. Oxford, UK: Rowman and Littlefield, 1999.

Anushiravani, Alireza, and Laleh Atashi. "Cultural Translation: A Critical Analysis of William Jones's Translation of Hafez." *Persian Literary Studies Journal* 1.1 (Autumn–Winter 2012): 41–58.

Appadurai, Arjun. *Modernity at Large: Cultural Dimensions of Globalization.* Minneapolis: University of Minnesota Press, 1996.

Apter, Emily. *The Translation Zone: A New Comparative Literature.* Princeton, NJ: Princeton University Press, 2006.

Arac, Jonathan. "Anglo-Globalism?" *New Left Review* 16 (July–August 2002): 35–45.

Arberry, A. J. *Asiatic Jones: The Life and Influence of Sir William Jones (1746–1794)*. New York: Longmans, Green, 1946.

———. *British Contributions to Persian Studies*. London: Longmans, Green, 1942.

———. "Orient Pearls at Random Strung." *BSOAS* 11.4 (1946): 699–712.

———. *The Seven Odes: The First Chapter in Arabic Literature*. London: Allen and Unwin, 1957.

Arendt, Hannah. *On Revolution*. New York: Penguin, 1990.

———. *The Origins of Totalitarianism*. New York: Harcourt Brace, 1973.

Arrighi, Giovanni. *The Long Twentieth Century: Money, Power, and the Origins of Our Times*. London: Verso, 1994.

Arvidsson, Stefan. *Aryan Idols: The Indo-European Mythology as Science and Ideology*. Chicago: University of Chicago Press, 2006.

Asad, Talal. *Formations of the Secular: Christianity, Islam, Modernity*. Stanford, CA: Stanford University Press, 2003.

Asani, Ali. "South Asian Literatures and the Qur'ān." In *Encyclopaedia of the Qur'ān*, edited by Jane Dammen McAuliffe, 5:93–98. Leiden: E. J. Brill, 2005.

Auerbach, Erich. "Epilegomena zu *Mimesis*." *Romanische Forschungen* 65, nos. 1/2 (1953): 1–18.

———. *Gesammelte Aufsätze zur romanischen Philologie*. Munich: Francke, 1967.

———. *Introduction aux études de philologie romane*. Frankfurt am Main: Vittorio Klostermann, 1949.

———. *Literary Language and Its Public in Late Latin Antiquity and in the Middle Ages*. Princeton, NJ: Princeton University Press, 1965.

———. *Mimesis: The Representation of Reality in Western Literature*. Princeton, NJ: Princeton University Press, 2003.

———. "Philology and *Weltliteratur*." *Centennial Review* 13.1 (Winter 1969): 1–17.

———. *Scenes from the Drama of European Literature: Six Essays*. Minneapolis: University of Minnesota Press, 1984.

Austin, J. L. *How to Do Things with Words*. Cambridge, MA: Harvard University Press, 1975.

Avery, Peter, trans., *The Collected Lyrics of Háfiz of Shíráz*. Cambridge, UK: Archetype, 2007.

Avery, Peter, and John Heath-Stubbs, trans. *Hafiz of Shiraz: Thirty Poems*. London: John Murray, 1952.

Badawi, M. M. "Abbasid Poetry and Its Antecedents." In *Abbasid Belles-Lettres*, edited by Julia Ashtiany, T. M. Johnstone, J. D. Latham, R. B. Serjeant, and G. Rex Smith, 146–66. Cambridge: Cambridge University Press, 1990.

Badiou, Alain. *Conditions*. London: Continuum, 2008.

———. *Ethics: An Essay on the Understanding of Evil*. London: Verso, 2001.

———. *Handbook of Inaesthetics*. Stanford, CA: Stanford University Press, 2004.

———. *Metapolitics*. London: Verso, 2005.

Baillie, Neil, trans. *A Digest of Moohummudan Law*. London: Smith, Elder, 1865.

Bal, Mieke. "Virginity: Toward a Feminist Philology." *Dispositio: Revista hispánica de semiótica literaria* 12 (1987): 30–82.

Balakrishnan, Gopal. *The Enemy: An Intellectual Portrait of Carl Schmitt*. London: Verso, 2000.

Balfour, Francis. *Inshā-yi Harkaran: The Forms of Herkern*. Calcutta: Charles Wilkins, 1781.

Ballantyne, Tony. *Orientalism and Race: Aryanism in the British Empire*. New York: Palgrave, 2002.

Bamyeh, Mohammed. *The Social Origins of Islam: Mind, Economy, Discourse*. Minneapolis: University of Minnesota Press, 1999.

Baran, Paul, and Paul Sweezy. *Monopoly Capital*. New York: Monthly Review Press, 1966.

Bashiri, Iraj. "Hafiz and the Sufic Ghazal." *Studies in Islam* (January 1979): 35–67.

———. "'Hafiz' Shirazi Turk': A Structuralist's Point of View." *Muslim World* 69 (1979): 178–97, 248–68.

Bates, David. *States of War: The Enlightenment Origins of the Political*. New York: Columbia University Press, 2011.

Bauer, Thomas, and Angelika Neuwirth, eds. *Ghazal as World Literature I: Transformations of a Literary Genre*. Würzburg: Ergon Verlag, 2005.

Baviskar, Amita. "Indian Indigeneities: Adivasi Engagements with Hindu Nationalism in India." In *Indigenous Experience Today*, edited by Marisol de la Cadena and Orin Starn, 275–303. New York: Berg, 2007.

Baxi, Upendra. "'The State's Emissary': The Place of Law in Subaltern Studies." In *Subaltern Studies VII*, edited by Partha Chatterjee and Gyanendra Pandey, 247–64. Delhi: Oxford University Press, 1992.

Bayly, C. A. *Indian Society and the Making of the British Empire*. Cambridge: Cambridge University Press, 1988.

Beecroft, Alexander. "The Sanskrit Ecumene." *New Left Review* 72 (November–December 2011): 153–60.

Bell, Gertrude, trans. *Poems from the Divan of Hafiz*. London: William Heinemann, 1897.

Benjamin, Walter. *Gesammelte Schriften*. 7 vols. Frankfurt am Main: Suhrkamp, 1974–89.

———. *Reflections*. New York: Schocken Books, 1986.

———. *Selected Writings*. Vol. 1, *1913–1926*. Cambridge, MA: Harvard University Press, 1996.

———. *Selected Writings*. Vol. 4, *1938–1940*. Cambridge, MA: Harvard University Press, 2003.

———. "The Translator's Task." *TTR: traduction, terminologie, redaction* 10.2 (1997): 151–65.

Benton, Lauren. *Law and Colonial Cultures: Legal Regimes in World History, 1400–1900*. Cambridge: Cambridge University Press, 2002.

Benveniste, Émile. *Indo-European Language and Society*. Coral Gables, FL: University of Miami Press, 1973.

Berg, Herbert. "Polysemy in the *Qur'ān*." In *Encyclopaedia of the Qur'ān*, edited by Jane Dammen McAuliffe, 4:155–58. Leiden: E. J. Brill, 2004.

Berkey, Jonathan. *The Formation of Islam: Religion and Society in the Near East, 600–1800*. Cambridge: Cambridge University Press, 2003.

———. *The Transmission of Knowledge in Medieval Cairo: A Social History of Islamic Education*. Princeton, NJ: Princeton University Press, 1992.

Bernal, Martin. *Black Athena: The Afroasiatic Roots of Classical Civilization*. Vol. 1, *The Fabrication of Ancient Greece 1785–1985*. New Brunswick, NJ: Rutgers University Press, 1987.

Béteille, André. "The Concept of Tribe with Special Reference to India." *European Journal of Sociology* 27.2 (1986): 297–318.

———. "The Idea of Indigenous People." *Current Anthropology* 39.2 (April 1998): 187–92.

Bhattacharyya-Panda, Nandini. *Appropriation and Invention of Tradition: The East India Company and Hindu Law in Early Colonial Bengal*. New Delhi: Oxford University Press, 2008.

Black, Joseph, Leonard Conolly, Kate Flint, Isobel Grundy, Don LePan, Roy Liuzza, Jerome McGann, Anne Lake Prescott, Barry Qualls, and Claire Waters, eds. *The Broadview Anthology of British Literature*. Vol. 4, *The Age of Romanticism*. Toronto: Broadview Press, 2010.

Bly, Robert, and Leonard Lewisohn, trans. *The Angels Knocking on the Tavern Door: Thirty Poems of Hafez*. New York: Harper, 2008.

Bopp, Franz. *A Comparative Grammar of Sanskrit, Zend, Greek, Latin, Lithuanian, Gothic, German, and Slavonic Languages*. 3 vols. London: Madden and Malcolm, 1845–53.

———. *Grammaire comparée des langues indo-européennes*. 5 vols. Paris: Imprimerie impériale, 1866–74.

Bose, Mandakranta. "Staging *Abhijñānaśākuntalam*." In *Revisiting Abhijñānaśākuntalam: Love, Lineage and Language in Kālidāsa's Nāṭaka*, edited by Saswati Sengupta and Deepika Tandon, 38–53. New Delhi: Orient BlackSwan, 2011.

Boyce, Mary, "A Novel Interpretation of Hafiz." *BSOAS* 15.2 (1953): 279–88.

Bremer, Jan. *Greek Religion*. Cambridge: Cambridge University Press, 2006.

Brennan, Timothy. *Borrowed Light: Vico, Hegel, and the Colonies*. Stanford, CA: Stanford University Press, 2014.

———. *Wars of Position: The Cultural Politics of Left and Right*. New York: Columbia University Press, 2006.

Brewer, John, and John Styles. *An Ungovernable People: The English and Their Law in the Seventeenth and Eighteenth Centuries*. London: Hutchinson, 1980.

Brown, Nathan. "Shari'a and State in the Modern Middle East." *International Journal of Middle East Studies* 29.3 (1997): 359–76.

Buck-Morss, Susan. *The Dialectics of Seeing: Walter Benjamin and the Arcades Project*. Cambridge, MA: MIT Press, 1989.

Burke, Edmund. *A Philosophical Enquiry into the Origin of Our Ideas of the Sublime and Beautiful*. London: Routledge and Kegan Paul, 1958.

Burnouf, Eugène. *Le lotus de la bonne loi*. Paris: L'Imprimerie nationale, 1852.

Butler, Judith. *Excitable Speech: The Politics of the Performative*. London: Routledge, 1997.

Campbell, Lyle. "The History of Linguistics." In *The Handbook of Linguistics*, edited by Mark Aronoff and Janie Rees-Miller, 81–104. Malden, MA: Blackwell, 2003.

Cannon, Garland. Introduction to *The Collected Works of Sir William Jones*, by William Jones, 1:xiii–lxi. Edited by Garland Cannon. New York: New York University Press, 1993.

———. *The Life and Mind of Oriental Jones*. Cambridge: Cambridge University Press, 1990.

———. *Oriental Jones: A Biography of Sir William Jones (1746–1794)*. London: Asia Publishing House, 1964.

———. "Sir William Jones and the Sakuntala." *Journal of the American Oriental Society* 73.4 (October/December 1953): 198–202.

———. "Sir William Jones, Persian, Sanskrit, and the Asiatic Society." *Historie Épistémologie Langage* 6.2 (1984): 83–94.

———. "Sir William Jones's Persian Linguistics." *Journal of the American Oriental Society* 78.4 (October/December 1958): 262–73.

———. "Sir William Jones's Summary of Sakuntala." *Journal of the American Oriental Society* 83.2 (April/June 1963): 241–43.

Cannon, Garland, and Siddheshwar Pandey. "Sir William Jones Revisited: On His Translation of the Śakuntalā." *Journal of the American Oriental Society* 96.4 (October/December 1976): 528–35.

Caton, Steven. *"Peaks of Yemen I Summon": Poetry as Cultural Practice in a North Yemeni Tribe*. Berkeley: University of California Press, 1993.

———. "Tribal Poetry as Political Rhetoric from Khawlan At-Tiyal, Yemen Arab Republic." PhD diss., University of Chicago, 1984.

Chadwick, Owen. *The Secularization of the European Mind in the Nineteenth Century*. Cambridge: Cambridge University Press, 1975.

Chakrabarty, Dipesh. *Provincializing Europe: Postcolonial Thought and Historical Difference*. Princeton, NJ: Princeton University Press, 2000.

———. "The Time of History and the Times of the Gods." In *The Politics of Culture in the Shadow of Capital*, edited by Lisa Lowe and David Lloyd, 35–60. Durham, NC: Duke University Press, 1997.

Chakravarti, Uma. "A Royal Hunt for Lineage: *Kshatriyas, Apsaras* and the *Ghandarva* Marriage." In *Revisiting Abhijñānaśākuntalam: Love, Lineage and Language in Kālidāsa's Nāṭaka*, edited by Saswati Sengupta and Deepika Tandon, 238–54. New Delhi: Orient BlackSwan, 2011.

Chamberlain, Michael. *Knowledge and Social Practice in Medieval Damascus*. Cambridge: Cambridge University Press, 1994.

Chandran, M. D. Subash, and J. Donald Hughes. "Sacred Groves and Conservation: The Comparative History of Traditional Reserves in the Mediterranean Area and in South India." *Environment and History* 6.2 (May 2000): 169–86.

———. "The Sacred Groves of South India: Ecology, Traditional Communities and Religious Change." *Social Compass* 44.3 (1997): 413–27.

Chatterjee, Partha. *The Black Hole of Empire: History of a Global Practice of Power*. Princeton, NJ: Princeton University Press, 2012.

Clastres, Pierre. *Archeology of Violence*. Los Angeles: Semiotexte, 2010.

———. *Society against the State: Essays in Political Anthropology*. New York: Zone Books, 1987.

Clines, David. "Philology and Power." In *On the Way to the Postmodern: Old Testament Essays, 1967–1998*, edited by David Clines, 2:613–30. Sheffield, UK: Sheffield Academic Press, 1998.

Cohn, Bernard. *An Anthropologist among the Historians and Other Essays*. Oxford: Oxford University Press, 1987.

———. *Colonialism and Its Forms of Knowledge: The British in India*. Princeton, NJ: Princeton University Press, 1996.

Colebrooke, H. T., trans. *A Digest of Hindu Law on Contracts and Successions*. 4 vols. Calcutta: The Honourable Company's Press, 1798.

———, trans. *A Digest of Hindu Law on Contracts and Successions*. 4th ed. 2 vols. Madras: Higginbotham and Company, 1874.

Comaroff, John. "Colonialism, Culture, and the Law: A Foreword." *Law & Social Inquiry* 26.2 (Spring 2001): 305–14.

Cooppan, Vilashini. "Ghosts in the Disciplinary Machine: The Uncanny Life of World Literature." *Comparative Literature Studies* 41 (2004): 10–36.

———. "World Literature and Global Theory: Comparative Literature for the New Millennium." *symplokē* 9, nos. 1/2 (2001): 15–43.

———. *Worlds Within: National Narratives and Global Connections in Postcolonial Writing*. Stanford, CA: Stanford University Press, 2009.

Copenhaver, Brian. "Valla Our Contemporary: Philosophy and Philology." *Journal of the History of Ideas* 66.4 (October 2005): 507–25.

Culler, Jonathan. "Anti-foundational Philology." In *On Philology*, edited by Jan Ziolkowski, 49–52. University Park: Penn State University Press, 1990.

———. "The Return to Philology." *Journal of Aesthetic Education* 36.3 (2002): 12–16.

Dabashi, Hamid. *Being a Muslim in the World*. New York: Palgrave, 2013.

Dalmia, Vasudha. *The Nationalisation of Hindu Traditions: Bhāratendu Hariśchandra and Nineteenth-Century Banaras*. Delhi: Oxford University Press, 1997.

Damrosch, David. *What Is World Literature?* Princeton, NJ: Princeton University Press, 2003.

Davis, Dick. "Persian: Literary Translations into English." In *Encyclopedia of Literary Translation into English*, edited by Olive Classe, 2:1057–60. Chicago: Fitzroy Dearborn, 2000.

de Certeau, Michel. *The Writing of History*. New York: Columbia University Press, 1992.

Deleuze, Gilles. *Difference and Repetition*. New York: Columbia University Press, 1994.

Deleuze, Gilles, and Félix Guattari. *Anti-Oedipus: Capitalism and Schizophrenia*. Minneapolis: University of Minnesota Press, 1983.

———. *A Thousand Plateaus: Capitalism and Schizophrenia*. London: Continuum, 1987.

Del Valle, José. "Language, Politics and History: Introductory Essay." In *A Political History of Spanish: The Making of a Language*, edited by José Del Valle, 3–20. Cambridge: Cambridge University Press, 2013.

De Man, Paul. "The Return to Philology." In *The Resistance to Theory*, 21–26. Minneapolis: University of Minnesota Press, 1986.

Denning, Michael. *Culture in the Age of Three Worlds*. London: Verso, 2004.

Derrett, J. D. M. *Essays in Classical and Modern Hindu Law*. Vol. 1, *Dharmaśāstra and Related Ideas*. Leiden: E. J. Brill, 1976.

Derrida, Jacques. *Demeure: Fiction and Testimony*. Stanford, CA: Stanford University Press, 2000.

———. *Demeure: Maurice Blanchot*. Paris: Galilée, 1998.

———. *Of Grammatology*. Baltimore: Johns Hopkins University Press, 1997.

———. *Monolingualism of the Other; or, The Prosthesis of Origin*. Stanford, CA: Stanford University Press, 1998.

———. *Psyché: Inventions de l'autre*. Paris: Galilée, 1987.

———. *Psyche: Inventions of the Other*. Vol. 1. Stanford, CA: Stanford University Press, 2007.

———. "Signature Event Context" in Jacques Derrida, *Margins of Philosophy* (Chicago: University of Chicago Press, 1982), 307–30.

de Sola Pinto, Vivian. "Sir William Jones and English Literature." *BSOAS* 11.4 (1946): 686–94.

Devji, Faisal. *Landscapes of Jihad: Militancy, Morality, Modernity*. London: Hurst, 2005.

———. *The Terrorist in Search of Humanity: Militant Islam and Global Politics*. New York: Columbia University Press, 2008.

Dharwadker, Vinay. "Orientalism and the Study of Indian Literatures." In *Orientalism and the Postcolonial Predicament*, edited by Carol Breckenridge and Peter van der Veer, 158–85. Philadelphia: University of Pennsylvania Press, 1993.

Dirks, Nicholas. *Castes of Mind: Colonialism and the Making of Modern India*. Princeton, NJ: Princeton University Press, 2001.

Doniger, Wendy. *The Hindus: An Alternative History*. Oxford: Oxford University Press, 2009.

———. Introduction to *The Laws of Manu*, translated by Wendy Doniger, xv–lxxviii. New York: Penguin, 1991.

Dow, Alexander. *The History of Hindostan*. Vol. 3. London: T. Becket and P. A. De Hondt, 1772.

Dumézil, Georges. "Civilization Indo-européene." *Cahiers du Sud* 34 (1951): 221–39.

———. *The Destiny of the Warrior*. Chicago: University of Chicago Press, 1970.

———. *Mitra-Varuna: An Essay on Two Indo-European Representations of Sovereignty*. New York: Zone Books, 1988.

Dumont, Louis. *Homo Hierarchicus: The Caste System and Its Implications*. Chicago: University of Chicago Press, 1980.

Eco, Umberto. *La ricerca della lingua perfetta nella cultura europea*. Rome: Laterza, 1993.

———. *The Search for the Perfect Language*. Oxford, UK: Blackwell, 1995.

Elst, Koenraad. "Manu as a Weapon against Egalitarianism: Nietzsche and Hindu Political Philosophy." In *Nietzsche, Power and Politics: Rethinking Nietzsche's Legacy for Political Thought*, edited by Herman Siemens and Vasti Roodt, 543–82. Berlin: de Gruyter, 2008.

Errington, Joseph. *Linguistics in a Colonial World: A Story of Language, Meaning, and Power*. Malden, MA: Blackwell, 2008.

Esterhammer, Angela. *The Romantic Performative: Language and Action in British and German Romanticism*. Stanford, CA: Stanford University Press, 2002.

Evans-Pritchard, E. E. *The Sanusi of Cyrenaica*. Oxford: Oxford University Press, 1949.

Finnegan, Ruth. *Oral Poetry: Its Nature, Significance, and Social Context*. Cambridge: Cambridge University Press, 1977.

Firoze, M. "Contribution of Jones to Persian Studies: A Reassessment." *Indo-Iranica* 41, nos. 1–4 (1988): 41–50.

Fisch, Jörg. "Law as a Means and as an End: Some Remarks on the Function of European and Non-European Law in the Process of European Expansion." In *European Expansion and Law: The Encounter of European and Indigenous Law in 19th- and 20th-Century Africa and Asia*, edited by W. J. Mommsen and J. A. De Moor, 15–38. New York: Berg, 1992.

Forrester, John. *Language and the Origins of Psychoanalysis*. New York: Columbia University Press, 1980.

Foucault, Michel. *Aesthetics, Method, and Epistemology*. New York: New Press, 1998.

———. *Language, Counter-Memory, Practice*. Ithaca, NY: Cornell University Press, 1997.

———. *Les mots et les choses: Une archéologie des sciences humaines*. Paris: Gallimard, 1966.

———. "Nietzsche, Genealogy, History." In *The Foucault Reader*, edited by Paul Rabinow, 76–100. New York: Pantheon, 1984.

———. *The Order of Things: An Archaeology of the Human Sciences.* New York: Vintage, 1973.

———. *Security, Territory, Population.* New York: Palgrave Macmillan, 2007.

———. "The Subject and Power." *Critical Inquiry* 8.4 (1982): 777–95.

———. "Two Lectures." In *Critique and Power: Recasting the Foucault/Habermas Debate,* edited by Michael Kelly, 17–46. Cambridge, MA: MIT Press, 1994.

Frank, André Gunder. *Capitalism and Underdevelopment in Latin America.* Harmondsworth, UK: Penguin, 1969.

Franklin, Michael. *Orientalist Jones: Sir William Jones, Poet, Lawyer, and Linguist, 1746–1794.* Oxford: Oxford University Press, 2011.

———, ed. *The European Discovery of India: Key Indological Sources of Romanticism.* 6 vols. London: Ganesha, 2001.

———, ed. *Representing India: Indian Culture and Imperial Control in Eighteenth-Century British Orientalist Discourse.* 9 vols. London: Routledge, 2000.

———, ed. *Sir William Jones: Selected Poetical and Prose Works.* Cardiff: University of Wales Press, 1995.

Freeman, J. R. "Gods, Groves and the Culture of Nature in Kerala." *Modern Asian Studies* 33.2 (May 1999): 257–302.

Fynes, Richard. "Sir William Jones and the Classical Tradition." In *Sir William Jones, 1746–94: A Commemoration,* edited by Alexander Murray, 43–65. Oxford: Oxford University Press, 1998.

Gadamer, Hans-George. *Truth and Method.* London: Continuum, 2004.

Gade, Anna. "Recitation of the Qur'ān." In *Encyclopaedia of the Qur'ān,* edited by Jane Dammen McAuliffe, 4:367–85. Leiden: E. J. Brill, 2004.

Gadgil, Madhav, and Ramachandra Guha. *The Fissured Land: An Ecological History of India.* Berkeley: University of California Press, 1993.

Gadgil, Madhav, and V. D. Vartak. "Sacred Groves of India—a Plea for Continued Conservation." *Journal of the Bombay Natural Historical Society* 72.2 (1975): 314–20.

Gaisser, Julia Haig. "Some Thoughts on Philology." *Transactions of the American Philological Association* 137 (2007): 477–81.

Gajula, Goutam. "Sacred Grove Lore and Laws: On the Beliefs of Ecologists, Environmentalist-Historians, and Others." *Indian Folklife* 26 (July 2007): 19–24.

Gandhi, Mahatma. *The Gandhi Reader: A Sourcebook of His Life and Writings.* New York: Grove Press, 1994.

Geertz, Clifford. *The Interpretation of Cultures: Selected Essays.* New York: Basic Books, 1973.

———. *Islam Observed: Religious Development in Morocco and Indonesia.* Chicago: University of Chicago Press, 1971.

Gellner, Ernest. *Nations and Nationalism.* Ithaca, NY: Cornell University Press, 1983.

Genette, Gérard. *Mimologics.* Lincoln: University of Nebraska Press, 1995.

Geoffrey, Éric. *Le soufisme en Égypt et en Syrie sous le dernier Mamelouks et les premiers Ottomans: Orientations spirituelles et enjeux culturels.* Damascus: Institut Français de Damas, 1995.

Gerow, Edwin. "Plot Structure and the Development of *Rasa* in the *Śakuntalā*." *Journal of the American Oriental Society* 99.4 (1979): 559–72; 100.3 (1980): 267–82.

Ghose, Aurobindo. *Speeches.* Calcutta: Arya, 1948.

Ghurye, G. S. *The Scheduled Tribes.* London: Transaction, 1980.

Gibb, A. R., and J. H. Kramers, eds. *The Shorter Encyclopedia of Islam.* Leiden: E. J. Brill, 1965.

Gilchrist, John. *A Dictionary, English and Hindustanee.* 2 vols. Calcutta: Stuart and Cooper, 1787–90.

Gladwin, Francis. *Ayeen Akbery; or, The Institutes of the Emperor Akber.* 3 vols. Calcutta: W. Mackay, 1783–86.

Gilsenan, Michael. *Lords of the Lebanese Marches.* Berkeley: University of California Press, 1996.

Gleig, G. R., ed. *Memoirs of the Life of the Right Hon. Warren Hastings, First Governor-General of Bengal.* 3 vols. London: R. Bentley, 1841.

Goethe, Johann Wolfgang von. *Conversations with Eckermann.* New York: M. Walter Dunne, 1901.

———. *Selected Poetry.* London: Penguin, 2005.

———. *Werke.* Vol. 1. Munich: C. H. Beck, 1996.

Graff, Gerald. *Professing Literature: An Institutional History.* Chicago: University of Chicago Press, 2007.

Grafton, Anthony. *Bring Out Your Dead: The Past as Revelation.* Cambridge, MA: Harvard University Press, 2001.

———. *Defenders of the Text: The Traditions of Scholarship in an Age of Science, 1450–1800.* Cambridge, MA: Harvard University Press, 1991.

———. *New Worlds, Ancient Texts: The Power of Tradition and the Shock of Discovery.* Cambridge, MA: Harvard University Press, 1992.

Grafton, Anthony, and Lisa Jardine. *From Humanism to the Humanities: Education and the Liberal Arts in Fifteenth- and Sixteenth-Century Europe.* Cambridge, MA: Harvard University Press, 1986.

Gramsci, Antonio. *The Gramsci Reader: Selected Writings, 1916–1935.* New York: New York University Press, 2000.

———. *Selections from the Cultural Writings.* Cambridge, MA: Harvard University Press, 1985.

Granqvist, Hilma. *Marriage Conditions in a Palestinian Village.* 2 vols. Helsinki: Sodorstrom, 1931, 1935.

Green, Nile. *Sufism: A Global History.* Oxford, UK: Blackwell, 2012.

Guha, Ranajit. "Chandra's Death." In *Subaltern Studies V,* edited by Ranajit Guha, 135–65. Delhi: Oxford University Press, 1986.

———. *Dominance without Hegemony: History and Power in Colonial India.* Cambridge, MA: Harvard University Press, 1997.

Guha, Sumit. *Environment and Ethnicity in South Asia 1200–1991.* Cambridge: Cambridge University Press, 1999.

Guillory, John. "Literary Study and the Modern System of the Disciplines." In *Disciplinarity at the Fin de Siècle,* edited by Amanda Anderson and Joseph Valente, 20–43. Princeton, NJ: Princeton University Press, 2002.

Gumbrecht, Hans Ulrich. *The Powers of Philology: Dynamics of Textual Scholarship.* Champaign: University of Illinois Press, 2003.

Gurd, Sean Alexander. *Iphigenias at Aulis: Textual Multiplicity, Radical Philology.* Ithaca, NY: Cornell University Press, 2005.

Hadley, George. *Grammatical Remarks on the Practical and Vulgar Dialect of the Indostan Language.* London: T. Cadell, 1772.

Halhed, N. B. *A Code of Gentoo Laws; or, Ordinations of the Pundits.* London: n.p., 1776.

———. *A Code of Gentoo Laws; or, Ordinations of the Pundits.* London: n.p., 1781.

———. *A Grammar of the Bengal Language.* Hooghly: Charles Wilkins, 1778.

Hallaq, Wael. *Authority, Continuity and Change in Islamic Law.* Cambridge: Cambridge University Press, 2001.

———. *A History of Islamic Legal Theories: An Introduction to Sunni Usul al-fiqh.* Cambridge: Cambridge University Press, 1999.

———. *Law and Legal Theory in Classical and Medieval Islam.* Aldershot, UK: Valorium Press, 1995.

———. *The Origins and Evolution of Islamic Law.* Cambridge: Cambridge University Press, 2004.

———. *Sharīʿa: Theory, Practice, Transformations.* Cambridge: Cambridge University Press, 2009.

———. "Was the Gate of Ijtihad Closed?" *International Journal of Middle East Studies* 16.1 (1984): 3–41.

Hamacher, Werner. "From '95 Theses on Philology.'" *PMLA* 125 (2010): 994–1001.

———. *Minima Philologica.* New York: Fordham University Press, 2015.

Hamilton, Charles. *The Hèdaya, or Guide: A Commentary on the Mussulman Laws.* London: T. Bensley, 1791.

Hammer-Purgstall, Joseph von, trans. *Der Diwan des Mohammed Schemsed-din Hafis.* 2 vols. Stuttgart: J. G. Cotta'schen Buchhandlung, 1812–13.

Hansen, Hans Lauge, ed. *Changing Philologies: Contributions to the Redefinition of Foreign Language Studies in the Age of Globalisation.* Copenhagen: Museum Tusculanum Press, University of Copenhagen, 2002.

Harpham, Geoffrey Galt. *The Humanities and the Dream of America.* Chicago: University of Chicago Press, 2011.

———. "Roots, Races, and the Return to Philology." *Representations* 106.1 (Spring 2009): 34–62.

Heesterman, Jan. *The Inner Conflict of Tradition: Essays in Indian Ritual, Kingship, and Society.* Chicago: University of Chicago Press, 1985.

Hefner, Robert. "Human Rights and Democracy in Islam: The Indonesian Case in Global Perspective." In *Religion and the Global Politics of Human Rights*, edited by Thomas Banchoff and Robert Wuthrow, 39–69. Oxford: Oxford University Press, 2011.

Hegel, G. W. F. *Aesthetics: Lectures on Fine Arts.* 2 vols. Oxford: Clarendon Press, 1975.

———. *Lectures on the Philosophy of History.* London: George Bell and Sons, 1902.

———. *Philosophie der Weltgeschichte.* Leipzig: Felix Meiner, 1923.

Heller-Roazen, Daniel. *Echolalias: On the Forgetting of Language.* New York: Zone Books, 2008.

———. "To Read What Was Never Written." Editor's introduction to *Potentialities: Collected Essays in Philosophy*, by Giorgio Agamben, 1–23. Stanford, CA: Stanford University Press, 1999.

Herder, Johann Gottfried. *Sämmtliche Werke.* Vol. 9. Tübingen: J. G. Cotta'schen Buchhandlung, 1807.

———. *Sämtliche Werke.* Edited by Bernhard Suphan. 33 vols. Hildesheim: Georg Olms Verlagsbuchhandlung, 1967.

Herling, Bradley. *The German Gita: Hermeneutics and Discipline in the Early German Reception of Indian Thought, 1778–1831.* London: Routledge, 2006.

Herzfeld, Michael. *Anthropology through the Looking-Glass: Critical Ethnography in the Margins of Europe.* Cambridge: Cambridge University Press, 1987.

Hilferding, Rudolf. *Finance Capital: A Study of the Latest Phase of Capitalist Development.* 1910. London: Routledge and Kegan Paul, 1981.

Hillmann, Michael. "Ḥāfeẓ's 'Turk of Shiraz' Again." *Iranian Studies* 8 (1975): 164–82.

———. "Pseudo-Scholarship in American Ḥāfeẓ Studies: A Comment." *Muslim World* 70 (1980): 267–70.

———. *Unity in the Ghazals of Hafez.* Chicago: Bibliotheca Islamica, 1976.

Hiltebeitel, Alf. *Dharma: Its Early History in Law, Religion, and Narrative.* Oxford: Oxford University Press, 2011.

Hobsbawm, Eric. *The Age of Revolution 1789–1848.* New York: Vintage, 1962.

Hobsbawm, Eric, and Terence Ranger, eds. *The Invention of Tradition.* Cambridge: Cambridge University Press, 1983.

Hodgson, Marshall. *The Venture of Islam.* Vol. 1, *The Classical Age of Islam.* Chicago: University of Chicago Press, 1958.

———. *The Venture of Islam.* Vol. 2, *The Expansion of Islam in the Middle Periods.* Chicago: University of Chicago Press, 1974.

Hoesel-Uhlig, Stefan. "Changing Fields: The Directions of Goethe's *Weltliteratur.*"

In *Debating World Literature*, edited by Christopher Prendergast, 26–53. London: Verso, 2004.

Holquist, Michael. "Why We Should Remember Philology." *Profession* (2002): 72–79.

Holwell, John Zephaniah. *Interesting Historical Events, Relative to the Provinces of Bengal, and the Empire of Indostan*. 3 vols. London: T. Becket and P. J. De Hondt, 1765–71.

Hopkins, E. Washburn. *Epic Mythology*. New York: Biblio and Tannen, 1969.

Human Rights Watch. *Getting Away with Murder: 50 years of the Armed Forces Special Powers Act*. New York: Human Rights Watch, 2008.

Humboldt, Wilhelm von. *On Language: The Diversity of Human Language Structure and Its Influence on the Mental Development of Mankind*. Cambridge: Cambridge University Press, 1988.

———. *Über die Verschiedenheit des menschlichen Sprachbaues und ihren Einfluß auf die geistige Entwickelung des Menschengeschlects*. Bonn: Ferd. Dümmlers, 1960.

Hussain, Nasser. *The Jurisprudence of Emergency: Colonialism and the Rule of Law*. Ann Arbor: University of Michigan Press, 2003.

Hutton, Christopher. *Linguistics and the Third Reich: Mother-Tongue Fascism, Race, and the Science of Language*. London: Routledge, 1999.

———. *Race and the Third Reich: Linguistics, Racial Anthropology and Genetics in the Dialectic of the Volk*. Cambridge, UK: Polity, 2005.

Ibbetson, David. "Sir William Jones and the Nature of Law." In *Mapping the Law: Essays in Memory of Peter Birks*, edited by Andrew Burrows and Alan Rodger, 619–40. Oxford: Oxford University Press, 2006.

———. "Sir William Jones as Comparative Lawyer." In *Sir William Jones, 1746–1794: A Commemoration*, edited by Alexander Murray and Richard Gombrich, 17–42. Oxford: Oxford University Press, 1998.

Inden, Ronald. *Imagining India*. Bloomington: Indiana University Press, 2000.

Inden, Ronald, and McKim Marriott. "Interpreting Indian Society: A Monistic Alternative to Dumont's Dualism." *Journal of Asian Studies* 36.1 (November 1976): 189–95.

Insler, Stanley. "The Shattered Head Split and the Epic Tale of Śakuntalā." *Bulletins d'études indiennes* 7–8 (1989–90): 97–139.

Irwin, Robert. *The Night and Horses and the Desert: An Anthology of Classical Arabic Literature*. Woodstock, NY: Overlook Press, 2000.

Jeremiás, Éva. "The Persian Grammar of Sir William Jones." In *History of Linguistics 1996*, vol. 1, *Traditions in Linguistics Worldwide*, edited by David Cram, Andrew Linn, and Elke Nowak, 277–88. Philadelphia: J. Benjamins, 1999.

Johnson, Barbara. "Philology: What Is at Stake?" *Comparative Literature Studies* 27.1 (1990): 26–30.

Johnson, W. J., trans. *Mahābhārata Book Three: The Forest, Volume Four*. New York: New York University Press, 2005.

Jones, Alan. "Sir William Jones as an Arabist." In *Sir William Jones, 1746–1794: A Commemoration*, edited by Alexander Murray and Richard Gombrich, 67–89. Oxford: Oxford University Press, 1998.

Jones, William, Sir. *The Collected Works of Sir William Jones*. Edited by Garland Cannon. 13 vols. New York: New York University Press, 1993.

———, trans. "Gítagóvinda; or, The Song of Jayadéva." In *Asiatick Researches; or, Transactions of the Society Instituted in Bengal for Inquiring into the History and Antiquities, the Arts, Sciences, and Literature, of Asia*, vol. 3, 185–207. Calcutta: T. Watley, at the Honourable Company's Printing Office; London: P. Elmsley, 1792.

———. *A Grammar of the Persian Language*. London: W. and J. Richardson, 1771.

———, trans. *Institutes of Hindu Law; or, The Ordinances of Menu*. Calcutta: Printed by order of the Government, 1794.

———, trans. *Institutes of Hindu Law; or, The Ordinances of Menu*. Calcutta: Printed by order of the Government; London: J. Sewell and J. Derrett, 1796.

———. *The Letters of Sir William Jones*. Edited by Garland Cannon. 2 vols. Oxford: Clarendon Press, 1970.

———, trans. *The Moallakát, or Seven Arabian Poems Which Were Suspended on the Temple at Mecca*. London: J. Nichols, 1782.

———, trans. *The Mahomedan Law of Succession to the Property of Intestates, in Arabick*. London: Dilly, 1782.

———. "Notes of legal cases argued in Bengal, 1783–89." Additional manuscript 8885. British Library, London.

———. *Poems Consisting Chiefly of Translations from the Asiatick Languages*. Oxford: Clarendon Press, 1772.

———, trans. *Sacontalá; or, The Fatal Ring*. In *Sir William Jones: Selected Poetical and Prose Works*, edited by Michael Franklin, 213–97. Cardiff: University of Wales Press, 1995.

———, trans. *Sacontalá; or, The Fatal Ring: An Indian Drama by Calidas*. Calcutta: Joseph Cooper, 1789; London: J. Cooper, 1790.

———. *Sacontala ossia L'anello fatale*. Translated by Luigi Doria. Darmstadt: n.p., 1815.

———. *Sacontala, ou L'anneau fatal*. Translated by A. Bruguière. Paris: Treuttel et Würtz, 1803.

———. *Sakontala; oder Der entschiedene Ring, ein indisches Schauspiel von Kalidas*. Translated by Georg Forster. Mainz: J. P. Fischer, 1791.

———, trans. *Al Sirájiyyah; or, The Mohammedan Law of Inheritance*. Calcutta: Joseph Cooper, 1792.

———. *The Works of Sir William Jones*. 13 vols. London: Stockdale, 1807.

Kadir, Djelal. *Memos from the Besieged City: Lifelines for Cultural Sustainability*. Stanford, CA: Stanford University Press, 2011.

Kaiwar, Vasant. "The Aryan Model of History and the Oriental Renaissance: The

Politics of Identity in an Age of Revolution, Colonialism, Nationalism." In *Antinomies of Modernity: Essays on Race, Orient, Nation*, edited by Vasant Kaiwar and Sucheta Mazumdar, 13–61. Durham, NC: Duke University Press, 2003.

Kaiwar, Vasant, and Sucheta Mazumdar. "Race, Orient, Nation in the Time-Space of Modernity." In *Antinomies of Modernity: Essays on Race, Orient, Nation*, edited by Kaiwar and Mazumdar, 261–98. Durham, NC: Duke University Press, 2003.

Kālidāsa. *Abhijñāna Śākuntalam*. In *Kālidāsa: The Loom of Time*, translated by Chandra Rajan, 165–281. London: Penguin, 1989.

———. *The Abhijñānaśākuntalam of Kālidāsa*. Edited by M. R. Kale. 1898. Bombay: Booksellers' Publishing Company, 1957.

———. *The Recognition of Śakuntalā*. Oxford: Oxford University Press, 2001.

Karamustafa, Ahmed. *God's Unruly Friends: Dervish Groups in the Islamic Later Middle Period 1200–1550*. Oxford, UK: Oneworld, 2006.

———. *Sufism: The Formative Period*. Edinburgh: Edinburgh University Press, 2007.

Kaufmann, Walter. *Nietzsche: Philosopher, Psychologist, Antichrist*. Princeton, NJ: Princeton University Press, 2013.

Keach, William. *Abitrary Power: Romanticism, Language, Politics*. Princeton, NJ: Princeton University Press, 2004.

Keith, Arthur Berriedale. *A History of Sanskrit Literature*. London: Oxford University Press, 1928.

Kemp, Tom. *Theories of Imperialism*. London: Dobson, 1967.

Kent, Eliza. *Sacred Groves and Local Gods: Religion and Environmentalism in South India*. New York: Oxford University Press, 2013.

Khānlarī, Parvīz Nātil, ed. *Dīwān-i Ḥāfiẓ*. Tehran: Kharazmi, 1983.

Khorramshahi, Baha'-al-Din. "Hafez (ii): Hafez's Life and Times." In *Encyclopædia Iranica*, 11:465–69. New York: Bibliotheca Persia, 2003.

Kierkegaard, Søren. *The Moment and Late Writings*. Princeton, NJ: Princeton University Press, 1998.

Kirkpatrick, William. *A Vocabulary, Persian, Arabic and English*. London: Joseph Cooper, 1785.

Kolff, D. H. A. "Indian and British Law Machines: Some Remarks on Law and Society in British India." In *European Expansion and Law: The Encounter of European and Indigenous Law in 19th- and 20th-Century Africa and Asia*, edited by W. J. Mommsen and J. A. De Moor, 201–36. New York: Berg, 1992.

Kosambi, D. D. "The Autochthonous Element in the Mahabharata." In *The Oxford India Kosambi: Combined Methods in Indology and Other Writings*, edited by B. D. Chattopadhyaya, 348–72. New Delhi: Oxford University Press, 2009.

———. "The Basis of Ancient Indian History." *Journal of the American Oriental Society* 75.1 (January–March 1955): 35–45.

Krishnamoorthy, K. *Kalidasa*. New York: Twayne, 1972.

Kristeva, Julia. *Language—the Unknown: An Initiation into Linguistics.* New York: Columbia University Press, 1989.

Kugle, Scott. "Framed, Blamed and Renamed: The Recasting of Islamic Jurisprudence in Colonial South Asia." *Modern Asian Studies* 35.2 (2001): 257–313.

———. *Homosexuality in Islam: Critical Reflection on Gay, Lesbian, and Transgender Muslims.* Oxford, UK: Oneworld, 2010.

Kuritz, Paul. *The Making of Theatre History.* Englewood Cliffs, NJ: Prentice Hall, 1988.

Laroche, Emmanuel. *Histoire de la racine* NEM- *en grec ancien.* Paris: Klincksieck, 1949.

Leemhuis, Frederik. "Readings of the Qur'ān." In *Encyclopaedia of the Qur'ān,* edited by Jane Dammen McAuliffe, 4:353–63. Leiden: E. J. Brill, 2004.

Le Gallienne, Richard. *Odes from the Divan of Hafiz.* London: Duckworth, 1905.

Lelyveld, David. *Aligarh's First Generation: Muslim Solidarity in British India.* (Princeton, NJ: Princeton University Press, 1978.

Lelyveld, Joseph. *Great Soul: Mahatma Gandhi and His Struggle with India.* New York: Vintage, 2012.

Lenin, V. I. *Imperialism, the Highest Stage of Capitalism: A Popular Outline.* 1916. New York: Penguin, 2010.

Lévi-Strauss, Claude. *The Savage Mind.* Chicago: University of Chicago Press, 1966.

Lewis, Franklin. "Hafez (viii): Hafez and *Rendi.*" In *Encyclopædia Iranica,* 11:483–91. New York: Bibliotheca Persia, 2003.

Lewisohn, Leonard. "Editor's Introduction and Acknowledgements." In *Hafiz and the Religion of Love in Classical Persian Poetry,* edited by Leonard Lewisohn, xxi–xxviii. London: I. B. Tauris, 2010.

———. "English Romantics and Sufi Poets: A Wellspring of Inspiration for American Transcendentalists." In *Sufism and American Literary Masters,* edited by Mehdi Aminrazavi, 15–52. Albany: State University of New York Press, 2015.

———. "Prolegomenon to the Study of Ḥāfiẓ 1: Socio-historical and Literary Contexts—Ḥāfiẓ in Shīrāz." In *Hafiz and the Religion of Love in Classical Persian Poetry,* edited by Leonard Lewisohn, 3–30. London: I. B. Tauris, 2010.

———. "Prolegomenon to the Study of Ḥāfiẓ 2: The Mystical Erotic Milieu—Ḥāfiẓ's Spirituality." In *Hafiz and the Religion of Love in Classical Persian Poetry,* edited by Leonard Lewisohn, 31–73. London: I. B. Tauris, 2010.

———. "The Religious Sources of Love and the Puritans of Islam: Sufi Sources of Hafiz's Anti-clericalism." In *Hafiz and the Religion of Love in Classical Persian Poetry,* edited by Leonard Lewisohn, 159–96. London: I. B. Tauris, 2010.

Limbert, John. *Shiraz in the Age of Hafiz: The Glory of a Medieval Persian City.* Seattle: University of Washington Press, 2004.

Lincoln, Bruce. *Theorizing Myth: Narrative, Ideology, and Scholarship.* Chicago: University of Chicago Press, 1999.

Lingat, Robert. *The Classical Law of India.* Berkeley: University of California Press, 1973.

Locke, John. *An Essay Concerning Human Understanding*. Oxford: Clarendon Press, 1975.
———. *Two Treatises of Government*. Cambridge: Cambridge University Press, 1970.
Loloi, Parvin. "Ḥāfiẓ and the Religion of Love in Nineteenth-Century English and American Poetry." In *Hafiz and the Religion of Love in Classical Persian Poetry*, edited by Leonard Lewisohn, 279–94. London: I. B. Tauris, 2010.
———. *Hâfiz, Master of Persian Poetry: A Critical Bibliography; English Translations since the Eighteenth Century*. London: I. B. Tauris, 2004.
Lukács, Georg. *The Theory of the Novel: A Historico-philosophical Essay on the Forms of Great Epic Literature*. Cambridge, MA: MIT Press, 1971.
Magdoff, Harry. *The Age of Imperialism*. New York: Monthly Review Press, 1969.
———. *Imperialism: From the Colonial Age to the Present*. New York: Monthly Review Press, 1979.
Mahadevan, Kanchana. "Gadamerian Hermeneutics: Between Strangers and Friends." In *Language and Interpretation: Hermeneutics from East-West Perspective*, edited by Manjulika Ghosh and Raghunath Ghosh, 91–124. New Delhi: Northern Book Centre, 2007.
Maine, Henry, Sir. *Village-Communities in the East and West*. New York: Henry Holt, 1876.
Majeed, Javed. *Ungoverned Imaginings: James Mill's "History of British India" and Orientalism*. Oxford: Clarendon Press, 1992.
Mamdani, Mahmood. *Define and Rule: Native as Political Identity*. Cambridge, MA: Harvard University Press, 2012.
Marriott, McKim, and Ronald Inden. "Caste Systems." In *Encyclopedia Britannica*, 3:982–91. Chicago: William Benton, 1974.
Marx, Karl, and Frederick Engels. *The Collected Works of Karl Marx and Frederick Engels*. Vol. 39, *Letters January 1852–December 1855*. Moscow: Progress Publishers, 1983.
Mauss, Marcel. *The Gift: Forms and Functions of Exchange in Archaic Societies*. London: Routledge, 1970.
Mbembe, Achille. *On the Postcolony*. Berkeley: University of California Press, 2001.
McFarland, James. *Constellation: Benjamin and Nietzsche in the Now-Time of History*. New York: Fordham University Press, 2012.
McGann, Jerome, ed. *The New Oxford Book of Romantic Period Verse*. Oxford: Oxford University Press, 1993.
———. "Philology in a New Key." *Critical Inquiry* 39.2 (2013): 327–46.
———. *The Poetics of Sensibility: A Revolution in Literary Style* (Oxford: Clarendon Press, 1996).
McGetchin, Douglas. *Indology, Indomania, and Orientalism: Ancient India's Rebirth in Modern Germany*. Madison, NJ: Fairleigh Dickinson University Press, 2009.
Meeker, Michael. *Literature and Violence in North Arabia*. Cambridge: Cambridge University Press, 1979.

Meisami, Julie Scott. *Medieval Persian Court Poetry*. Princeton, NJ: Princeton University Press, 1987.

———. "Persona and Generic Conventions in Medieval Persian Lyric, with Illustration." *Comparative Criticism* 12 (1990): 125–51.

———. *Structure and Meaning in Medieval Arabic and Persian Poetry: Orient Pearls*. New York: RoutledgeCurzon, 2003.

Melas, Natalie. *All the Difference in the World: Postcoloniality and the Ends of Comparison*. Stanford, CA: Stanford University Press, 2006.

Melchert, Christopher, and Asma Afsaruddin. "Reciters of the Qurʾān." In *Encyclopaedia of the Qurʾān*, edited by Jane Dammen McAuliffe, 4:386–92. Leiden: E. J. Brill, 2004.

Meri, Joseph. *The Cult of Saints among Muslims and Jews in Medieval Syria*. Oxford: Oxford University Press, 2002.

Messick, Brinkley. *Calligraphic State: Textual Domination and History in a Muslim Society*. Berkeley: University of California Press, 1996.

Metcalf, Barbara. *Islamic Contestations: Essays on Muslims in India and Pakistan*. Oxford: Oxford University Press, 2004.

———. *Islamic Revival in British India: Deoband, 1860–1900*. Princeton, NJ: Princeton University Press, 1982.

———. *"Traditionalist" Islamic Activism: Deoband, Tablighis, and Talibs*. ISIM Papers IV. Leiden: International Institute for the Study of Islam in the Modern World, 2002.

Miège, J.-L. "Legal Developments in the Maghrib, 1830–1930." In *European Expansion and Law: The Encounter of European and Indigenous Law in 19th- and 20th-Century Africa and Asia*, edited by W. J. Mommsen and J. A. De Moor, 101–9. New York: Berg, 1992.

Mignolo, Walter. *The Darker Side of the Renaissance: Literacy, Territoriality, and Colonization*. Ann Arbor: University of Michigan Press, 2003.

Mill, James. *The History of British India*. 6 vols. London: Baldwin, Cradock, and Joy, 1820.

———. *The History of British India*. 5th ed., with notes and continuation by Horace Hayman Wilson. 10 vols. London: James Maddon, 1858.

Miller, Barbara Stoler. Preface to *Theater of Memory: The Plays of Kalidasa*, edited by Barbara Stoler Miller, ix–xii. New York: Columbia University Press, 1984.

Momma, Haruko. *From Philology to English Studies: Language and Culture in the Nineteenth Century*. Cambridge: Cambridge University Press, 2013.

———. "A Man on the Cusp: Sir William Jones's 'Philology' and 'Oriental Studies.'" *Texas Studies in Literature and Language* 41.2 (Summer 1999): 160–79.

Monier-Williams, Monier. "Introduction to *Śakoontalá or The Lost Ring* (1856)." In *Śakuntalā: Texts, Readings, Histories*, by Romila Thapar, 219–32. New York: Columbia University Press, 2011.

———. *Sakoontala*. London: Routledge and Sons, 1898.

Moretti, Franco. "Conjectures on World Literature." *New Left Review* 1 (January–February 2000): 54–68.

Morris, James. "Transfiguring Love: Perspective Shifts and the Contextualization of Experience in the Ghazals of Hafiz." In *Hafiz and the Religion of Love in Classical Persian Poetry*, edited by Leonard Lewisohn, 227–50. London: I. B. Tauris, 2010.

Morton, Stephen. *States of Emergency: Colonialism, Literature and Law*. Liverpool, UK: Liverpool University Press, 2013.

Mufti, Aamir. "Auerbach in Istanbul: Edward Said, Secular Criticism, and the Question of Minority Culture." *Critical Inquiry* 25 (1998): 95–125.

———. "Orientalism and the Institution of World Literatures." *Critical Inquiry* 36 (Spring 2010): 458–93.

Müller, Friedrich Max. *A History of Ancient Sanskrit Literature So Far as It Illustrates the Primitive Religion of the Brahmans*. London: Williams and Norgate, 1860.

———. *The Science of Language: Founded on Lectures Delivered at the Royal Institution in 1861 and 1863*. 2 vols. New York: Scribner's, 1891.

Musil, Alois. *The Manners and Customs of Rwala Bedouins*. New York: American Geographical Society, 1928.

Nair, P. T. "Calcutta's Contribution to Persian Studies." *Indo-Iranica* 55.1–4 (2002): 18–35.

Negri, Antonio. *Insurgencies: Constituent Power and the Modern State*. Minneapolis: University of Minnesota Press, 1999.

Nehru, Jawaharlal. *The Discovery of India*. Oxford: Oxford University Press, 1989.

Neuwirth, Angelika, Michael Hess, Judith Pfeiffer, and Börte Sagaster, eds. *Ghazal as World Literature II: From a Literary Genre to a Great Tradition*. Würzburg: Ergon Verlag, 2006.

Nichols, Stephen. "Introduction: Philology in a Manuscript Culture." *Speculum* 65 (1990): 1–10.

Nietzsche, Friedrich. *The Anti-Christ, Ecce Homo, Twilight of the Idols, and Other Writings*. Cambridge: Cambridge University Press, 2005.

———. *Briefwechsel*. 24 vols. Berlin: de Gruyter, 1975–2004.

———. *Fragmente 1884–85*. Vol. 5. Hamburg: Tredition, 2012.

———. *The Gay Science*. New York: Vintage, 1974.

———. *On the Genealogy of Morality and Other Writings*. Cambridge: Cambridge University Press, 2007.

———. *Philosophical Writings*. New York: Continuum, 1997.

———. *Sämtliche Werke: Kritische Studienausgabe*. 15 vols. Berlin: de Gruyter, 1988.

———. *The Twilight of the Idols and the Anti-Christ*. London: Penguin, 1990.

———. *Untimely Meditations*. Cambridge: Cambridge University Press, 1997.

———. *The Will to Power*. New York: Vintage, 1968.

Nkrumah, Kwame. *Neo-colonialism: The Last Stage of Capitalism*. New York: International Publishers, 1965.

Nöldeke, Theodor. *Beiträge zur Kenntnis der Poesie der alten Araber.* Hannover: Carl Rümpler, 1864.

Nwyia, Paul, ed. *Ibn 'Aṭā' Allāh et la naissance de la confrèrie šādilite.* Beirut: Dar el-Machreq, 1970.

O'Grady, Desmond, trans. *The Golden Odes of Love: Al-Mu'allaqat.* Cairo: American University in Cairo Press, 1997.

O'Hanlon, Rosalind, and David Washbrook. "Histories in Transition: Approaches to the Study of Colonialism and Culture in India." *History Workshop Journal* 32.1 (1991): 110–27.

Olender, Maurice. *The Languages of Paradise: Race, Religion and Philology in the Nineteenth Century.* New York: Other Press, 2002.

———. *Les langues du Paradis: Aryens et sémites, un couple providentiel.* Paris: Éditions du Seuil, 1989.

Olivelle, Patrick. Introduction to *The Law Code of Manu,* translated by Patrick Olivelle, xvi–xlv. Oxford: Oxford University Press, 2004.

———, ed. *Manu's Code of Law: A Critical Edition and Translation of the Mānava-Dharmásāstra.* Oxford: Oxford University Press, 2005.

———. "The Semantic History of Dharma: The Middle and Late Vedic Periods." *Journal of Indian Philosophy* 32.5 (December 2004): 491–511.

Ordoubadian, Reza, trans. *The Poems of Hafez.* Bethesda, MD: Ibex, 2006.

Ostwald, Martin. *Nomos and the Beginnings of the Athenian Democracy.* Oxford: Oxford University Press, 1969.

Padel, Felix, and Samarendra Das. *Out of This Earth: East India Adivasis and the Aluminium Cartel.* New Delhi: Orient BlackSwan, 2010.

Paden, W. D. "Tennyson and Persian Poetry, Again." *Modern Language Notes* 58.8 (December 1943): 652–56.

Parry, Jonathan. "The Brahmanical Tradition and the Technology of the Intellect." In *Reason and Morality,* edited by Joanna Overing, 200–225. London: Tavistock, 1985.

Patterson, Lee. "The Return to Philology." In *The Past and Future of Medieval Studies,* edited by John van Engen, 231–44. Notre Dame, IN: University of Notre Dame Press, 1994.

Payne, John, trans. *The Poems of Shemsuddin Mohammed Hafiz of Shiraz.* London: Villon Society, 1901.

Pictet, Adolphe. *Les origines indo-européennes, ou les Aryas primitifs: Essai de paléontologie linguistique.* 3 vols. Paris: Sandoz et Fischbacher, 1877.

Pirbhai, M. Reza. *Reconsidering Islam in a South Asian Context.* Leiden: E. J. Brill, 2009.

Poliakov, Leon. *The Aryan Myth: A History of Racist and Nationalistic Ideas in Europe.* New York: Barnes and Noble, 1996.

Pollock, Sheldon. "Future Philology? The Fate of a Soft Science in a Hard World." *Critical Inquiry* 35 (Summer 2009): 931–61.

————. *Language of the Gods in the World of Men: Sanskrit, Culture, and Power in Pre-modern India*. Berkeley: University of California Press, 2006.

————. "Ramayana and Political Imagination in India." *Journal of Asian Studies* 52.2 (1993): 261–97.

Porter, James. Introduction to *Time, History, and Literature: Selected Essays of Erich Auerbach*, ix–xlv. Princeton, NJ: Princeton University Press, 2013.

Pouzet, Louis. *Damas aux VII/XIII siècle: Vie et structures religieuses d'une métropole islamique*. Beirut: Dar al-Mashreq, 1988.

Povinelli, Elizabeth. *The Cunning of Recognition: Indigenous Alterities and the Making of Australian Multiculturalism*. Durham, NC: Duke University Press, 2002.

Prasad, Archana. *Against Ecological Romanticism: Verrier Elwin and the Making of Antimodern Tribal Identity*. Delhi: Three Essays Collective, 2003.

Price, Pamela. "The 'Popularity' of the Imperial Courts of Law: Three Views of the Anglo-Indian Legal Encounter." In *European Expansion and Law: The Encounter of European and Indigenous Law in 19th- and 20th-Century Africa and Asia*, edited by W. J. Mommsen and J. A. De Moor, 179–200. London: Berg, 1992.

Pritchett, Francis. "Orient Pearls Unstrung: The Quest for Unity in the Ghazal." *Edebiyât* 4 (1993): 199–235.

Proceedings of the Governor and Council at Fort William, Respecting the Administration of Justice amongst the Natives in Bengal. Calcutta: n.p., 1776.

Rahman, Tariq. "British Language Policies and Imperialism in India." *Language Problems and Languge Planning* 20.2 (1996): 91–115.

————. "Decline of Persian in British India." *South Asia: Journal of South Asian Studies* 22.1 (1999): 47–62.

————. *Language, Ideology, and Power: Language Learning among Muslims of Pakistan and North India*. Oxford: Oxford University Press, 2002.

Raman, Bhavani. "Law in Times of Counterinsurgency." In *Iterations of Law in South Asia: Legal Histories from India*, edited by Aparna Balachandran, Rashmi Pant, and Bhavani Raman (Oxford: Oxford University Press, 2018).

Rancière, Jacques. *Dissensus: On Politics and Aesthetics*. London: Continuum, 2010.

————. *La mésentente*. Paris: Galilée, 1995.

————. *The Politics of Literature*. Cambridge, UK: Polity, 2011.

Redford, Kent. "The Ecologically Noble Savage." *Cultural Survival Quarterly* 15.1 (1991): 46–48.

Rehder, Robert. "The Unity of the *Ghazals* of Ḥāfiẓ." *Der Islam* 51 (1974): 55–96.

Reid, Megan. *Law and Piety in Medieval Islam*. Cambridge: Cambridge University Press, 2013.

Renan, Ernest. *Questions contemporaines*. Paris: Michel Lévy Frères, 1868.

Restall, Matthew. "A History of the New Philology and the New Philology in History." *Latin American Research Review* 38.1 (2003): 113–34.

Reynolds, Dwight. *Heroic Poets, Poetic Heroes*. Ithaca, NY: Cornell University Press, 1995.

Reyntjens, Filip. "The Development of the Dual Legal System in Former Belgian Central Africa (Zaire-Rwanda-Burundi)." In *European Expansion and Law: The Encounter of European and Indigenous Law in 19th- and 20th-Century Africa and Asia*, edited by W. J. Mommsen and J. A. De Moor, 111–27. New York: Berg, 1992.

Richardson, John. *A Dictionary, English, Persian and Arabic*. Oxford: Clarendon Press, 1780.

Rocher, Rosane. "British Orientalism in the Eighteenth Century: The Dialectics of Knowledge and Government." In *Orientalism and the Postcolonial Predicament: Perspectives on South Asia*, edited by Carol Breckenridge and Peter van der Veer, 215–49. Philadelphia: University of Pennsylvania Press, 1993.

———. "Weaving Knowledge: Sir William Jones and Indian Pandits." In *Objects of Enquiry: The Life, Contributions, and Influence of Sir William Jones (1746–1794)*, edited by Garland Cannon and Kevin Brine, 51–79. New York: New York University Press, 1995.

Roy, Arundhati. *Capitalism: A Ghost Story*. Chicago: Haymarket Books, 2014.

Roy, Kumkum. *The Emergence of Monarchy in North India 800–400 BC*. Delhi: Oxford University Press, 1994.

Said, Edward. *Beginnings: Intention and Method*. New York: Basic Books, 1975.

———. *Culture and Imperialism*. New York: Alfred A. Knopf, 1993.

———. "Erich Auerbach, Critic of the Earthly World." *boundary 2* 31.2 (2004): 11–34.

———. "Introduction to the Fiftieth-Anniversary Edition." In *Mimesis: the Representation of Reality in Western Literature*, by Erich Auerbach, ix–xxxii. Princeton, NJ: Princeton University Press, 2003.

———. *Orientalism*. Twenty-fifth anniversary edition. New York: Vintage, 2003.

———. *Reflections on Exile and Other Essays*. Cambridge, MA: Harvard University Press, 2000.

———. "The Return to Philology." In *Humanism and Democratic Criticism*, 57–84. New York: Columbia University Press, 2004.

———. *The World, the Text and the Critic*. Cambridge, MA: Harvard University Press, 1983.

Saraswati, Dayananda. *The Light of Truth: English Translation of Swami Dayananda's Satyaartha Prakasha*. Allahabad: Kala, 1960.

Saussure, Ferdinand de. *Recueil des publications scientifiques de Ferdinand de Saussure*. Geneva: Éditions Sonor, 1922.

Savarkar, Vinayak Damodar. *Hindutva: Who Is a Hindu?* Bombay: Veer Savarkar Prakashan, 1969.

Sawhney, Simona. *The Modernity of Sanskrit*. Minneapolis: University of Minnesota Press, 2009.

———. "Who Is Kalidasa? Sanskrit Poetry in Modern India." *Postcolonial Studies* 7.3 (2004): 295–312.

Schimmel, Annemarie. "Ḥāfiẓ and His Critics." *Studies in Islam* 16 (January 1979): 1–33.

Schlegel, August Wilhelm, and Friedrich Schlegel. *Athenäum, eine Zeitschrift*. Vol. 3. Berlin: Heinrich Erdlich, 1800.

Schlegel, Friedrich. *Kritische Ausgabe seiner Werke*. Vol. 14. Paderborn: Schöningh, 1960.

———. *Über die Sprache und Weisheit der Indier: Ein Beitrag zur Begrundung der Altertumskunde*. 1808. Amsterdam: John Benjamins, 1977.

Schmitt, Carl. *The Nomos of the Earth in the International Law of the Jus Publicum Europaeum*. New York: Telos Press, 2003.

———. *Political Theology: Four Chapters on the Concept of Sovereignty*. Chicago: University of Chicago Press, 2005.

———. *Politische Theologie: Vier Kapitel zur Lehre von der Souveränität*. Berlin: Duncker und Humblot, 1996.

———. *Roman Catholicism and Political Form*. Westport, CT: Greenwood Press, 1996.

Schwab, Raymond. *The Oriental Renaissance: Europe's Rediscovery of India and the East, 1680–1880*. New York: Columbia University Press, 1984.

Searle, John. *Intentionality: An Essay in the Philosophy of Language*. Cambridge: Cambridge University Press, 1983.

———. *Speech Acts: An Essay in the Philosophy of Language*. Cambridge: Cambridge University Press, 1969.

Sedlar, Jean. *India in the Mind of Germany: Schelling, Schopenhauer, and Their Times*. Washington, DC: University Press of America, 1982.

Seebohm, T. M. *Hermeneutics: Method and Methodology*. London: Kluwer Academic Publishers, 2004.

Sengupta, Saswati, and Sharmila Purkayastha. "When the King Is the Subject: The Play of Power in Kālidāsa's *Abhijñānaśākuntalam*." In *Revisiting Abhijñānaśākuntalam: Love, Lineage and Language in Kālidāsa's Nāṭaka*, edited by Saswati Sengupta and Deepika Tandon, 148–66. New Delhi: Orient BlackSwan, 2011.

Sengupta, Saswati, and Deepika Tandon. Introduction to *Revisiting Abhijñānaśākuntalam: Love, Lineage and Language in Kālidāsa's Nāṭaka*, edited by Saswati Sengupta and Deepika Tandon, 1–14. New Delhi: Orient BlackSwan, 2011.

Shryock, Andrew. *Nationalism and the Genealogical Imagination*. Berkeley: University of California Press, 1997.

Singha, Radhika. *A Despotism of Law: Crime and Justice in Early Colonial India*. Delhi: Oxford University Press, 1998.

Skaria, Ajay. *Hybrid Histories: Forests, Frontiers and Wildness in Western India*. Delhi: Oxford University Press, 1999.

Slyomovics, Susan. *The Merchant of Art*. Berkeley: University of California Press, 1987.

Smith, Brian. "Eaters, Food and Social Hierarchy in Ancient India: A Dietary Guide to a Revolution of Values." *Journal of the American Academy of Religion* 50.2 (Summer 1990): 201–29.

Smith, John, trans. *The Mahābhārata*. London: Penguin, 2009.

Sowayan, Saad Abdullah. *Nabati Poetry: The Oral Poetry of Arabia*. Berkeley: University of California Press, 1985.

Spivak, Gayatri Chakravorty. *An Aesthetic Education in the Era of Globalization*. Cambridge, MA: Harvard University Press, 2012.

———. *A Critique of Postcolonial Reason: Toward a History of the Vanishing Present*. Cambridge, MA: Harvard University Press, 1999.

———. *Death of a Discipline*. New York: Columbia University Press, 2003.

Steiner, George. *After Babel: Aspects of Language and Translation*. New York: Oxford University Press, 1975.

Stetkevych, Jaroslav. *Arabic Poetry and Orientalism*. Oxford: St. John's College Research Centre, 2004.

Stetkevych, Suzanne Pinckney. *The Mantle Odes: Arabic Praise Poems to the Prophet Muhammad*. Bloomington: Indiana University Press, 2010.

———. *The Mute Immortals Speak: Pre-Islamic Poetry and the Poetics of Ritual*. Ithaca, NY: Cornell University Press, 1993.

Stokes, Eric. *The English Utilitarians and India*. Oxford: Oxford University Press, 1989.

Strawson, John. "Islamic Law and English Texts." In *Laws of the Postcolonial*, edited by Eve Darian-Smith and Peter Fitzpatrick, 109–26. Ann Arbor: University of Michigan Press.

Sundar, Nandini. *Subalterns and Sovereigns: An Anthropological History of Bastar, 1854–1996*. New York: Oxford University Press, 1998.

Tagore, Rabindranath. "Sakuntala: Its Inner Meaning." In *Sakuntala*, by Kalidasa, edited by Kedar Nath Das Gupta and Laurence Binyon, xiii–xxix. London: Macmillan, 1920.

Talmon-Heller, Daniella. *Islamic Piety in Medieval Syria: Mosques, Cemeteries and Sermons under the Zangids and the Ayyubids (1146–1260)*. Leiden: E. J. Brill, 2008.

Taylor, Charles. *Sources of the Self: The Making of the Modern Identity*. Cambridge, MA: Harvard University Press, 1989.

Thapar, Romila. *Aśoka and the Decline of the Mauryas*. Oxford: Oxford University Press, 1961.

———. "Creating Traditions through Narration: The Case of Śakuntalā." In *Boundaries, Dynamics and Construction of Traditions in South Asia*, edited by Federico Squarcini, 159–73. London: Anthem Press, 2011.

———. *Early India: From the Origins to AD 1300*. Berkeley: University of California Press, 2002.

———. "Forests and Settlements." In *Environmental Issues in India: A Reader*, edited by Mahesh Rangarajan, 33–41. Delhi: Pearson Longman, 2007.

———. "Sacrifice, Surplus and the Soul." In *Cultural Pasts: Essays in Early Indian History*, 809–31. New Delhi: Oxford University Press, 2000.

———. *Śakuntalā: Texts, Readings, Histories.* New York: Columbia University Press, 2011.

Thompson, E. P. *Customs in Common: Studies in Traditional Popular Culture.* New York: New Press, 1993.

———. *Whigs and Hunters: The Origins of the Black Act.* London: Breviary Stuff, 2013.

Tiedemann, Rolf. "Historical Materialism or Political Messianism? An Interpretation of the Theses 'On the Concept of History.'" *Philosophical Review* 15.1–2 (Fall/Winter 1983–84): 71–104.

Tilak, Bal Gangadhar. *The Orion; Or, Researches into the Antiquity of the Vedas.* 1893. Poona: Tilak, 1955.

Trautmann, Thomas. *Aryans and British India.* Berkeley University of California Press, 1997.

———, ed. *The Aryan Debate.* Delhi: Oxford University Press, 2005.

———. "The Lives of Sir William Jones." In *Sir William Jones, 1746–1794: A Commemoration,* edited by Alexander Murray and Richard Gombrich, 91–121. Oxford: Oxford University Press, 1998.

Tuetey, Charles Greville, trans. *Classical Arabic Poetry: 162 Poems from Imrulkais to Ma'arri.* London: Routledge and Kegan Paul, 1985.

Turner, James. *Philology: The Forgotten Origins of the Modern Humanities.* Princeton, NJ: Princeton University Press, 2014.

Vernant, Jean-Pierre. Foreword to *The Languages of Paradise: Race, Religion and Philology in the Nineteenth Century,* by Maurice Olender, vii–xi. New York: Other Press, 2002.

Vernant, Jean-Pierre, and Pierre Vidal-Naquet. *Myth and Tragedy in Ancient Greece.* New York: Zone Books, 1990.

Vesey-FitzGerald, S. G. "Sir William Jones, the Jurist." *BSOAS* 11.4 (1946): 807–17.

Vikor, Knut. "The Shari'a and the Nation-State: Who Can Codify the Divine Law?" In *The Middle East in a Globalized World,* edited by Bjorn Utvik and Knut Vikor, 220–50. Bergen: Nordic Society for Middle Eastern Studies, 2000.

Viswanathan, Gauri. *Masks of Conquest: Literary Study and British Rule in India.* New York: Columbia University Press, 2015.

Volosinov, V. N. *Marxism and the Philosophy of Language.* Cambridge, MA: Harvard University Press, 1986.

Warner, Michael. "Professionalization and the Rewards of Literature: 1875–1900." *Criticism* 27 (Winter 1985): 1–28.

Washbrook, David. "Law, State and Agrarian Society in Colonial India." *Modern Asian Studies* 15.3 (1981): 649–721.

———. "Sovereignty, Property, Land and Labour in Colonial South India." In *Constituting Modernity: Private Property in the East and West,* edited by Huri Islamoglu, 69–99. London: I. B. Tauris, 2004.

Waterhouse, Eric. "Secularism." In *Encyclopaedia of Religion and Ethics,* edited by James Hastings, 11:347–50. New York: Scribner's, 1921.

Weber, Max. *Economy and Society: An Outline of Interpretive Sociology.* 2 vols. Berkeley: University of California Press, 1978.

Wellek, René. "Literature and Its Cognates." In *Dictionary of the History of Ideas,* edited by Philip Weiner, 3:81–89. New York: Charles Scribner's, 1974.

———. *The Rise of English Literary History.* Chapel Hill: University of North Carolina Press, 1941.

Wellhausen, Julius. *Skizzen und Vorarbeiten: Erstes Heft.* Berlin: Georg Reimer, 1884.

Wenzel, Siegfried. "Reflections on (New) Philology." *Speculum* 65 (1990): 11–18.

White, Hayden. *Figural Realism: Studies in the Mimesis Effect.* Baltimore: Johns Hopkins University Press, 1999.

Wickens, G. M. "An Analysis of the Primary and Secondary Significance in the Third Ghazal of Hafiz." *BSOAS* 14 (1952): 627–38.

Wilkins, Charles. *The Bhagvat-Geeta, or Dialogues of Kreeshna and Arjoon.* London: C. Nourse, 1785.

———. *The Heetopades of Veeshnoo-Sarma, in a Series of Connected Fables, Interspersed with Moral, Prudential and Political Maxims.* Bath: n.p., 1787.

Williams, Raymond. *Keywords: A Vocabulary of Culture and Society.* New York: Oxford University Press, 1983.

Williamson, George. *The Longing for Myth in Germany: Religion and Aesthetic Culture from Romanticism to Nietzsche.* Chicago: University of Chicago Press, 2004.

Wilmot, Paul, trans. *Mahābhārata Book Two: The Great Hall.* New York: New York University Press, 2006.

Wilson, A. Leslie. *A Mythical Image: The Ideal of India in German Romanticism.* Durham, NC: Duke University Press, 1964.

Wilson, Jon. *Domination of Strangers: Modern Governance in Eastern India, 1780–1835.* New York: Palgrave, 2008.

Windfuhr, Gernot. *Persian Grammar: History and State of Its Study.* Stuttgart: de Gruyter, 2011.

Winternitz, Moriz. *A History of Indian Literature.* Vol. 1. New York: Russell and Russell, 1972.

Wood, Ellen Meiksins. *Citizens to Lords: A Social History of Western Political Thought from Antiquity to the Late Middle Ages.* London: Verso, 2012.

Wordsworth, William, and Samuel Taylor Coleridge. *Lyrical Ballads: 1798 and 1802.* Oxford: Oxford University Press, 2013.

Yarshater, Ehsan. "Hafez (i): An Overview." In *Encyclopædia Iranica,* 11:461–65. New York: Bibliotheca Persia, 2003.

Young, Robert. *Postcolonialism: An Historical Introduction.* Oxford, UK: Blackwell, 2001.

Zaman, Muhammad Qasim. *The Ulama in Contemporary Islam: Custodians of Change.* Princeton, NJ: Princeton University Press, 2002.

Zimmerman, Francis. *The Jungle and the Aroma of Meats: An Ecological Theme in Hindu Medicine*. Berkeley: University of California Press, 1987.

Ziolkowski, Jan, ed. *On Philology*. University Park: Penn State University Press, 1990.

Žižek, Slavoj. *The Ticklish Subject: The Absent Centre of Political Ontology*. London: Verso, 1999.

Zvelebil, Kamil. *Tamil Literature*. Wiesbaden: Otto Harrassowitz, 1974.

Zwettler, Michael. *The Oral Tradition of Classical Arabic Poetry: Its Character and Implications*. Columbus: Ohio State University Press, 1978.

INDEX